1415

The Purple Heart Throbs

Also by Rachel Anderson

Fiction

PINEAPPLE

The Purple Heart Throbs

the sub-literature of love

by

RACHEL ANDERSON

HODDER AND STOUGHTON
LONDON SYDNEY AUCKLAND TORONTO

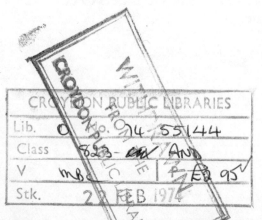
Extracts from the works of Elinor Glyn are quoted by permission of
Gerald Duckworth & Co., Ltd. Extracts from the works of Ethel
M. Dell are quoted by permission of A. P. Watt & Son. Extracts
from the works of Berta Ruck are quoted by permission of the author.

to Bertha and Edward Bradby

Contents

Illustrations

I

Yet Love Remains

TWENTY-FIVE MILLION new romantic novels a year are sold in this country. Each of those twenty-five million is read by more than one person, and usually by several people several times. A recent survey showed that people who buy romances themselves lend them to five or six friends to read; the public libraries lend them to many more.

A popular romantic novel is easily recognisable from the outside by its title and its distinctive cover. The coloured illustration on the front usually shows two people, one of each sex, who, by their expressions of pensive intensity and their desperate gestures, are seen to be having an Important Human Relationship.

The titles of popular romantic novels make frequent use of the key words love, hearts, heaven (and sometimes, more dangerously, Eden): *Yet Love Remains, My Heart's a Dancer, No Heart is Free, The Hazard of Hearts, Fever of Love, Fool's Heaven, A Man to Protect You, Kiss in Sunlight, Heart of Paris*. Sometimes there are wild animals and birds in the title, which refer to the primeval nature of the heroes: *Who rides a Tiger, An Eagle Swooped, Love is an Eagle, The Way of an Eagle*.

Not only do these popular romantic novels sell in large numbers, but also their authors are extremely prolific. Denise Robins has published 162 books and is said to sell 300,000 paperback copies each year. She claims that her novels are translated into 'all European languages, all have been serial-ised, and I now have an American market. Hardcover sales about 6,000, paperback 40,000 first print, many reprinted four to five times.' Barbara Cartland has published 135 books and is said to have sold altogether fourteen million of them. Ursula Bloom has written 468 books, and published 420, for which she features in *The Guinness Book of Records* as the authoress with the greatest total of published books.

But the wide readership and extraordinary sales of popular romantic fiction is no new phenomenon, and the productiveness of present-day authors is equalled by many of the earlier romantic novelists. Ruby M. Ayres, who pub-lished her first novel in 1917, wrote 143 novels, many of which are still selling. Annie S. Swan wrote 183, as well as innumerable short stories and tales for young people. *The Sorrows of Satan,* by Marie Corelli, was first published in 1895, and twenty years later was into its fifty-sixth edition and still selling. *Three Weeks*, by Elinor Glyn, published in 1907, sold five million copies in the first fourteen years. *The Rosary*, by Florence Barclay, sold well over 150,000 hard-back copies within the first nine months of its publication in 1909, and in 1928 was still a best-seller and also running as a serial in a magazine, *Woman's World*, 'the Favourite Paper of a Million Homes'.

Some of the romantic novelists who have been especially prolific published their novels under several names. Ursula Bloom is also Sheila Burns; Maysie Greig wrote also as Jen-nifer Ames, Ann Barclay and Mary D. Warre; Major Charles Mason writes under the names Elaine Carr, Phyllis Marlow, Caroline Homes and Margaret Stanley.

The general, hazy impression of popular romantic fiction, by those who do not read it, is of something poorly written and cheaply produced, whose contents, presumed to be endless repetitions of the same love-story, hover impossibly somewhere between searing passion and relentless prudery. As such, it is usually condescendingly dismissed by those with highbrow pretensions as being harmless wish-fulfilment for ageing spinsters, or relatively harmless escapism for the ill-educated masses. 'But at least it's not dirty, dear.'

Strangely, even though this type of light reading matter has been written and read in vast quantities for over a hundred years, very little attention has been paid to it, except by those who read it. This omission of serious study of romantic fiction is, according to Peter Mann, a sociologist at Sheffield University, in itself quite an odd social phenomenon:

In these days which we are constantly being told are so permissive, people who are happy to talk about obscenity and pornography, and who quite openly espouse its dissemination, seem to be embarrassed by suggestions of disseminating simple romantic novels of impeccable moral purity. This itself is an interesting social situation which is not easy to explain.

Books, Borrowers, and Buyers (1971)

The word romance has had a long and lively etymological history. Its meaning has changed, and to some extent deteriorated, frequently over the centuries, so that today it conveys a variety of different ideas to different people. The pronunciation of the word, too, can affect how it will be interpreted; stress on the first half of the word, *ro*-mance, implies something of less literary value than does ro-*mance*. Used as an adjective—romantic—the word can be pejorative or derogatory, to imply that something is untrue or exaggeratedly idealistic.

To the medieval scholar, romance probably means a verse tale about chivalry written in Old French or Provençal; to the linguist, a romance language means any of the European vernacular languages which developed from the spoken Latin of ancient Rome; to the newsagent who sells it or the young girl who buys it, a romance means a weekly semi-pictorial publication, such as *Romance, Loving, Mirabelle, Valentine*, which recounts love-tales either in strip form with balloons coming out of the lovers' mouths or, at a less wholly pictorial level, in 'real-life' case-history style, illustrated with photographs posed by models. The word can also mean a late

eighteenth-century 'Gothic' novel about fear, innocence, the
supernatural, dark forests and swiftly falling twilights, written by Horace Walpole or Mrs. Anne Radcliffe, like *The
Romance of the Forest* (1791), *A Sicilian Romance* (1790).

I shall not attempt to study any of these. In the terms of
this book romance means the branch of fiction consisting of
lightweight, but full-length, novels of no great literary qualities, which appeal to a wide popular audience which, though
not so highbrow as the medieval scholar, is not so lowbrow
as the reader of weekly pictorial love-stories.

This book will attempt to follow the development of this
branch of light reading-matter from its beginnings in the
1850s, and to trace how the sentimental early Victorian romance has changed through 120 years to become the modern
romantic novel of today, seeing how the hero, heroine and
subject matter have altered over the years, and how the
motives and attitudes of the novelists themselves have
changed.

Today's romantic novelists see themselves as maintaining,
even defending, the most noble status of romance. One writer
of romantic fiction, Anne Maybury, has, in defence of her
craft, summarised the meaning of romance:

> The trouble with 'romance' is that it has moved away from
> its original meaning. True romance is not something gentle
> and rose-tinted, it is Arthurian, Brontëan, full of action,
> desire, tension. Unfortunately, it has taken on an entirely
> different meaning and has become, for many, a word to
> giggle over.

The romantic novelists' own explanations for the success of
their subject-matter have often seemed absurd, either endowing their novels with inflated literary merits, or else being
so whimsical about romance as to be meaningless. And yet
the sales figures through the decades do have meaning.
Reading-matter which can continue to attract readers in such
numbers must have some importance. Vapid or shallow as
some of the romantic novels may seem on first sight, they

do have some irresistible quality, a quality which Q. D. Leavis, in *Fiction and The Reading Public* (1932), defined as vitality:

> Even the most critical reader who brings only an ironical appreciation to their work cannot avoid noticing a certain power, the secret of their success with the majority. Bad writing, false sentiment, sheer silliness, and a preposterous narrative are all carried along by the magnificent vitality of the author, as they are in *Jane Eyre*.

Popular romance is now, and always has been, both mocked and ignored by the serious literary critics. And yet, despite this, and despite the authors' and publishers' gloomy forebodings about dropping sales, the genre has survived; the novels have continued to sell; the romantic novelists have continued to write. The one thing they all have in common is a belief in the universal importance of their chosen subject. Denise Robins states firmly:

> The magic, the very breath of romance, is still in the air. And to my mind there is no literary revolution that can entirely disparage or annihilate romance.
> It is indestructible.

The aim of this book is to account for that 'indestructible magic'.

2

Readers who Rank by Millions

THE BEST-SELLER, or the popular novel, is a comparatively
recent innovation. Before the beginning of the nineteenth
century there was no such thing as popular fiction for,
on the whole, the populace could not or did not read. But
during the early nineteenth century there were many changes
and improvements in education, and also improvements in
the techniques of papermaking and printing. The gradual
movement of the working population from the country to
the towns also helped towards an increased reading population, for in the new urban districts there was, in comparison
with the recreations and community activities of village and
country life, very little in the way of laid-on entertainment.
Reading became a national habit, almost a craze. The number of people who could read in Britain increased between
1780 and 1830 nearly six times, from one and a half million
to nearly eight million. But just because they could read,
it didn't necessarily follow that they were educated:

> Our modern system of proper education was indeed in-
> dispensable and has conferred great benefits on the
> country; but it has been a disappointment in some impor-
> tant respects ... it has produced a vast population able to
> read but unable to distinguish what is worth reading, an
> easy prey to sensations and cheap appeals. Consequently
> both literature and journalism have been to a large extent

debased since 1870, because they now cater for millions of half-educated and quarter-educated people, whose fore-bears, not being able to read at all, were not the patrons of newspapers or of books. The small highly educated class no longer sets the standards to the extent that it used to do, and tends to adopt the standards of the majority.

G. M. Trevelyan, *The Illustrated History of England*

There were various writers and publishers who quickly be-came aware of the voracious appetite for easy reading-matter of the new reading public, among them Wilkie Collins who wrote novels specifically aimed at this lowbrow semi-educated readership, but whose view of his readers, though well-intentioned, was somewhat idealistic:

It is perhaps hardly too much to say that the future of English fiction may rest with this Unknown Public—a reading public of three millions which lies right out of the pale of true literary civilisation—which is now waiting to be taught the difference between a good book and a bad. It is probably a question of time only. The largest audience for periodical literature, in this age of periodicals, must obey the universal law of progress, and must, sooner or later, learn to discriminate. When that period comes, the readers who rank by millions will be the readers who give the widest reputations, who return the richest rewards, and will therefore command the services of the best writers of their time. A great, an unparalleled prospect awaits, perhaps, the coming generation of English novelists. To the penny journals of the present time belongs the credit of having discovered a new public!

Wilkie Collins was of course right in predicting an un-paralleled prospect for novelists, though they were not necessarily all 'the best writers of their time'. There were a great many people jumping on the reading-bandwagon during the mid-nineteenth century, and all forms of litera-ture and sub-literature flourished. Wilkie Collins saw the

Unknown Public as possessing rather more innate discrimination than it did, for some very nasty and gruesome tales were highly popular—stories of melodramatic, supernatural horror, with vampires and lots of blood. There was also a taste for crime, depravity and rape, culminating in detailed accounts of the executions and hangings of the criminals, as, for instance, some of the novels of Bracebridge Hemyng, *The Prostitute Class Generally* (1861), *Revelations by a Private Policeman* (1884), *The Orange Girl, A Romance of the London Streets*, or *The Women of Paris: a Romance*, a novel of backstreet sin and harlots, featuring 'that hump back abortion', the hunchback of Rue d'Enfer, who has a terrible tendency to kiss any pretty woman he sees, and who, in a chapter entitled 'How Throats Are Cut' murders a young woman by slicing through her jugular vein. Miss Braddon who, besides being a very prolific romantic novelist, was forced at one time to write serials for the penny dreadfuls (possibly in order to pay off secret debts she had incurred), noted in a letter to a friend, 'The amount of crime, tragedy, murder, slow poisoning and general infamy required by the halfpenny reader is something terrible. I am just going to do a little parricide for this week's supply.'

George Ponderevo, narrator of H. G. Wells' *Tono-Bungay* (1909), relates how as a boy his chief reading-matter was the *Police News* 'in which vilely-drawn pictures brought home to the dullest intelligence an interminable succession of squalid crimes, women murdered and put into boxes, buried under floors, old men bludgeoned at midnight by robbers, people thrust suddenly out of trains, happy lovers shot, vitriolated, and so forth by rivals'.

Higher up the scale from the 'Penny Dreadfuls' or the *Police News* was the reading matter that Wilkie Collins and Charles Reade formulated as being both suitable for the masses and able to hold their attention. They were consciously catering for the masses, and their stories were carefully thought out, rather than gushing straight from the heart.

Novels were normally published in three-volume sets costing 31/6d., which priced them out of the range of the common reader. But the novels of such writers as Wilkie Collins, Charles Reade and Dickens, which were aimed specifically at the lower-paid people, were made available to them by being published in monthly parts at a shilling a time, in such periodicals as *Household Words*.

To cater for those readers who were above buying their reading-matter in monthly parts, but too poor to pay a guinea and a half for a three-tier novel, Charles Edward Mudie opened his Select Library in 1842. For a subscription of a guinea a year, a reader could borrow any three-volume novel which Mudie had in stock. There were soon a great many imitators of the circulating library and dozens of novel- ists writing to supply this particular demand. 'Anybody can write a three-volume novel. It merely requires a complete ignorance of both life and literature,' wrote Oscar Wilde in *The Critic as Artist*.

As the craze for reading grew, new places and times for doing it were sought. In 1848 W. H. Smith bookstalls first started appearing on railway stations so that 'from now on all who ride may read'. Railway novels had brightly coloured covers, often yellow (hence the term 'yellow back') in order to catch the eye of the traveller, and garishly coloured jacket illustrations.

The reading of novels—and railway novels in particular —was considered by some to be a sinful degrading pastime, apparently for no better reason than that a lot of people were doing it a lot of the time. It was 'a capital excuse for laziness; a powerful anodyne for conscience; a reason for putting off the reading of the Bible; an easy way of teaching slang, cant, etc., to the rising generation; an introduction for our daughters to low society of both sexes'.

Most publishers, though, were certainly doing everything to try to keep the books clean and wholesome. Mudie's Select Library claimed to issue nothing that was unsuitable to be in the hands of young girls of sixteen, and 'The Run and Read Library, for Railway, Road and River' consisted of 'Tales uniting Taste, Humour and Sound Principles, written by competent Christian writers with a view to elevating the character of our popular fiction'. It was felt that 'light literature should be used to carry pleasantly to the minds of the young, germs of precious truth, which time and the blessing of heaven may cause to take root and spring up to the present and future well-being of the soul'.

This kind of selling-line would not have been considered unnecessarily smug or pious, for religion was still part of people's everyday lives; even in the penny dreadfuls, the fundamentals of Christian morality had to be observed, and the villain had to hang in the end. 'The good ended happily, and the bad unhappily. That is what Fiction means,' said Miss Prism of her own (unpublished) three-volume novel, in *The Importance of Being Earnest*. God was still very much in evidence in all forms of popular fiction in the 1850s, as Margaret Dalziel has shown in *Popular Fiction 100 Years Ago*:

> Innumerable references, some of them very brief and slight, others more substantial, make it clear that the existence of God is taken for granted. Almost always it is clear that the conception of God is definitely Christian, though not necessarily Christian in the most orthodox sense. The characters who are meant to attract the reader's sympathy are usually represented as pious, at any rate in the sense of showing deference to the deity. Heroines in particular have recourse to prayer, and there is a good deal of rolling of eyes to heaven in a more or less prayerful way. Sorrows and joys are commonly regarded as sent from on high, moral laws are given a religious foundation, and moral decisions are based on religious considerations.

Mudie's Select Library reached the peak of its triumph in the 1870s and 1880s, but the whole fifty-year period from the library's opening in 1842 to its decline at the end of the century can, in literary terms, be called The Age of Mudie. Mudie's had the power to make or break an author by inclusion or rejection of a novel in its lists. Popular fiction and

Mudie's were synonymous, and the circulating library revolutionised the reading habits of the middle classes. Mudie's library shelves in Southampton Row were both the incentive and the outlet for the works of dozens of mediocre novelists. The immense popularity of the more well-known and successful writers, far from lessening the chances of literary success of other would-be novelists, seemed instead to increase the general demand for more and more light, entertaining reading-matter.

By the 1870s there were a great many popular lady authors working away to fulfil the demand that had been created: Anne Manning, Mrs. Alexander, Charlotte Tucker, Mrs. Lynn Linton, Jean Inglow, Julia Kavanagh, Amelia Edwards, Annie Edwardes, Miss Betham-Edwards, Mrs. Craik, Mrs. Marshall, Mrs. Hungerford, Mrs. Riddell, Charlotte Dempster, Harriet Parr, Hesba Stretton, Mrs. Archer Clive, Rosa Carey, Rosa Kettle, Mrs. Linnaeus Banks, Florence Maryat, Jessie Forthergill, Sarah Tytler, Eleanor Pynter, Anne Thackeray, Mrs. De Courcy Laffan, to name but a few.

There were several imitators of Mudie's circulating library —Bull's, Saunders', Otley's, Churton's, Thomas Hookham's, The Library Company Limited of Pall Mall—but none could compete for price, or for the number of volumes kept in stock. A year's subscription cost only one guinea, and by the end of the nineteenth century there were over seven and a half million volumes to choose from. With branches opening up all over the country in provincial libraries and clubs, with a fleet of horse-drawn vans delivering books all over London, and with a 'mail-order' system which packed books into brass-bound boxes and sent them to country districts and overseas, Mudie's became part of the way of life of the middle classes. 'We have become a novel-reading people, from the Prime Minister down to the last-appointed scullery-maid,' wrote Antony Trollope in 1870. 'Poetry we also read, and history, biography and the social and political news of the day. But all our reading together hardly amounts to what we read in novels.' And Edmund Gosse in 1892 summed up that 'the Victorian has been primarily an age of the triumph of fiction'.

But whether it really was a triumph of fiction, or just a flood
of fiction, was a debatable point. According to one high-
minded critic, the kind of fiction which, 'securely packed in
tin-cornered boxes, is sent from the London depot and scat-
tered through the drawingrooms of the United Kingdom' was
no triumph at all, but a 'headless, trunkless, limbless ...
pulseless non-vertebrate, jelly-fish sort of thing'.

But this is not to say that the novelists were *all* writing
headless, limbless stories concerned with nothing but the
frivolity of love. Some of the lady authors whose books were
distributed by the circulating libraries were trying hard to
be serious. There were, for instance, the polemical novels of
the matronly, free-thinking Communist Mrs. Lynn Linton
which discussed the 'Woman Question' and other 'contemporary controversies' be they of a religious, political or social
nature; there were the 'domestic' sagas and supernatural
novels of the very prolific Mrs. Oliphant, who struggled to
support all her own and her brother's children by her
writing; there were the didactic novels of Mrs. Humphry
Ward. Unfortunately, earnestness and good intention do not
necessarily win the reward of immortality and posterity, and
most of these ladies' 'important' novels, though of interest
to researchers of sociology, make dull reading today compared to the frivolous raptures of, say, a Rhoda Broughton
love-story.

In the later years of the century the great tide of religious
fervour was beginning to ebb and there was increasing scepticism, brought about partly by the wave of scientific discoveries. With typically Victorian thoroughness, the new absence
of belief was discussed as seriously as belief had been. Victorian agnostics and humanists revelled in religion as much
as did the believers. One example of this change of interest
from earnest religious feeling to earnest religious doubt is
shown in Mrs. Humphry Ward's *Robert Elsmere* (published in 1888). Although it was in no way sensational or
daring in the manner of Ouida, it was quite notorious in its
time for its open discussion of the problem of loss of faith.
A clergyman, Robert Elsmere, and his wife, both of them

fervent, young, enthusiastic and happy in their devoted parish work, meet a brilliant non-believer who destroys Robert's faith. He gives up his living and goes with his now heart-broken wife to preach his new agnostic ideals to working-men's clubs and soon dies of overwork.

Mrs. Humphry Ward's novels were always *about* something; she presented life as a series of abstract problems which, through the novel, could be discussed. While this kind of solid and well-intentioned approach to the uses of fiction had many enthusiastic supporters, there were many other readers who did not want to be instructed but just wanted to be entertained. For them there were other lady authors, perhaps less well-educated, less intellectual, but with more unharnessed vitality, more frivolous creative energy, who were fulfilling the ever-present demand for love, with all the variations on the theme of secret weddings, bigamy, deserted sweethearts, unfaithful husbands, wicked brothers and mistaken identities that could be worked in.

The titles of many of the novels of this period proclaim clearly the melodramatic nature of their contents. Annie Thomas wrote such novels as *Blotted Out, 'He Cometh not', She Said, Called to Account, No Alternative, A Passion in Tatters, A Narrow Escape.* Mrs. Riddell wrote *Forewarned, Forearmed, The Earl's Promise, Too Much Alone, 'Home Sweet Home'.* And Mrs. Forrester, author of *Fair Women* and *Dolores*, wrote the stunner *From Olympus to Hades*, which title refers to the far-reaching extremes of emotion of the heroine, Olive. Loved by simple Mr. Alan, but herself in love with Sir George, Olive's sensibilities soar up to the 'Olympus of rapture' only then to plummet down to the 'Hades of despair'.

Geraldine Jewsbury was a publisher's reader for Bentley's and, because of that firm's close association with Mudie's, she had a certain amount of influence over what reading-matter became available to the library. She was a critic with some very forthright views on what constituted a good novel; although she strongly disapproved of novels which were in any way 'disagreeable', 'unpleasant' or 'immoral', she appreciated fully the 'eternal importance of love in the financial and popular success of a novel'. But love in its straightforward form did not make for interesting reading, and all possible complications of love were popular, both in its pre- and post-marital form. Married partners in novels might indulge in almost any sins *provided* that the final tone of the story was spiritually edifying. Geraldine Jewsbury's own first novel *Zoe*, although it did not sink to bigamy, was on the similar and equally popular theme of the wife who marries the wrong person and then finds someone else who is more *worthy* of her love. Zoe is a beautiful Greek girl who marries a man much older than herself because she thinks it is the only way she can find her freedom. Then she meets a priest who falls in love with her and resigns his priesthood. But he is converted to Protestantism and leaves Zoe, to practise his new belief among the miners. Both Zoe's husband and the priest die, leaving Zoe alone to care for her two children.

> Under the influence of her love for the priest, Zoe had become a woman changed for the better, so that the final effect was uplifting. This was important for Mudie's readers: matrimonial errors might form the material of the book but its message should be optimistic.
> Guinevere Griest, *Mudie's Circulating Library*

Geraldine Jewsbury was known to have rejected a manuscript because there was 'a total absence of anything noble ... It would *never* help a struggling person but might injure by depressing their faith and ... bewildering their principle of right and wrong.'

The literature purveyed and controlled by the circulating libraries was a product of its age, and concerned with moral or religious precept and resolutely 'noble'.

3

Reverential Love and Ever-Increasing Honour

POPULAR ROMANTIC FICTION began in 1853 with the publication of *The Heir of Redclyffe* by Charlotte M. Yonge. She
discussed, by means of a popular story, whether or not the
sins of the fathers are necessarily visited upon the sons even
to the fourth and fifth generations.

Such a lofty subject may not sound like the basis for a
romantic story at all. But, contrary to the common miscon-
ception that romantic novelists are stirred by erotic fantasies
and wish fulfilments, they are more often driven by a semi-
religious, vaguely spiritual conviction or belief which they
wish to expound to the public. The religious 'messages' of
subsequent romantic novelists have become gradually less
clearly defined, often being no more than vague beliefs in
some general all-purpose Goodness, but in the 1850s, the
ethics of Charlotte M. Yonge and her contemporaries were
founded firmly on God-fearing, bible-reading Christianity.

What marks out *The Heir of Redclyffe* as the forerunner
of popular romantic fiction, and different from the 'didactic'
novels of the time, is its combination of the important message with the author's own emotional involvement with her
hero, her heroine, her theme and her readers. It is emotional
intensity which makes a good romance.

The story of *The Heir of Redclyffe* is by no means secondary or extraneous to the discussion of inherited sins. The two
are linked. Miss Yonge offers a delightful, soft, affectionate,

modest heroine, Amabel, with whom readers can identify, and a noble-hearted, well-intentioned, misunderstood hero, the heir of the title, inheritor both to Redclyffe estate and to some appalling family sins, whom the reader can admire as, he manages to overcome the sins with love. And, when this hero risks his life for the villain and dies of the fever seven chapters before the end of the book, the reader can also share vicariously in the sacrifice of martyrdom.

If love is an important component of romantic fiction, so, too, is death. For, traditionally, the truest, purest romantic love is a fatal love. Ever since Tristan, in the early medieval Romance of *Tristan and Iseult* (on which the entire western concept of romantic love is based), first drank the *lovendrinc* and fell fatefully in love with Iseult, romantic love has been in its very essence a tragic, impossible love, a fatal love which must end in death.

> Love and death, a fatal love—in these phrases is summed up, if not the whole of poetry, at least whatever is popular, whatever is universally moving in European literature, alike as regards the oldest legends and the sweetest songs.
>   Denis de Rougement, *Passion and Society*

The story of *The Heir of Redclyffe* opens when its young hero, nineteen-year-old Sir Guy, already tragically orphaned in infancy, is bereft of his grandfather and goes to live with his uncle's family, the Edmonstones, and his four cousins. He takes his dog Bustle with him. In her enthusiasm to show that he is the hero, Miss Yonge makes Sir Guy almost too handsome and too virtuous to be true. In appearance, he had 'a frank open face and lustrous hazel eyes'. Moreover, 'There was no lounging in his attitude, and at the first summons he roused up with an air of alert attention that recalled to mind the eager head of a listening greyhound'. He also had uncommonly thick black lashes, and 'light, loose, soft and wavy hair'. The women of the family are particularly enamoured of Sir Guy, as indeed almost the entire British nation soon learned to be.

'He is so entertaining', said Charlotte.
'He sings so beautifully', said Amabel.
'He is so right-minded', said Mrs. Edmonstone.
'So well-informed', said Laura.
Then it all began again.
'He plays chess so well', said Amy.
'Bustle is such a dear dog', said Charlotte.
'He is so attentive to Charlie', said Mrs. Edmonstone, going into the drawing room to her son.
'Papa says he will make up for the faults of all his ancestors', said Amabel.

For this lustrous-eyed, listening, greyhound-like young man has one serious drawback—he comes of very bad stock.

Miss Yonge describes the dreadful faults of Sir Guy's ancestors with as much enthusiasm as she has his virtues. The skeletons in Guy's family cupboard are myriad for, though his ancestors were undoubtedly of the aristocracy, they were 'a fiery violent race'. There were duels, murders and plottings. With relish, Miss Yonge tells her readers how one ancestor even went so far as to force a lady to marry him against her will, and shut up in a turret the man she really loved; he then had him condemned to death, and took his wife to watch the execution. The sins of young Sir Guy's recently deceased grandfather are 'particularly odious', and Miss Yonge spares us no pains in describing them. There was 'the idleness and insubordination at first, then the reckless pursuit of pleasure, the craving for excitement, the defiance of rule and authority, till folly had become vice, and vice led to crime ... In conclusion, his life was stained with sin.'

The awareness that he probably has all these family vices running in his blood makes Sir Guy feel downhearted:

His grandfather a blood-stained remorseful man! The doom complete, himself heir to the curse of Sir Hugh, and fated to run the same career; and as he knew full well, with the tendency to the family character strong within him, the germs of these hateful passions ready to take root downwards and bear fruit upwards, with the very countenance of Sir Hugh, and the same darkening, kindling eyes.

So he resolves to find himself a classical tutor in order to 'study grammar and Greek roots', and thus to keep himself in check by hard work.

' "I have been leading too smooth a life with you," he confides to his aunt as they are out riding together in the phaeton. "I want something unpleasant to keep me in order. Something famously horrid," repeated he, smacking the whip with relish, as if he would have applied that if he could have found nothing else.'

The Edmonstone family passes its time in the kind of dull wholesome way that Miss Yonge clearly enjoyed and thought everybody else should, too—in singing, talking, reading and gardening. While watching his cousin Amabel (known as Amy) playing the piano, Guy falls in love with her; though his inner life is still 'full of grief and doom' he finds that when in her company, 'sunshine penetrated those inmost recesses of his soul and made them glance and sparkle, and clear and limpid'. Music, especially piano-playing, has a way of bringing out the best in romantic heroes. It is often a way of sorting the sheep from the goats; villains tend to be insensitive to music whereas true heroes are moved deeply by it.

Guy worships his cousin desperately and tenderly from afar. But at last after pages of doubt and confusion and after hours of pacing up and down the garden, he is driven to declare his love for her:

If ever there is to be happiness for me on earth, it must be through you; as you, for the last three years, have been all my brightness here. What I feel for you is beyond all power of telling you, Amy! But I know full well all there is against me—I know I am untried, and how can I dare to ask one born to brightness and happiness to share the doom of my family?

But Amy is prepared to share his doom, and Guy as a lover shows considerable restraint and self-discipline:

> Guy was a very chivalrous lover; the polish and courtesy that sat so well on his frank truthful manners were even more remarkable in his courtship ... It was as if he hardly dared to believe that she could really be his own, and treated her with a sort of reverential love and gentleness, while she looked up to him with ever-increasing honour.

Noble and lustrous-eyed as the hero clearly is, it is hard for a modern reader to imagine him ever experiencing physical desire for Amy.

She too is an exemplary character; she is a girl of 'shrinking modesty and maidenly feeling'; when her mother says she has spent too much time piano-playing and gardening with Guy, she is so ashamed of herself for 'flirting' that she hurries to her bedroom and prays about it; when Guy speaks to her she blushes all over, and when he finally proposes, she is so overcome that she rushes to her mother and buries her face in her mother's lap.

In a tale of romantic love, many hardships, complications and misunderstandings must come between the lovers before they can be united. Moreover, Miss Yonge is writing not only about love, but about sins and the powers of love to conquer sins. As the reader soon gathers, the representative of sin is not Sir Guy at all, but a cousin called Philip. None of the characters suspect him of being a villain, because he is not a descendant from the 'fiery violent' Redclyffe branch of the family, but it is clear to the reader, for 'a smile curls over his lip' in an obviously villainous way, as he controls his temper. Philip announces that he has noticed that the well-known and odious family sins have already taken root in Sir Guy and begun to show themselves. But in reality Philip, is racked with jealousy of that paragon of virtue, cousin Guy, and denounces him to their mutual uncle, Mr. Edmonstone, as having gambled away a fortune at Oxford. While Guy represents the virtues of the code of courtly behaviour, Philip stands for treachery, considered by that code to be the worst of crimes.

As the reader knows, Guy is no gambler, and the family fortune was spent on paying off a disreputable relation's debts, but rather than admit this and dishonour the relation, Guy sacrifices his own reputation. He is banished for ever from the Edmonstone household, his engagement is broken off and his horse is sold. His now ex-fiancée is especially upset by the departure of the horse.

Guy suffers many hardships but, after an episode in which he bravely rescues some shipwrecked sailors, his true nature is revealed to the Edmonstones and he is reinstated in the bosom of the family.

When Guy and Amy marry, the congregation in the church see only 'the radiance, purity and innocence of Amy's bridal appearance', but for the family, it appears from Miss Yonge's description to have been an occasion of considerable distress.

Amabel, of course, went with her parents. Poor child! Her tears flowed freely on the way, and Mr. Edmonstone, now that it had really come to the point of parting with his little Amy, was very much overcome, while his wife, hardly refraining from tears, could only hold her hand very close.

The regular morning service was a great comfort, by restoring their tranquillity, and by the time it was ended, Amabel's countenance had settled into its own calm expression of trust and serenity. She scarcely even trembled when her father led her forward; her hand did not shake, and her voice, though very low, was firm and audible; while Guy's deep, sweet tones had a sort of thrill and quiver of intense feeling.

Guy wants to spend the honeymoon 'touring all the cathedral towns of England', which caused a contemporary romantic novelist, Rhoda Broughton, to remark that 'she-novelists' men were like old governesses in trousers'. Instead, they go for two months to Switzerland, and while Amy is gathering purple saxifrage she slips halfway down a mountain. Having created this moment of intense drama, which a more dramatic writer would have used to the full, Miss Yonge throws it away by letting Guy once again prove his reverent love by immediately rescuing her. The moment has not yet come for the death scene.

During their honeymoon, Amy and Guy by chance encounter their cousin Philip who has gone from bad to worse. When warned that there is an epidemic of malaria at nearby Sandrio and that he should keep away, he obstinately goes there nonetheless. Inevitably, he catches the fever and is soon on his death-bed.

Amy and Guy abandon their honeymoon and nobly rush into the fever-ridden area to nurse Philip. For three weeks he is close to death, and 'home' is the word oftenest on his lips. When he is slightly recovered he and Guy have a death-bed reconciliation: Guy cries a bit and then catches the fever. Soon it is Philip's turn to sit by the sick bed. Guy, who really is dying, now makes his confession to a passing English clergyman who, in an aside to Amy, declares from the very fullness of his heart, that it is quite the best confession he has ever heard.

Guy takes several pages to die. 'We have been very happy together,' he tells Amy, and she recites a suitable poem, 'When death is coming near', to him. Then he says he did not think it would have been so soon.

> Morning light came on—the church bell rang out matins —the white hills were tipped with rosy light. His pulse was almost gone—his hand was cold. At last he opened his eyes.
>
> 'Amy!' he said, as if bewildered, or in pain.
>
> 'Here, dearest!'
>
> 'I don't see.'
>
> At that moment the sun was rising, and the light

streamed in at the open window, and over the bed; but it was 'another dawn than ours' that he beheld, as his most beautiful of all smiles beamed over his face, and he said, 'Glory in the Highest!—peace—good-will'—A struggle for breath gave an instant's look of pain; then he whispered so that she could just hear—'The last Prayer'.

She wipes the death-damp from his brow and he dies very beautifully, as beautifully as he had lived, with a smile on his face. 'She closed the dark fringed eyelids—saw him look more beautiful than in sleep—then, laying her face down on the bed, she knelt on. She took no heed of time, no heed of ought that was earthly.'

The novel should really have ended here, leaving the reader at the highest emotional point. But Miss Yonge is anxious to ensure that her message about the power of Guy's love to overcome all things, and the importance of giving and receiving forgiveness, is fully appreciated, and so she takes the reader on for several more chapters to show how things are resolved between Amy and Philip. Although a return to the Edmonstone household comes as rather an anticlimax, it is reassuring to know that Amy does not grieve for too long and that Philip becomes reformed.

Amy gives birth to a daughter, so there is no direct heir to Redclyffe. Philip, now contrite as well he might be, becomes godfather to Amy's baby, marries Amy's sister Laura, and, with terrible irony, inherits Redclyffe. Amy decides that she and the baby will go and live with her crippled brother, Charlie. And so, all the ends are tied up and Miss Yonge has proved her point that love resolves all things.

4

O Prosper Thou our Handywork or The Trial of One's Life

The Heir of Redclyffe was an enormous success with all levels of readers. It was read by young ladies, by undergraduates, by soldiers fighting in the Crimean War, by parsons and high church officials and by members of the Pre-Raphaelite Movement, who saw its insipid young hero, Sir Guy, as 'the spirit of the modern crusader'. Sir Guy even became a popular cult figure; he represented many of the medieval qualities of the 'verray parfit gentil knight',—chivalry, loyalty, fidelity—but with that sugar-coating of Victorian middle-class pacifism and gentility.

Miss Yonge's message was not seen to be outstandingly pious, for religion was still part of most people's daily lives. Sunday observance, bible-reading and family prayers were still common till the end of last century.

But, though the novel's content was acceptable, the writing of it was not. Writing for profit was held to be a bold and disreputable activity for ladies. However, Charlotte Yonge managed to come outside this criticism, as the money earned by her novel's success all went to local church funds, and her motives for writing it stemmed from high principles.

Charlotte M. Yonge was born in 1823 in Hampshire. Her life at home with her parents was uneventful and pious; she was educated by her father in Latin, Greek, French, Ger-

man, History, Italian, Mathematics and Nature Study and it
was probably this broad education which prevented her from
becoming a complete full-blown 'novelist of the heart'. She
was, like all romance-writers, teased in her time, most of all
by a contemporary writer, Rhoda Broughton; but the mock-
ery was provoked not so much by the love content of Miss
Yonge's stories as by their purity and wholesomeness. As a
young girl, she fell under the influence of John Keble,
initiator of the Oxford Movement in the 1820s; he was vicar
of the next-door parish and became her mentor and spiritual
guide. After meeting him for the first time she 'fell headlong
in love with religion' and was involved with the Oxford Movement and high-church matters all her life.

At the age of fifteen, Charlotte Yonge published her first
book *Le Chateau de Melville*, children's stories written in
French. She did a lot of parish work and edited, and wrote
stories and serials for, various religious magazines like *The
Monthly Packet* and *The Magazine for the Young*. *The Heir
of Redclyffe* was her first novel, but she did not step lightly
into professional authorship.

When she had finished writing *The Heir of Redclyffe* her
family, the parish and John Keble met together to discuss
whether it was appropriate for the book to be published. They
decided it was, and to save Charlotte from the sordid business
of involvement with publishers, her father took the manuscript to London.

But although she was thus protected from some of the
problems of successful authorship, she was not saved from
them all.

The success of her novel caused Miss Yonge to become very
worried about the sin of pride. She consulted her mentor,
John Keble, about it and he offered her this advice:

He told me 'a successful book might be the trial of one's
life'; showed me how work (even of this sort) might be
dedicated; how, whenever it was possible, I could explain
how the real pith of the work came from another mind;
and dismissed me with the concluding words of the 90th

psalm (the which has most thankfully, I own, so far been realised).

(The concluding words of the 90th psalm are 'Prosper thou the work of our hands upon us, O prosper thou our handy-work').

Miss Yonge remained a popular and very prolific writer, but none of her subsequent books, of which there were over a hundred, had quite the same impact as the first. Her later novels—tales of devout family life and selfless schoolgirl heroines, admired for their ability to 'mould the mind of the English girl into high standards of grace and gentleness'—have a certain, if long-winded, charm about them, but they were not in any way romantic novels. Miss Yonge's strongly felt beliefs in the virtues of self-discipline and subordination to husbands, were eventually superseded by the audacity and amorous intensity of later, more daring Victorian romantic novelists. But this did not prevent there also being a great quantity of light fiction which, following on from the success of *The Heir of Redclyffe*, used a love-story to make religion seem palatable to the young and vulnerable mind.

The Religious Tract Society and the Home Words publishing company were among the better-known publishing houses which issued this type of fiction—novels of love and marriage with a high moral content—and they continued to be popular right through till the end of Queen Victoria's reign. There was, for instance, *The Shadow Lifted* (1899), by Annie Lucas ('The special purpose of this tale is to promote home happiness, and throw light upon the "shadows" of home discipline—the "clouds" which so often break with blessing'), or *No Ambition* (1895), by Adeline Sergeant, in which Valentine (who is plain but has 'inner beauty') has no ambition and stays unenterprisingly at home, nursing her invalid mother, while her brothers and sisters achieve marital and artistic successes in the world. But in the end, their lives result in tragedy, suicide and untimely death, whereas Valentine, who has been making remarks like 'There are things more worth having than happiness', finds a like-minded hus-

band with whom she can share her belief that worldly aspirations are of no use, and that one must set one's ambitions
on things above this earth.

Only a Girl-Wife, by Ruth Lamb (1889) (author also of
A Wilful Ward (1900), *Not Quite a Lady* (1896), *Thoughtful
Joe and How He Gained his Name* (1880)), and published
by the Religious Tract Society is a romance of the domestic
and spiritual life of a young country doctor and his wilful
'girl-wife'. The couple's courtship and love-affair take up
only a short part of the novel, the rest being concerned with
their ups and downs in marriage. The religious message is
quite straightforward. Mrs. Lamb states plainly that young
wives who do not accept their Saviour will make selfish partners in marriage and will be unhappy themselves, whereas
those who are converted to Christianity are happier and
more useful both to their husbands and to the community.

Andrew Crawford is the tolerant, virtuous, bible-reading,
God-fearing doctor-hero who goes out to India shortly before
the Mutiny and on the very day of his arrival in India falls
in love with orphaned, eighteen-year-old Ida. There is no
description of Ida's physical appeal beyond that she was 'a
pretty young creature'. But anyway, it is not her beauty that
has attracted him. He is attracted towards her 'as a brave
man's sympathies are sure to be in the direction of one who
is fighting an unequal battle'. And Ida is certainly fighting
an unequal battle. She lives with her brother and sister-in-
law Beatrice, who, jealous of Ida's beauty, makes her life
one continual misery by spreading false rumours about her.
Sister-in-law Beatrice is the nearest Mrs. Lamb comes to portraying a wicked character, for in this world, characters are
divided, not into heroes and villains, but more clearly, into
the converted and the un-converted.

Young Ida, cruelly plagued by Beatrice, spends most of
her time crying in her bedroom in the dark. On just such
an occasion Dr. Andrew finds her when everybody else is at
the ball.

As he passed the door of a room which was almost in dark-

ness, he heard a faint sob. He gave a slight tap, and Ida
said, 'Come in', thinking it was a servant with lights.

The girl gave a little cry, half of shame, half of glad-
ness as the doctor entered. She was rejoiced at the sight of
a friend's face, yet eager to wipe away the bitter tears
which were streaming down her cheeks. She looked so sad
and lonely in the dim light, that Dr. Crawford's heart beat
fast from a combination of feelings. How could he help
trying to comfort her? For what else, indeed, had he
come?

Dr. Andrew reveals 'his hidden secret from the innermost
chamber of his heart'. Ida, 'with quivering lips and her sweet
eyes humid and downcast', accepts his declaration.

Soon Dr. Andrew's adoptive father dies and on his death-
bed delivers a brief sermon to Andrew in which, using a
wide assortment of metaphors and similes (the narrow path;
does her heart burn within her; is there a spark to kindle
into the very glow of Christian love; the light that shines;
walking with the Holy Spirit) he expresses the hope that
Andrew has chosen for his bride a Christian with the many
qualities of his own wife, Grace.

The dying sermon is the first ominous hint that Ida is not
all she seems. But it is not until she and Andrew have set
off on their honeymoon that Andrew learns the truth that,
despite her fair outside and winsome ways, she is totally indifferent to her Saviour. He is deeply shocked and 'her light
musical laugh which had always sounded so pleasantly in his
ears' now jars sadly.

Their relationship goes from bad to worse. Ida will not
read her Bible every day, nor does she show any desire to
go and visit the local poor. She pains her husband still further
by refusing to call their first child after her virtuous deceased
step-mother-in-law, Grace. Andrew struggles on for four
years and three hundred pages, trying to lead her towards
'the throne of grace', but it is not till Ida is rather less of a
girl-wife, and her children have all been drugged with laud-
anum by a drunken nurse, that she finally starts to 'look

beyond earthly joys and sorrows towards eternal aims and hopes'. Then she speedily takes up her loving ministrations amongst the young, the poor and the sick, and Andrew at last sees the light in her face which tells of the divine light in her soul. Together they can go 'forward into maturer years sharing the same blessed source of strength'. As for the near-villainess, Beatrice, having spent the sub-plot scheming to get at Ida's inheritance, she too becomes converted in the end, thanks to a tragedy. Her son is accidentally shot by a fellow-sportsman during a shooting excursion. He dies three days later, and Ida and Beatrice are united as they mourn together over the grave.

Mrs. Lamb's picture of perfect marriage as a succession of loving ministrations amongst the poor, though doubtless very character-forming, is rather dreary, and it was basically against such morally exemplary, but unexciting, romantic fiction as this that romantic novelists like Ouida and Rhoda Broughton felt it necessary to rebel. However, Mrs. Lamb's story showing the advantages of Christian marriage seems positively frivolous when compared to a love-story hung around the 'problem' of the Thirty-Nine Articles, which is what Mrs. Eliza Vaughan Stannard managed to do in *The Soul of the Bishop* (1893).

She was an extremely prolific writer of the 1880s and 1890s, one of her specialities being military romances; under the name of John Strange Winter she produced dozens, with such titles as *Cavalry Life* (1881), *Regimental Legends* (1882), *In Quarters* (1885), *A Born Soldier* (1894). 'We know of no books of military life which can compare with Mr. Winter's for a combination of perfect realism and romantic flavour,' said the *Country Gentleman* reviewing *Army Society* (1886). She also wrote perky romantic tales such as *That Imp!* (1887) and *That Mrs. Smith!* (1888), *Three Girls* (1892), *Aunt Johnnie* (1893), fresh, bright and essentially harmless stories. 'Clean, healthy and pure, without being the least bit tiresome or mawkish,' wrote the *Star* of *Bootles' Children*.

Compared to these essentially light and charming romantic tales, Mrs. Stannard's romance about the Thirty-Nine Articles seems especially strange. As a reviewer in the *Standard* wrote at the time, 'The last person from whom we should have expected a religious novel is the writer who signs herself "John Strange Winter"'. *The Soul of the Bishop* was none-theless felt to be 'by far the best and most thoughtful' of her novels, and 'the best and strongest work she has ever done'.

Against a background of the society life of Blankhampton, *The Soul of the Bishop* traces the romance of Miss Cecil Constable and the Rev. Archibald Netherby at two levels, on the one hand the outward aspect, as seen by the local Blankhampton people, while on the other hand, we are shown into the depths of the lovers' souls. There is suspense and intrigue and gossip about the whys and hows of the affair—has the bishop, or has he not, yet proposed? Is Miss Cecil marrying for position or money? Did the bishop kiss her last night beneath the potted palm? Only the reader knows the full truth: that the unhappy lovers are being torn about by the differences of their religious beliefs, and it is eventually their differing interpretations of the Thirty-Nine Articles which wreck their hope of happiness together.

Though the treatment of the theme is in no way irreligious or irreverent—indeed, Mrs. Stannard copes as seriously as she is able with the 'problem' she has set herself—there is all the same a certain delicious audacity in revealing to the general public the contents of a bishop's soul. It is rather like discussing his knees, or some other part which is nor-mally kept covered. And the idea of a bishop being young and falling in love has a certain daring appeal, too. The Reverend Archibald is no clerical eunuch. He is as manly as any other romantic hero:

Imagine a man of forty, big, strong, athletic and alert, with a quick, clean gait and a keen, interested, everyday sort of manner. He was fair of complexion, was clean shaven— and his thick, light-brown hair was cut as closely as any soldier's up at the barracks. His eyes were very blue and looked at you in a straight and frank manner. For the rest, his nose was straight, his mouth pleasant enough, and his chin firm and square, with a cleft in the middle of it.

Archibald first notices Miss Cecil one Sunday when he is preaching in the cathedral:

> On that particular occasion, when there was everything to arouse a feeling of fervour in the hearts of both preacher and people—glorious sunshine, rich and stately surroundings, entrancing music, and almost perfect singing—the Bishop of Blankhampton found his attention gradually rivetting itself upon one of the faces just across the choir, framed as in a shrine of dark oak.

Some months later he catches another fleeting glimpse of the lady through the elaborate table decorations, during the fourth course of a big dinner party and 'his heart seemed suddenly to stand still within him'.

By the end of the evening he has been introduced, noted every detail of her face and figure and found her excessively handsome, with her dark abundant hair in soft rings on her brow and her eyelashes as black as night, her teeth as white as pearls, her dignity and self-possession, and 'her absolutely clear enunciation'.

As in so many romances, music is the catalyst which makes love possible. While it may not be universally true that people fall in love *because* of music, in romantic fiction, the common ground of music—whether piano-playing, or singing duets or, in more recent romantic fiction, a visit to the ballet or the Proms—very frequently provides the shared emotional experience which leads on to love.

At the bishop's request, Miss Cecil sings him an outrageously sentimental song about broken love, which is quoted in full in the text, all five verses. 'The music was passionately dreamy and the words despairingly tender.' She sings it with her soft, rich, sympathetic and beautiful voice and the bishop is so entranced that 'his soul goes into his blue eyes', which blaze with love. On the very next occasion that they meet, which happens to be at a ball in the Blank-hampton Assembly Rooms (this bishop not only attends ecclesiastical meetings but is also quite a party man), he seizes hold of Miss Constable's slender hands, imprisons them in his great strong clasp, and proposes. Miss Cecil flushes vivid, painful scarlet and later grows ghastly pale, as might any girl who is proposed to by a bishop. But the bishop is passion-ately in earnest, and draws her little white-gloved hands up against his breast. After this, and after the word has spread round the town that the bishop tried to kiss her, she is more or less forced to accept his offer. There follow the many misunderstandings and complications of romance, plus a few special ones engendered by his vocation. The bishop is un-able, for instance, to dine out during Lent, even to attend (to Cecil's annoyance) the dinner-party given by her father to celebrate the engagement.

'I don't quite see, Archie,' she said (she had long ago taken to calling him Archie), 'I don't quite see what Lent has to do with your going to a dinner-party.'

'But,' he answered, 'I have never gone out to entertain-ments during Lent in my life.'

'But surely this is a separate occasion,' she urged.

'Well, that is so, but I really can't—at least, I don't see how I could—break my rule. If there is any good in keep-ing Lent at all, there must be more reason now than ever for not breaking my regular habit.'

'But you want to come, don't you?' she asked.

'Yes, I would like to come, of course I would like to come; but that is the more reason why I should not do so.' ...

'I don't think,' she said thoughtfully, 'that you ought to have engaged yourself to me just before Lent if you meant Lent to interfere with proper attention to me, and it is a proper attention to me that you should meet my friends and my father's friends as my future husband.'

Mrs. Stannard hammers home the many difficulties of loving

a bishop, and the dichotomies that arise between vocation and true love. Cecil observes that if only Archie had not been a bishop 'we could have got married and it would not have mattered so much, whether I accepted or denied certain things, we could have agreed to differ on those points.'

But when it comes to the question of the Thirty-Nine Articles, they cannot agree to differ. Cecil more or less accuses her betrothed of hypocrisy, for preaching one thing while believing another. In an aside to the reader, Mrs. Stannard criticises churchmen who are neither *High* nor *Low* but so *Broad* that they, like Archie Netherby, will swallow the Thirty-Nine Articles in a lump, as one tries to swallow a pill without tasting it. 'We know there are all sorts of horrible things in it, but some of them seem to do us good and so we don't enquire too closely into the internal composition.'

The suspense of the story is maintained by the device of Cecil continually breaking off and reaffirming her engagement to the bishop as the battle of wills rages on. The engagement is finally broken off irrevocably and the novel ends on a note of high passionate tragedy when Cecil goes to hear him preach for the last time.

Across the crowd of men and women, two souls stood face to face, two hearts lay bare, one before the other—the palpitating, bleeding, passionate, eager heart of the one, the crushed, aching, hopeless, despairing, lonely heart of the other...

So they stood, this man and this woman, who loved each other beyond all the world, who loved each other for time and for eternity and who yet were utterly and irrevocably apart for ever ... So they stood, the Bishop with his eyes and head and heart on fire, wrestling with God and Satan both for the light to be let in on this one precious soul ... And she, hope all dead, life all blasted, love starved, and heart desolate though so full, gave up from that moment even the one little thread of joy in loving him which had seemed to keep her woman's heart alive.

Then the Bishop uttered the words which gave the glory

of his heart's agony to God above; and the choir chanted
Amen!

The idea is very fine: that a young girl's faith and love of
truth should be stronger even than any mortal love, even to
the extent that she is prepared to 'blast her life' for it. And
doubtless there are young couples who discuss the Thirty-
Nine Articles before entering into marriage. But Mrs. Stannard's discussion is not the intellectual one she sees it as, but
is more of an emotional appeal. In her attacks on *'Broad'*
churchmen's hypocrisies she is only skimming over the surface, and her arguments, as voiced by Cecil, are wholly emotive. The emotional intensity engendered by Mrs. Stannard
on behalf of her desolated heroine makes some present-day
heroines seem positively apathetic in their reactions to the
sufferings of love.

The settings for this type of romantic novel tended
to be fairly domestic, with heroines living at home with
parents or guardians in upper-class England. Readers had
not yet started demanding something new or different or
amazingly exotic for their settings and heroines. Even the
religion, passionately felt though it is, is always orthodox. It
was not till the twentieth century that romantic novelists
began to develop and expound their own wildly unconven-
tional religious views, or, like Marie Corelli, to invent their
own explanations of divine matters.

5

The Desire to be Loved is Strong

WHAT THE WRITERS of the romance-plus-a-moral novel lacked was the ability to let themselves go, to enter totally into the love aspect of their stories, to identify completely with their young wives in love. True deep happiness in marriage sprang, in their view, from being obedient to your husband rather than from kissing him. The embraces of lovers were almost completely ignored.

In *The Heir of Redclyffe* there are no kisses, except when Amy kisses her little girl at the end; in *The Soul of the Bishop*, the Bishop once bends down to kiss Cecil behind the potted palms but he is interrupted and, though his eyes blaze with love more than once, he never apparently attempts to kiss her again. In *Probation* (c.1880) by Jessie Fothergill, there are two kisses, but one of these is renunciatory rather than passionate. In *Only a Girl-Wife*, when the engaged couple are reunited, having been apart for a whole year, all Dr. Andrew can say is: 'You are changed, Ida.' Though we are not told if he kisses her, Mrs. Lamb does remark, rather coyly, that 'Ida was not at arms' length as Andrew said this'.

It was not so much prudishness that lead these writers to leave out kissing, as that they were so busy with their themes that they forgot, or else did not have much time to concentrate on, the physical side of love.

Rhoda Broughton however, soon broke through the kissless barrier. She was mad keen on kisses. In her novels, kisses were, as one contemporary reader said, 'as multitudinous as dewdrops at daybreak on a briar rose'. She was love-obsessed; she saw embraces everywhere. She even describes 'A lane where trees entwined their lissom arms together, and kissed each other lovingly over the way'. It was partly all this kissing, rather than any real immorality, which gave her her early reputation for unrestraint and naughtiness. She makes it clear right from the start, where her priorities lie. 'I am not going to instruct anyone on religion or trains,' she states firmly if oddly, at the beginning of *Red As a Rose is She* (1870). 'So I may as well make up my mind to a more limited audience.' And in the opening of *Not Wisely But Too Well* (1867) she delivers a eulogy to love, taking as her 'text' Keats's line, 'A thing of beauty is a joy for ever,' and the underlying theme of the mystical correlation between earthly sexual love and divine worship is one held, expounded and confused by many later romantic novelists:

> The subject I am going to write about is to my mind 'a thing of beauty'; for what is more pre-eminently so than a tender, loving, passionate, human soul, made more tender, more loving, by many a sore grief, by many a growing sorrow, till towards the hour of its setting, whether calm or whelmed to the last in stormclouds, it shines with a chaste mellow radiance such as our earth lamps do not afford us here, borrowed (oh, priceless loan!) from the fountains of light above? Love in such a soul, growing purified from the drossy, worthless part of earthly passion which oftentimes forms the largest share of it, is raised higher and higher above this world's low level, above its dull swampy flats, till it merges in that better, boundless love which is the essence of the Deity, a love free from the sharp sting of disappointment, free from the mortal taint of satiety, and which decay is powerless to soil with its foul, polluting fingers.

It seems surprising today that a writer offering such an idealistic view of love should have been considered dangerous, and been a forbidden author. But there is, of course, a certain voluptuousness and lasciviousness in her style, even when describing the wicked world with 'its drossy worthless passion'. Moreover, she tossed off daring generalisations about love and women whose flippancy many Victorians doubtless found offensive. 'In the summer time most women like to have a lover; it is almost as necessary to them as warm clothes at Christmas.' Or

> A woman's soul is such a small room that it has only space for one idea at a time; consequently, if a passion, a desire, an impulse lays hold of her, it possesses her with infinitely more force and concentration than it would a man in like case. A woman in love thinks of nothing but her love; a man in love thinks of his love parenthetically, episodically; it shares his thoughts with his horses, his trade, his books, his dinner.

Rhoda Broughton started writing her first novel, *Not Wisely But Too Well*, when she was twenty-two, one wet Sunday afternoon, as a relief from the tedium of reading the Bible or other improving literature, which was all that was allowed during Sunday observance. The first publisher it was sent to turned it down, shocked by its tone and subject. When it *was* published—anonymously—Rhoda Broughton's father (a Welsh parson) is reputed to have forbidden her to read it, considering it to be too shocking. By today's standards it does not seem to be in the least bit improper, and even in her own lifetime, Rhoda Broughton saw her early reputation for audacity taken from her by a younger generation of even more daring writers. She summarised her life, self-mockingly, 'I began my life as Zola, I finish it as Miss Yonge'.

What her writing really shows, more than any impropriety, is a complete lack of restraint. She writes about love with youthful enthusiasm, enters into it with spontaneity and obvious enjoyment. She lets herself feel free even in writing the simple phrase, Once upon a time:

> Once upon a time—I like that old time-honoured opening;

it makes one so nobly free, gives one so much room to stretch one's wings in, ties one down to no king's reign, no hampering, clogging century—once upon a time there was a valley in Taffyland:

so nobly free, in fact, that, quite apart from becoming long-winded, her sentence becomes virtually meaningless.

The love interest of her first novel *Not Wisely But Too Well* is between soft-eyed, soft-fleshed, twenty-year-old Kate and Captain Dare Stamer, who is an absolute rotter, a roué, a cheat, a seducer of women, and who, it is eventually revealed, is already married. But he has certain irresistible charms. He is rugged, has world-marked features, herculean shoulders, a thick moustache, and yet is not so powerful as to have dominated all passionate feelings:

The flood was rising up in him—higher, higher—taking giant steps fiercer than ever it surged and boiled; he *could* not stand it any longer. It was stronger than he. Devils are mightier than men. What good wasting one's strength wrestling with them? He gave in.

He kisses her against her will, or rather, such are his irresistible charms, he persuades her that she *wants* to be kissed.

'Don't you think, Kate,' he said—and the mounting flood made his voice very husky, 'that as we are going to part so soon we had better say good-bye now?' ... 'And how do friends bid each other good-bye, Kate?' asked Dare again.

He could not speak above a deep whisper now, and the light he had been keeping out of his eyes with such difficulty blazed full in them; lurid, like a watchfire on a dark night.

'I don't know,' said Kate mistily, with the shade of something that was coming dim on her soul.

'Is it this way, Kate?' came the low whisper, shaken and hurried; and off went the last rag of restraint, and he wrapped his arms around her as she stood before him,

tighter, tighter, and bent down his head from its stately
height to her small uplifted face, nearer, nearer, till their
lips met, and were joined in a wedlock so fast, so long
enduring, so firm, that it seemed as if they would never
be divorced again.

Captain Dare marks the advent of a new kind of romantic
hero. His appeal is not that of the 'parfit gentil knight' but
of the big tough guy who has repressed passions, and power
over women. Captain Dare, far from treating Kate with
'honour and reverential gentleness' as Sir Guy had treated
Amy, treats her abominably. He lies to her, walks out on
her, extracts impossible promises from her, and carries on
with other women; but the power of this lean-flanked, vast-
chested man is so strong, almost hypnotic, that Kate, who
hitherto has led a carefree happy and girlish life with her
brother and her dog, falls in love with him with 'all the un-
developed passion in her young soul'. Her frantic passion is
utterly uncurbed, and the appeal of those world-marked
features is so strong, that Captain Dare is able to lead her into
sin. First, he merely persuades her to go for clandestine evening walks with him and to lie to her family about it afterwards. Later he persuades her to elope and to blaspheme.
She admits, for instance, that she loves Dare even more than
her own soul, and when he has abandoned her for the first
time she tells God in a weeping prayer that she would do
anything in the world, even something really wicked, just to
have the man back.

In one of the love scenes, Captain Dare admits to loving
Kate so much 'that I'd cut your dear little soft white throat
here, this very minute, if I thought any other man would
ever kiss you again as I have done today'.

At one level this slightly bloodthirsty touch stems from
Rhoda Broughton's simple pubescent delight in suggesting
horrible things, but, as well, it is yet another indication that
part of the appeal of Captain Dare—for Kate and for the
author—lies in this brutal and dangerous streak in him. Kate
has surrendered herself to his charms and his violence; she

is totally dominated by the brute. Despite the many attempts to persuade women to liberate themselves from the tyrannical domination of men, there were then and are still now women who wish to be trapped beneath man's domination, for whom part of the erotic thrill is the inability to escape, the terrible risk that perhaps one *might* have to die for love. Captain Dare in *Not Wisely But Too Well* did not actually do violence to Kate, but he opened the way to more extreme forms of violence in later heroes.

Although Rhoda Broughton abandoned, or even reversed, the idea of the chivalrous knight in favour of a violent knight, the novel still retains one element of the ancient idea of courtly love, which is the hopelessness of Kate's love. It is a fatal love, closer to death than to life.

> Happy love has no history. Romance only comes into existence where love is fatal, frowned upon and doomed by life itself. What stirs lyrical poets to their finest flights is neither the delight of the senses nor the fruitful contentment of the settled couple; not the satisfaction of love, but its *passion*. And passion means suffering. There we have the fundamental fact.
>
> Denis de Rougement, *Passion and Society*

Although Denis de Rougement was not applying his theories in *Passion and Society* to these lower levels of sub-literature, the necessity for the 'sufferings of love' is still to be found in romantic fiction. A convention of a happy ending, rather than a fatal one, later developed; but what still gives the story its interest is the sufferings of the heroine, either through loving the wrong man, or through loving the right man but being separated, or through not knowing whether the love is requited.

Rhoda Broughton was fully aware of the ultimately fatal nature of the love she had inflicted on Kate. After some more kissing she suddenly seemed to despair, 'I've done. I'm tired of writing about love-making. When two people have climbed up to the extremest pinnacle of insane bliss, it is best to leave them alone there. They come tumbling down quick enough, without anyone's help.'

Kate, having lost all for Captain Dare, is a ruined woman and sets out on philanthropic visits among the dregs of humanity, where she meets a clergyman called James, who falls in love with her. But his love for Kate is 'pure, deep, utterly unselfish ... a love which, well hidden, was killing him by inches', and she cannot accept this kind of love. She is still yearning for the 'wild beast passion' of the perfidious Captain Dare.

She catches brain-fever, recovers, discovers that the clergyman James has died of malaria, so resolves to become a nun. The night before doing so she goes to a ball with her family. Captain Dare hurries to the ball to see her but his carriage overturns outside the assembly hall and, although not quite dead, he is 'crushed internally' and survives just one night, lying on a sofa with Kate by his side. She realises what a sinner he is, and tries to convert him as he lies dying. Throughout the night she nags at him about it not being too late; the gate of mercy is still open if he wishes to enter in.

> But her voice broke down, choked with overwhelming emotion; her whole soul went out in that passionate pleading. But she spoke to inattentive ears ... so they sat, the dying and the living, hand-in-hand, through the short, hot summer night.

Dare dies, unrepentant, and all the chambermaids weep copiously, though Miss Broughton points out with some contempt that 'the tears of the uneducated are proverbially near their eyes'. Kate returns to doing acts of kindness in the reeking back streets of London and, very soon, dies.

This novel, besides being read fervently and furtively by thousands, also brought Rhoda Broughton abuse and notoriety. And yet, in the portrayal of Kate's desperate and hapless love for the villainous Captain Dare, Rhoda Broughton takes a firm moral line. Dare must die and Kate, as the result of her one youthful fling, must suffer for the rest of her life:

The desire to be loved is strong enough in us all; in this girl it amounted to madness; it is the key to all the foolish, wicked, senseless things you will find her doing through this history's short course.

Kate's long struggle between her passion for Dare and the pure love of clergyman James shows the reader clearly how love is ultimately, even if only in heavenly values, the winner and how passion, however sweet at the time, is the destroyer.

The background to Rhoda Broughton's tales of fatal passions are filled in with some delightful observations of everyday life as she saw it around her, with descriptions of childhood visits to the seaside, or country activities like hay-making or feeding the hens.

Any lapses into bad taste she makes seem to be not so much from the undecorous behaviour of her heroines, as from the unashamedly enthusiastic way she writes about it, sprinkling her amorous prose with French phrases and half-remembered quotations, for no particular reason except to show that she knows them. 'The temptation being mighty, he flings his arms, *sans ceremonie* about her supple body, and strains her to his breast.' As the critic, Michael Sadleir, said of her, she is slapdash, often clumsy and quite indifferent to the texture of her style:

> Absurd, utterly absurd, both of them (*Red As a Rose is She* and *Not Wisely But Too Well*). And yet—with all their callowness and snobbery and silly ostentatious swagger, with all their French words and tags of verse and rhetoric and overwhelming egotism ... the books are alive. If they have the rawness and sham cleverness of youth, they have also its freshness.

Rhoda Broughton's preoccupations with unhappy love are said to result from an unsuccessful and very youthful love affair of her own. Michael Sadleir, in *Things Past*, says:

> There can be no shadow of doubt that the ill-fated love-

affair of Char and Bill Drinkwater in *A Fool in Her Folly*
is the love-affair of Nell and Dick McGregor in *Cometh
Up*, of Kate and Dare Stamer in *Not Wisely*, and of Rhoda
herself in her excited book-stimulated teens, and some dis-
creditable unknown ... The heartbreak of her deserted
girls was, for all its exaggerations, written from experience
and not imagined.

Rhoda Broughton, unlike some of her contemporaries, did
not see herself as a great contributor to English literature.
Her chief aim was simply to please herself and to entertain.
In *Red As a Rose is She* (1870), she is shamelessly sentimental in the use of her metaphor of the rose to describe
her heroine.

> There is a great pot, full and brimming over with roses—
> a beanpot our forefathers would have called it—in the
> middle of the table. They were plucked but half an hour
> ago, and their faces were still wet with the dew-tears that
> they wept at being torn away from their brothers and
> sisters on the old gnarled rose trees up the kitchen-garden
> walk.
>   But the freshest, the sweetest, the largest of the roses is
> not in the beanpot with the others; it is on a chair by
> itself; there are no dew-tears on its cheeks, it has no prickles
> and its name is Esther.

As in her first novel, Rhoda Broughton sees sex everywhere,
in everything she describes, from Esther lying in a haystack:

> The hay moulds itself pliably into a soft arm-chair for her
> young slight figure, and the big hay spiders walk up her
> back at their leisure, and explore the virgin forests of her
> thick dusky hair

to a description of the rising of the sun, where the sun is
personified as a kind of Louis XIV lover:

> Morning has come again. The sun cannot bear to be long
> away from his young sweetheart, the earth, so he has come

back hasting, with royal pomp, with his crown of gay gold
beams on his head, with his flame-cloak about his strong
shoulders, and with a great troop of light, flaky clouds—
each with a reflex of his red smile on its courtier face—
at his back. He has come back to see himself in the laughing blue eyes of her seas and streams, and to rest at noon-
tide, like a sleepy giant, on her warm green lap.

Esther, the rose heroine, with her 'soft plenitude of dusky
love-knots' and 'the velvet rose leaf of her cheek', is continually being proposed to by a huge rustic oaf, with bright
blue eyes, a yellow beard and big feet who, nonetheless, has
a certain 'vigorous rustic comeliness'. Esther does not wish
to marry him but accepts his offer of marriage 'on the same
principle as some people give babies gin'. It is not good for
them but it keeps them quiet. Being engaged to Esther will
not be very good for Robert the rustic oaf, as she does not
intend to keep her promise, but at least it will keep him quiet.
Esther goes away to be governess in a large rich house where
she manages to fall off a horse and hurt her foot, so her
companion, the knight's son, St. John, has to pick her up.
In order to convey the full emotional intensity of the moment,
Rhoda Broughton recounts it in the historic present:

> He stoops and lifts her gently. He is not Samson or a
> prize-fighter, and well grown young women of seventeen
> are not generally feather-weights; but it seems to him that
> the second occupied in raising her from the ground and
> placing her in the saddle was shorter than other seconds. A
> man's arms are not sticks or bits of iron, that they can hold
> a beautiful woman without feeling it. St. John's blood is
> giving little quick throbs of pleasure. His arms seem to
> feel the pleasure of that pleasant burden long after they
> have been emptied of it.

Esther faints while on the horse that St. John has lifted her
on to, and from then on love burgeons, on both sides. 'Those
glances of hers, they give a man odd sensations about the

midriff; they inspire in him a greedy, covetous desire for more of them.' One may be surprised that St. John should feel desire in his midriff but, as he admits to Esther, he once had an unhappy affair with a deceitful woman, and so now he doesn't really care for women. However, he manages to care for Esther, and when she is wandering about the garden in the moonlight gathering stones, while the rest of the household are at a ball, he kisses her—again in the historic present:

> Not speaking, he takes the little pink palm, stones and all, into his hand, and looks into her face; and then, as if yielding to a temptation he hates, that he would fain resist, and to which, being over-strong he' must yet succumb, he snatches her to his breast, and kisses her fiercely—eyelids, lips and neck with a violence he is himself scarcely conscious of.

The passion that Esther feels is always sudden and surprising, which somehow, by implication, makes it seem all the more wicked, for it shows she is not exercising any of the self-control or self-discipline over her emotions that Miss Yonge would have advocated. Esther's heart suddenly gives a 'great boundless throb', and there are 'hard quick pulsings which are but poorly concealed by the thin muslin of her dress' and her breast 'heaves up and down in angry quick pants'. But despite Esther's throbbings and St. John's odd sensations in the midriff, love cannot go ahead too smoothly between them. Many tears must glisten, 'like dew on the grass, on her long swart lashes', many complications and misunderstandings have to be waded through before they can find true happiness. Many of the predicaments that arise between them are entirely self-made. She refuses, for instance, to accept St. John's sincerely offered proposal of marriage because she believes her name is 'sullied' by her earlier engagement to the comely rustic Robert, and she cannot let St. John suffer the humiliation of marrying a woman with a sullied name. She causes them both considerable distress by her insistence on this sacrifice.

It is, of course, essential to romantic fiction that the lovers' paths be strewn with difficulties and misunderstandings, and where these do not arise naturally out of the narrative, they must be invented by the lovers. In *Tristan and Iseult* 'the romance is given its motive power by the repeated partings and reunions of the lovers'. Without these partings, there would be no suffering. Suspense and suffering are the heroine's lot. Algernon in Oscar Wilde's *The Importance of Being Earnest* summed it up when giving advice to earnest Jack:

> 'I really don't see anything romantic in proposing. It is very romantic to be in love. But there is nothing romantic about a definite proposal. Why, one may be accepted. One usually is, I believe. Then the excitement is all over. The very essence of romance is uncertainty.'

The 'uncertainties' experienced by popular romantic heroines often seem far too slight to cause the torments and near-tragedies that they do, except in extremely neurotic people. But lovers in romantic fiction *are* slightly neurotic.

In *Red As a Rose is She* St. John reacts so acutely and sensitively to the misunderstandings that occur between himself and Esther that he becomes speechless, or shaky, or 'quavers like an hysterical woman or a paralytic old man', and spurns Esther terribly:

> 'If I were a thief or a murderer,' she says indignantly, withdrawing her hands, 'you could not turn from me with greater loathing!'
> 'You are a murderer!' he answers, with a fierce vehemence, looking at her once again as she had asked him, but not kindly. 'You have murdered my whole future—my hope, my belief in women, my truth—my everything of life but what is merely animal. If you had murdered my body I could have forgiven you more easily.'

The knowledge that a girl can have a highly volatile power

over men obviously pleased Rhoda Broughton for, having allowed her heroine to reduce St. John to the state of 'an hysterical woman', she then allows Esther to give her ex-fiancé, the comely rustic Robert, a quick kiss to apologise for the broken engagement. Esther, in all innocence, intends it to be of an entirely sisterly nature, but Rhoda Broughton knows that even friendly kisses can have an inflammable effect on men.

> At the touch of her soft mouth, that has been to him hitherto, despite his nominal betrothal, a sealed book, his steadfast heart begins to pulse frantically fast; if a river of flame instead of blood were poured through his veins, they could not have throbbed with insaner heat.

Miss Broughton goes on for a whole page to explain the astounding effect this kiss has on Robert, and then concludes:

> But the paroxysm is short. Before she who has caused it has guessed at its existence, it is put down, held down strongly. Women are very often like naughty children, putting a lighted match to a train of gunpowder, and then surprised and frightened because there is an explosion.

On hearing that Esther is in love with another, Robert does the manly thing and goes off to be a soldier. In order to delay still further the union of her heroine and hero, Rhoda Broughton sends Esther off to become companion to a senile, deaf old man to whom she must read aloud from *The Times*, and *Justice of the Peace* hour after hour, and pick up his wife's dropped stitches. There is every imaginable horror in the new job, including rats under the bed. Esther develops a nasty 'churchyard' cough and is soon dying through neglect and undernourishment. Luckily St. John turns up again, so that when Esther faints he is there to catch her and lay her on a convenient handy bed.

> Her head is thrown back, and her round chin slightly

raised. Over the tossed pillow wander the tangled riches of her swart hair; nerveless on the counterpane lie the white carven hands and blue-veined wrists, on which the faint blue lines make a tender network. Half-shadowed by her dressing-gown, half-emerging from it gleam bare feet. He leans over her, gazing with passionate admiration mixed with sharp pain; for he can see, plainer now in this long quiet look than in the hasty stolen glances he has hitherto given her, the purple stains under closed eyes... The temptation being mighty, he flings his arms *sans ceremonie* about her supple body, and strains her to his heart ... For one moment Esther lies passive in her lover's arms, yielding to the bliss of that rough embrace ... then her recollected resolution comes back. 'Let me go,' she says, faintly; 'this is not right!'

Esther then endures a tragic death-bed sequence at her bedside, with the doctor, the hurriedly summoned priest, and St. John. Her imminent death offers an opportunity for some final sexual satisfaction. She allows St. John to kiss her, knowing that it cannot cast any lasting slur on her character.

His lips cling to hers in the wild silence of a solemn last farewell ... then, her arms slacken their clasp about his bronzed neck, and her head droops heavy and inert about his shoulder. And so they find them half an hour later; he, like one crazed, with a face as ashen-white as her own, clasping a lifeless woman to his breast.

Here the chapter ends and, seemingly, Esther's life. But Rhoda Broughton was in advance of her time as regards a clinical definition of death. At the beginning of the next chapter, Rhoda Broughton carefully explains that there are two kinds of lifelessness—the one from which there is no back-coming, and another from which there is. Esther has luckily succumbed to the latter, revives, and is able to marry St. John. But the last word is with the vigorous comely rustic. While fighting under foreign skies he catches bubonic plague

and, with the vision of the girl he always loved, 'the innocent-
est, freshest, shyest, rose-bud face', on his face, he dies, and

> Surrenders his fair soul
> Unto his Captain—Christ!

Among her other well-known titles are *Goodbye Sweetheart!*
(1872), *Cometh up as a Flower* (1867), *Second Thoughts* (1880),
Doctor Cupid (1886), *A Waif's Progress* (1905). Her later
novels became gradually less risqué than the early ones. It
was not only that attitudes were changing so that they seemed
less offensive in a more liberal climate. They actually were
less and less fired by the youthful, if agonised, exuberance of
young love, and their themes were increasingly gloomy and
pessimistic. *Scylla and Charybdis* (1899) tells how Honor
steers her love between the twin dangers of Scylla, the rock
of her own mother's jealousy, and Charybdis, the whirlpool
of her lover's probable madness. The hero discovers that
there is inherited lunacy in his family; his father died in the
madhouse, having first attempted to murder his mother. So
did his grandfather, and his father before that. By marrying
Honor, he runs the risk of murdering her too. This inevitably results in a very gloomy story with none of those careless moments of enraptured bliss that were possible in the
earlier, and equally unhappy, stories such as *Not Wisely But
Too Well*.

With the exception of her first two novels which were
published anonymously, Rhoda Broughton was not afraid to
write under her own name, even though writing popular
novels was hardly a respectable occupation for a middle-class
lady. Many other writers wrote anonymously or under men's
names. A contemporary romantic novelist, Mrs. Eliza Margaret Humphreys, who wrote in very similar vein to Rhoda
Broughton, preferred to hide behind the safety of her pseudonym, 'Rita'.

Her daring treatment of love in such novels as *Peg, the
Rake* (1894), *My Lady Coquette* (1881), *My Lord Conceit*
(1884), *The Doctor's Secret* (1890), or the rather more pro-

saic *Betty Brent, Typist* (1908), which heralded the beginnings of heroine's emancipation, was read assiduously by 'Rita's' clandestine middle-class admirers.

Although Rita was not so enthusiastic about kissing as Rhoda Broughton, she was just as ready to break the bounds of convention. In *Two Bad Blue Eyes* (1884), there are few kisses, but there is an adulterous embrace.

Predicaments on themes of enforced weddings, unconsummated marriages, the honour or dishonour of heroes, slurs on heroines' reputations, were all popular with romantic novelists of the nineteenth century, and *Two Bad Blue Eyes* opens with what is almost a classic situation for the popular romantic novel. On the morning of her marriage to a man she does not love, the heroine learns of the return of her long-lost sweetheart.

The unhappy union in *Two Bad Blue Eyes*, between lovely Lauraine and debauched old Sir Francis, has been arranged by Lauraine's mother who cares less for her daughter's happiness than for the sum of money she will receive from the arranged marriage. But she is an unsubtle schemer:

'How thankful I am that I have secured so excellent a future for her ... Sir Francis will have to manage her now; she's off my hands, thank goodness! It is a pity he is such a brute; but then he is such a good match, and I am fearfully in debt ... All danger is over now. Do not all novels end with a wedding? Are not all Society's daughters considered settled and established, once the ring is on and the rice and slippers thrown?'

This ingenuous sinner had not bargained for the return of her daughter's Mr. Right. Though Keith arrives too late to marry Lauraine, he can at least admire her 'in her filmy lace headdress which seems to float like a transparent cloud and envelop the lovely figure in its misty folds', and take her in his arms for that adulterous embrace:

Then there comes a faint rustle of silken skirts, the door

opens, there is a sweet subtle perfume of orange-flowers
and roses, and before him stands the loveliest vision of
womanhood that his eyes have ever rested on.

One moment he looks at her, and all his anger melts
away, and an unutterable reproach speaks in his eyes, that
are 'bad' blue eyes no longer, but only very sad and very
haunting.

'Oh Lauraine!' he says, and his arms go out to clasp her
as in the old sweet days that are gone forever, and sobbing
wildly, the girl falls upon his breast ... her beauty mad-
dens him, and he is longing with all the wildest and most
passionate longing of his hot-blooded southern nature to
fold that lovely figure in his arms, to rain kisses on the
sweet quivering lips, to call her his—his own—his love,
though a hundred laws of right and honour barred the
way.

The unhappy lovers, Lauraine and Keith, obey these hundred laws and, still yearning, go their separate ways. As Sir
Francis's wife, Lauraine enters Society which, as depicted by
Rita, is full of scoundrels, plotting to put each others' names
into disrepute. There are wicked women who, when thwarted
in their schemings, 'clench their teeth like a vice'. It must
have offered at least some self-righteous comfort to middle-
class readers with aspirations for the high life, to read that
Society was only full of wicked people.

Lauraine and Keith are kept apart for many years of suffering and misfortune. Then, at last, Lauraine is finally faced
with a real moment of choice. Both the men in her life lie
dying: her faithless husband, Sir Francis, is in Italy with
typhoid fever; Keith, her 'two bad blue eyes', lies dying of a
duel-wound in Paris. Lauraine is caught between two death-
beds. To which one shall she fly?

Her perfidious husband, in the wild ravings of his
delirium, repeatedly calls out for her:

He knows his own hours are numbered, despite the hopes
held out. He knows that to have her with him during the

dreadful ordeal through which he has to pass would be the only comfort that life has in it. He shudders as he lies there face to face with death, as the cold waters of the great river seem to flow on—on—up to his very feet; and in that awful passage there will be no voice to whisper comfort, no prayers from that low, sweet woman's voice to tell of peace, of hope, of the gates of mercy standing open yet, even to the greatest of sinners.

It is to his bedside, treacherous, faithless and wicked though he is, that Lauraine hurries; it is to the husband to whom she made solemn vows before God so long ago to love, cherish and obey in sickness and in health, that she must go in his final hour of need.

Sir Francis, much comforted by her presence, hurriedly repents his sins and dies a saved man.

Lauraine is thus freed to rush up to Paris to the other deathbed, where she faints over the patient's body.

'The shock is enough to kill him,' remarks one of the society ladies who happen to be participating in the death scene. But it does not. Lauraine's presence helps two bad blue eyes to recover and the sundered lives are joined at last. Rita ends the novel as Rhoda Broughton ended *Red As a Rose is She*, on a note of thankful prayer,

> Trust in the Lord; wait patiently for Him,
> and He will give thee thy heart's desire,

which seems to suggest that the Lord's main concern is to bring lovers together.

6

Certain Fine and Nasty Books

OUIDA SHARED WITH Rhoda Broughton the reputation for being one of the most daring and outrageous writers of the 1860s and 1870s.

While Rhoda Broughton managed to strike a balance between passionate involvement with her absurdly silly stories, and self-mockery, Ouida took her work immensely seriously. But then, she did not consider she was writing romantic fiction in the first place. She believed her work to be that of a genius. She held herself to be one of the 'last great writers of English prose', and believed each successive book was greater than the last.

Shortly after the death of George Eliot, she wrote to one of her publishers, 'English Literature is very sorry stuff nowadays. You must make much of me, for now George Eliot is gone there is no one else who can write English.' She was, as she described one of her characters, 'blinded by the mufflers of her vanity and inordinate belief in herself'.

Her belief in her own greatness led her to be obsessed with a fear that other people were trying to steal the plots of her stories. She made elaborate plans to prevent this. She never handed over the complete manuscript of a new novel to her publishers until they had paid all the money due for it; she never revealed any details of its title, setting or story until the novel was definitely accepted; and she sent the manuscript to the copyist one page at a time, in random order, so that no one except herself could work out what the plot was. In fact, the ability to concoct a good plot was not one of her strong points, and her novels ramble and roar along, piling one situation on to another to produce a colourful, rapid and cinematic effect. Perhaps Ouida got her random pages mixed up too.

While Rhoda Broughton was rebelling against the pruderies and conventions of young ladies in love, Ouida's rebellion extended to cover not only contemporary conventional morality, but almost all aspects of novel-writing as well— plot, characterisation, theme, accuracy, realism.

Ouida was said to have written the 'naughtiest' novel of the 60s; *Under Two Flags* (1867) was called 'a very immoral book written on the pattern of French novels', and her work was also accused of being full of vice, and out to poison people's minds—all of which, far from diminishing her success, encouraged her readers to have their minds still further poisoned.

The critics, both in her own time and subsequently, have never quite been able to make up their minds about her. Perhaps her own insistence on her genius, the way she behaved like a *grande dame* of literature, and the fact that she wrote at times for the more serious critical reviews and periodicals, were confusing to the critics. Some mocked and derided her work, while others enthused.

> We do feel ourselves capable of noticing ... certain fine and nasty books, signed with the name of a certain Ouida ... They are so fine as to be unreadable, and consequently we should hope could do little harm, the diction being too gorgeous for merely human faculties

wrote Mrs. Oliphant of Ouida in *Blackwoods Magazine* in 1867, while the editor of *New Monthly* exclaimed that

> Few periodical writers have suddenly achieved a greater success than the contributor who has chosen the fanciful designation of Ouida, whose sketches of society, both in

England and on the Continent, are as graceful as they are accurate.

The *Contemporary* periodical thanked Ouida in 1869 for transporting her readers into 'regions fairer and more intense than the everyday pettiness of fashionable realism'. And the *Spectator*, reviewing *Pascarel* in 1875, remarked, with a somewhat double-edged observation, that it is 'preposterous, wild, luscious and beautiful'. One of today's best known romantic novelists, Denise Robins, maintains that everybody ought to read Ouida or they will not begin to understand romantic fiction. And certainly it is true that many subsequent romantic novelists have tried to capture the extravagance and colourfulness of Ouida's style. Her novels have been called the 'voluptuous daydreams of a flamboyant romancer'. She wrote, as various critics have pointed out, with a mixture of 'romantic absurdity, sentimental extravagance, exaggerated inaccuracy; garish sentimentality and blatant melodramatic effects'; G. K. Chesterton said, 'Though it is impossible not to smile at Ouida, it is equally impossible not to read her'. In her biography, *Ouida, a Study in Ostentation*, Yvonne ffrench summarised the secret of Ouida's appeal:

> Although she was never a realist, she was real. She wrote as she pleased, and she had the power to communicate her feelings. For no other novelists could impress by sheer force of strong feeling the passion and the fire, the pathos and sincerity, the splendid careless touches of generosity and extravagance that amazed a susceptible public, so well as Ouida.

Ouida's real name was Marie Louise Ramé. She was born in 1839; her mother was English and her father, Louis Ramé, was a French political refugee who gave French lessons in Bury St. Edmunds. He was frequently leaving home mysteriously while Ouida was a girl, finally disappeared altogether at the time of the Paris Commune in 1871, and was probably

killed in the street fighting in Paris. But such real-life home-
bred drama as this did not interest Ouida so much as what
she invented herself. The political intrigue, battles and the
high-society life, as revealed in her novels, is less about how
life really was than about how Ouida would have liked it to
be. But not only did she invent in her novels an absurdly
exaggerated way of life; she also proceeded to live her life
as though her ostentatious aristocracy really existed.

She was rather plain, but self-centred, vain and spoilt. She
dressed very showily, usually in expensive dresses by Worth
specially cut to reveal her small feet of which she was very
proud. Even at the age of forty-seven, when one observer
described her as having 'a hideous and deformed body', she
continued to wear youthfully styled and coloured silk dresses.
She was described by the poet William Allingham in 1869 as
being 'in green silk, sinister, clever face, hair down, small
hands and feet, voice like a carving knife'.

When playing the role of the famous lady writer, she
would receive visitors to her soireés with her feet stretched
out in front of her on a footstool so that everybody could
admire them. These noticeably small feet reappear on one of
her characters. 'Lady Dolly had lovely feet, and could afford
to uncover them; very few of her rivals could do so ... She
always gave her miniature feet and arched insteps their
natural play.'

In her mid-thirties, Ouida settled in a villa near Florence
and lived in Italy for the rest of her life. She frequently
fell in love with members of English or Italian aristocracy
and wrote most of these would-be lovers into her novels. Her
pseudonym, Ouida, was derived, with typical interest in
infantile things, from her own childhood attempts to pro-
nounce her name, Louise. She was keen on developing the
French half of herself and also called herself *La Ramé*, and
later *de la Ramée*. She also added the honorary title *Madame*
to her name, though in fact she never married.

Although Ouida liked to think she had a full understanding of political matters, of social injustices and hypocrisies,
she really had no notable great ideas beyond a desire to rep-

resent fashionable love-life as she liked to see it. Her real gift was imagination, uncontrolled by culture, reason or intellect. She knew how to write readably and entertainingly; she had a wide and versatile vocabulary and a dexterous handling of words. Even when describing minor details in her narrative, she let her fancy soar. Here, for instance, is the smoking-room:

> (he) entered the warm full light of that chamber of liberty, that sanctuary of the persecuted, that temple of refuge, thrice blessed in all its forms throughout the land, that consecrated Mecca of every true believer in the divinity of the meerschaum, and the paradise of the narghile—the smoking room.

Part of her appeal was that she dared to write about things and places that had hitherto been exclusively male territory. She let readers into the sacred secrets of the smoking-room, the barracks, the steeplechase; threw them into the midst of the gory battle or the gaming-room, allowed them a long lingering glimpse of what men in love think about women, and revealed the intimacies of bachelor life, or at any rate *her* idea of the luxurious style in which bachelors lived. Even if her vision of male behaviour was not strictly accurate, it was a vision her readers liked enough to believe in. Her young-men heroes are handsome, strong and brave. They are at times listless, languid and apparently indifferent. But, when necessary, they have it in them also to be loyal and true, and to make huge sacrifices for one another. Despite their nonchalant outward appearances, most of her heroes have soft sensitive centres, which are capable of showing great tenderness towards animals, and an appreciation and depth of understanding of the arts and music. But her lovers do not really conform to the courtly myth, for it is the men who are on pedestals and are worshipped and adored by their female admirers. There is, for instance, Clyde Suddeley, 'before whom all women go down, and for whom little notes are piled a foot high at the Guards and the Trovelleri, and who counts himself the Richelieu of our day'. There is also Bertie Cecil, hero of *Under Two Flags* (1867), who is more or less the same person as Bertie Erroll, hero of *The Last Coquetry of Lady Caprice* (1862), who is also Hilarion, hero of *Ariadne* (1877). In the role of Bertie Cecil, this man is so strong that 'with a single straightening of his left arm he felled the detective to earth like a bullock'. But despite this strength, he also has a face 'of as much delicacy and brilliancy as a woman's, handsome, thoro'bred, languid, nonchalant, with a certain latent recklessness under the impassive calm of habit, and a singular softness given to the large, dark hazel eyes by the unusual length of the lashes over them'.

Her first novel, *Held in Bondage* (1861), is about the loves, follies and adventures of a group of cavalry officers, the hero being Granville deVigne, and his mate, Sabretasche of the Dashers. In describing her heroes, the highest praise Ouida can bestow on them is that they should be like animals, especially dogs. Bertie Cecil has eyes like a spaniel; elsewhere in the same novel, another character has tiny white teeth that are, again, like a spaniel's.

Women are more often likened to members of the vegetable kingdom; one young girl is said to be 'like a hare-bell', another has an exquisite face, 'with that lovely tint like the wild white rose'. If they are older, they are some-times likened to insects. Here is a fashionable lady on the beach at Trouville:

> Lady Dolly in a penthouse-like erection of straw above her head to keep the sun off, and her body tightly encased in black and yellow stripes, looked like a wasp—if a wasp had ever possessed snowy arms quite bare and bare white legs.

Ouida had an almost obsessive love for animals, especially dogs, besides being rather fond of Italian peasants. She was known in Italy as *La Signora Dei Cani*, The Dog Lady, be-cause of her habit of taking in strays, and there were some thirty stray dogs in her home when she died. When her first dog, Beausire, died, both Ouida and her mother were so ill with grief that they had to take to their beds. Characterful dogs feature in nearly all her books. Lady Marabout crimples the ears of Bijou; Lady Caprice shares her breakfast with a Maltese; Avarina Sansreproche has a terrier named Azar, and Bertie Cecil is accompanied on his soldiering in North Africa by a poodle called Flick-Flack. Ouida herself wore a locket round her neck with a portrait of her Newfoundland dog, Sulla, in it, and one of her novels, *Puck*, is narrated, in the first person, by one dog and is dedicated to another. Ouida's powers of description reach their emotive heights when she is describing her animal friends.

Here is an account of Forest King, one of the noble heroes in *Under Two Flags*, whose attributes are dealt with even more lovingly than Bertie Cecil's. It is the night before the Grand Military, a steeplechase in which Bertie Cecil and Forest King are to take part for the honour of the Guards of England.

Serenely as Wellington, another hero slept profoundly, on the eve of a great event—of a great contest to be met when the day should break—of a critical victory, depending on him alone to save the Guards of England from defeat and shame; their honour and their hopes rested on his solitary head; by him they would be lost or saved; but unharassed by the magnitude of the stake at issue, unhaunted by the past, unfretted by the future, he slumbered the slumber of the just. Not Sir Tristam, Sir Caledore, Sir Launcelot— no, nor Arthur himself, was ever truer knight, ever gentler, braver, bolder, more staunch of heart, more loyal of soul, than he to whom the glory of the Brigades was trusted now; never was there spirit more dauntless and fiery in the field; never temper kindlier and more generous with friends and foes ... but he took his rest like the cracker he was—standing as though he were on guard, and steady as a steel-grey in colour, darkening well at all points, shining and soft as satin, with the firm muscles quivering beneath rock, a hero every inch of him. For he was Forest King ...

at the first touch of excitement to the high mettle and finely strung organisation; the head small, lean, racer-like, 'blood' all over, with the delicate taper ears, almost transparent in full light; well ribbed up, fine shoulders.

Not only is this horse a perfect physical specimen, he also has a wonderful temperament:

Awake only could you tell the generous and gallant promise of his perfect temper; for there are no eyes that speak more truly, none on earth that are so beautiful as the eyes of a horse. Forest King's were dark as a gazelle's, soft as a woman's, brilliant as stars, a little dreamy and mournful, and as infinitely caressing when he looked at what he loved, as they could blaze full of light and fire when danger was near and rivalry against him.

Under Two Flags (filmed in 1936 with Ronald Coleman and Claudette Colbert) was first written for a military periodical and in a slightly self-important *Avis au Lecteur*, Ouida warns the general public that there are many French phrases in the book, some of them the slang of the Algerian Army, and that when English translations are offered, they will be idiomatic rather than literal. In fact, much of the French argot tends to be of an exclamatory nature which is more or less self-explanatory. '*"Dame!"* he growled fiercely', or '*"Sang de Dieu!"* fiercely swore a Zouave', or '*"Tiens! tiens!* I did him wrong"', or simply, '*Pouf!*'

The basic story of *Under Two Flags* is that Bertie, in order to save his brother's honour, takes his brother's name, leaves England, the aristocratic woman he is infatuated with, and his dear horse Forest King, and flees across Europe, joining up with the Algerian Army. The complicated plot is of little importance to the book, for it is more a series of vividly recounted set-pieces, with Bertie, in various roles as society beau, jockey, hunted man, near-corpse, warrior, featuring in each of them. Ouida's plots were generally improbable, and she was inaccurate about court etiquette, about the geographical situations of her action, and about the rules of the various athletic sports her heroes engage in. But she is never slow or dull, and her stories proceed at a rattling good pace.

While Bertie is in North Africa, fighting some somewhat undefined Arabs, he meets the swearing, killing, fighting, laughing, dancing bastard heroine, Cigarette, one of Ouida's strangest and more endearing characters. Cigarette is a sort of girl soldier cum mascot cum camp-follower. She has a heart like a kitten, yet fights like a hawk. Bertie first sees her when she is dancing a can-can in the music-hall of a café for the common soldiers. She will not dance for officers, even if they bribe her, but for her *gros bébés*, war-worn, dust-covered, weary with toil and stiff with wounds, she would do anything.

And she was dancing for them now.

Her soft short curls all fluttering, her cheeks all bright with a scarlet flush, her eyes as black as night, and full of fire, her gay little uniform, with its scarlet and purple, making her look like a fuschia-bell tossed by the wind to and fro ever so lightly on its delicate swaying stem, Cigarette danced with the wild grace of an Almeh, of a Bayadère, of a Nautch girl, as untutored and instinctive in her as its song to a bird, as its swiftness to the chamois. To see Cigarette was like drinking light fiery wines, whose intoxication was gay as mischief, and sparkling as themselves. All the warmth of Africa, all the wit of France, all the bohemianism of the Flag, all the caprices of her sex, were in that bewitching dancing. Flashing, fluttering, circling, whirling, glancing, like a sabre's gleam, tossing like a flower's head, bounding like an antelope, launching like an arrow, darting like a falcon, skimming like a swallow; then for an instant resting as indolently, as languidly, as voluptuously, as a water-lily rests on the water's breast; Cigarette en Bacchante no man could resist.

Little Cigarette understands so well the soldier's mentality and comes out with little maxims like, '*Quand la parse est vide, l'épee mange vite*', meaning that when the soldiers are hungry, they kill so much better.

Ouida writes excitingly and grippingly about the dangers that face Bertie and Cigarette in the North African deserts, and her idea of army life, exaggerated and wild though it may be, certainly had glamour. She does occasionally linger a little too lovingly and with relish over the more gruesome horrors of battle, describing the Arab corpses piled up one upon another, the severed limbs and heads of both sides, and how Bertie, fully conscious, has a stray bullet, which has lodged beneath his breast-bone, gouged out with a knife. In the last great battle, Bertie has two horses killed under him, but still he fights on courageously, even though the situation seems hopeless; in one hand he holds his sword, hacking down the oncoming flood of Bedouins, and in the other hand he holds high the flag of the eagle of the Bonapartes.

> It was bitter, stifling, cruel work; with their mouths choked with sand, with their throats caked with thirst, with their eyes blind with smoke; cramped as in a vice, scorched with the blaze of powder, covered with blood and dust; while the steel was thrust through nerve and sinew, or the shot ploughed through bone and flesh.

Cigarette falls in love with Bertie between and during these wild battles, but is too proud to admit it. Instead, she saves his life several times, arriving with reinforcements in the nick of time, or dragging his half-dead body out from beneath a suffocating pile of corpses. In her final life-saving bid, she sacrifices her own life for his, in a complete reversal of the code of chivalry. Bertie, owing to the unjust workings of Justice, is condemned to death by firing squad. As he is about to be executed—he himself gives the orders to the soldiers to fire—Cigarette appears on the horizon, breathless and staggering. 'Wait! in the name of France', she cries and throws herself in front of Cecil so that her warm young body receives the bullets. 'O God! my child! they have killed you!'

says Bertie, as Cigarette sinks to the earth at his feet. But she is not quite dead. There is still enough breath in her to declare her passionate, hopeless, imperishable love for him.

'My darling!—my darling! what have I done to be worthy of such love?' he murmured, while the tears fell from his blinded eyes, and his head drooped until his lips met hers. At the first utterance of that word between them, at the unconscious tenderness of his kisses that had the anguish of farewell in them, the colour suddenly flushed all over her blanched face; she trembled in his arms, and a great shivering sigh ran through her. It came too late, this warmth of love. She learned what its sweetness might have been only when her lips grew numb, and her eyes sightless and her heart without pulse, and her senses without consciousness.

'If I could only see France once more! France—'

It was the last word upon her utterance; her eyes met Cecil's in one fleeting upward glance of unutterable tenderness then with her hands still stretched out westward to where her country was, and with the dauntless heroism of her smile upon her face like light, she gave a tired sigh as of a child that sinks to sleep, and in the midst of her Army of Africa the Little One lay dead.

This is a fine example of a hopeless fatal love. But even if she had lived, it is doubtful if Cigarette would have been happy with Bertie Cecil, for despite all his protestations of love to the dying Cigarette, he returns to England and, with little more than an aching heart, promptly marries his aristocratic girlfriend. But the real hero of the story, anyway, is the amazing horse, Forest King, who, despite years of separation, instantly recognises his master on his return.

Sleeping—with the sun on his grey silken skin, and the flies driven off with a dreamy switch of his tail, and the grasses odorous about his hoofs, with dog-violets, and cowslips, and wild thyme—sleeping, yet not so surely but at one voice he started and raised his head with all the eager grace of his youth, and gave a murmuring noise of welcome and delight. He had known that voice in an instant, though for so many years his ear had never thrilled to it; Forest King had never forgotten. Now, scarce a day passed but what it spoke to him some word of greeting or of affection, and his black soft eyes would gleam with their old fire.

When Ouida wrote *Moths* (1880), in many ways her most successful novel, she abandoned the blood and thunder of battle and concentrated on revealing the 'true iniquities' of high society. The moths of the title are the fashionable international society ladies who, for all their gentle fluttering beauty, eat away at the 'ermine' of life, destroying all that is good and pure.

Ouida explains how 'one weeps for the death of children, but perhaps the change of them into callow men and worldly women is a sadder thing to see after all'.

She contrasts the follies, depravities, hypocrisies and sins of her continental aristocracy with scenes of Normandy peasants, showing the reader all the beauty, truth and simplicity of that bucolic bliss; it is almost as though she is trying to persuade herself, more than the reader, of the purity of simple rustic life when her real desire is to be in the midst of the sumptuous life of the rich.

The queen moth is Lady Dolly and Ouida opens the novel with an ironical account of Lady Dolly's distressed state of mind. 'Lady Dolly ought to have been perfectly happy. She had everything that can constitute the joys of a woman of her epoch.' Ouida catalogues the trite pleasures of this fashionable lady—among them, that she has seen her chief rival looking bilious in an unbecoming gown, that she has heard from her husband that he is going away to South America, that she has a new dress and many admirers, that she has been told a state secret by a minister, that she has had a new French play read to her three months before it is to be played in Paris, that she had seen her dearest friend cheating at cards, and above all, the prime joy of a woman of her epoch, she is staying at the smart seaside resort of Trouville.

There was a charming blue sea beside her; a balmy fluttering breeze around her, a crowd of the most fashionable sunshades of Europe before her like a bed of full-blown anemones. She had floated and bobbed and swum and splashed semi-nude, with all the other mermaids *à la mode*, and had shown that she must still be a pretty woman, pretty even in daylight, or the men would not have looked at her so; and yet with all this she was not enjoying herself. It was very hard.

The reason for Lady Dolly's distress is that her nubile sixteen-year-old daughter, Vere, is coming to stay with her and Lady Dolly fears it will upset her own fun. For a start, the presence of a sixteen-year-old daughter will make it abundantly clear that Lady Dolly is rather older than she has been pretending she is. Furthermore, Lady Dolly sees her daughter as being a possible threat to her own amorous intrigues. But when Vere arrives it is clear that she is in no way part of society.

Lady Dolly stands for all that is corrupt and artificial. Vere on the other hand is a child of nature and represents purity and innocence. Her face is quite colourless, with a complexion like the leaf of a white rose. 'Her fair hair was cut square over her brows, and loosely knotted behind; she had a beautiful serious mouth, not so small as her mother's, and serene eyes, as grey as night, contemplative, yet wistful.' She is, in summary, 'like Burne-Jones's things and all that'. To illustrate further the natural wholesomeness that Vere stands for, in contrast to her mother's society pastimes, Vere is shown to be interested in healthy, outdoor—but definitely boyish—activities: she can ride, shoot, row, sail and steer a boat; moreover, best of all she likes Greek, and after that, music. Vere causes a riot in Trouville society with her odd, *ingénue* appearance and her unsophisticated ways. Lady Dolly is particularly upset when her daughter is seen on the beach, barefooted, dressed in a coarse unbleached holland dress:

> It was brown holland, naked and not ashamed, unadorned and barbaric, without any attempt at disguise of itself, and looking wet and wrinkled from sea-water, and very brown indeed beside the fresh and ethereal costumes of the ladies gathered there, that looked like bubbles just blown in a thousand hues to float upon the breeze.

Lady Dolly tries half-heartedly to make her bizarre daughter socially acceptable, but the relationship between them goes badly from the start.

> 'Dear me! What a pity!—You might have come and jumped about tonight if you had only had something to wear. Of course you like dancing?'
> 'I dislike it very much.'
> 'Dear me! Ah well! You won't say so after a cotillon or two. You shall have a cotillon that Zouroff leads; there is nobody better. Good night, my sweet Vera. Mind, I shall always call you Vera. It sounds so Russian and nice, and is much prettier than Vere.'
> 'I do not think so, mother, and I am not Russian.'
> 'You are very contradictory and opinionated; much too opinionated for a girl. It is horrid in a girl to have opinions.'

In order to rid herself of this embarrassing progeny, Lady Dolly plans to marry her off to the Russian Prince Zouroff, a rich brute of a man who has, in the past, been Lady Dolly's own lover. It was this particular aspect of Ouida's immorality that her generation found especially shocking and exciting. Even by today's standards, it is not very acceptable for a woman to sell her nubile daughter to an ex-lover. Vere, however, falls in love with de Corrèze, a famous opera-singer (based on Mario, the world-renowned opera-singer of Ouida's time, with whom she believed herself to be madly in love).

It is, of course, music which brings Vere and de Corrèze together, and which, moreover, symbolises the purity of their love. Vere is going for an early morning walk beside the sea when she comes across de Corrèze, who is practising his arias on a rock at dawn.

> Suddenly a voice from the waves, as it seemed, began to chaunt parts of the Requiem of Mozart. It was a voice pure as a lark's, rich as an organ's swell, tender as love's first embrace, marvellously melodious, in a word, that rarity which the earth is seldom blessed enough to hear from more than one mortal throat in any century: it was a perfectly beautiful tenor voice.

Ouida tries hard, piling up metaphors and similes to convey the effect that the emotional experience of listening to music can have on a sensitive person. The effect it has on Vere on this particular occasion as she sits wistfully on her rock, 'entranced by the surpassing beauty and melody of his singing' is rather bizarre. She is struck dumb, her eyes dilate, and she almost stops breathing. But this is nothing to the effect de Corrèze's singing has on her when she hears him some years later, singing in the Paris Opera House:

> It thrilled through the house, that exquisite and mysterious music of the human voice, seeming to bring with it the echo of a heaven for ever lost ... Vere's heart stood still; then seemed to leap in her breast as with a throb of new warm life ... The ear has its ecstasy as have other senses, and this ecstasy for the moment held in suspense all other emotion, all other memory.

Music, as de Corrèze explains to Vere, can only have a transitory value:

> 'After all, the fame of a singer can never be but a breath, a sound through a reed. When our lips are once shut there is on us for ever eternal silence. Who can remember a

summer-breeze when it has passed by, or tell in any after-time how a laugh or a sigh sounded?'

But Ouida attempts to give it permanency (the inventions for recording sounds were still only in their infancy in the 1880s) by her emotive and lyrical descriptions of how Vere hears it. When Vere listens to de Corrèze singing the songs of Gounod's Romeo, 'the passionate music bursts into the very silence', 'seems to pierce the very heavens' and finally, 'sinks as low and sweet and soft as a lover's sigh of joy'. When it stops Vere gives a great breathless cry 'as if something beautiful were dead'.

Vere, sitting on her rock listening to de Corrèze, is cut off from the mainland by the tide, and when he has led her to safety, they fall in love. Their love represents the purity and innocence of the natural world, and to indicate this, Ouida shows the simple rustic things they do together: when Vere (who has lost her shoes) cuts her feet, de Corrèze teaches her the country art of binding grass around them; then they go to a simple village full of pure, happy peasants and eat a meal of simple homely food—a wooden bowl of milk, honey, brown bread, cherries.

Although his love stands for purity, de Corrèze also stands for musical sensitivity, and this gives him immunity from the contaminations of the high-society world in which, as an opera singer, he has to mix. He manages to be in that world, but not of it. Only he, of all the characters in the novel, really appreciates the true wickedness of society. He fears for Vere's innocence, and in a speech which comes with al-most hysterical sincerity straight from Ouida's own heart, he tries to warn Vere:

'This world you will be launched in does no woman good. It is a world of moths. Half the moths are burning them-selves in feverish frailty, the other half are corroding and consuming all that they touch. Do not become of either kind. You are made for something better than a moth.

You will be tempted; you will be laughed at; you will be surrounded with the most insidious sort of evil example, namely that which does not look like evil one whit more than the belladonna berry looks like death. The women of your time are not, perhaps, the worst the world has seen, but they are certainly the most contemptible. They have dethroned grace; they have driven out honour; they have succeeded in making men ashamed of the sex of their mothers; and they have set up nothing in the stead of all they have destroyed except a feverish frenzy for amusement and an idiotic imitation of vice. You cannot understand me now, but you will see it—too soon. They will try to make you like them. Do not let them succeed. You have truth, innocence, and serenity—treasure them. The women of your day will ridicule you, and tell you it is an old-fashioned triad, out of date, like the Graces; but do not listen. It is a triad without which no woman is truly beautiful, and without which no man's love for her can be pure. I would fain say more to you, but I am afraid to tell you what you do not know; and woe to those by whom such knowledge comes first! *Mon enfant,* adieu.'

All de Corrèze's worst predictions come true. Vere is quickly married off to the barbarian Russian, Prince Zouroff. It is as though 'her girlhood had been killed in her as a spring blossom is crushed by a rough hot hand that, meaning to caress it, kills it'. A mere week after the marriage, Zouroff is crashing about tearing roses to pieces in his anger at having married a sullen unco-operative wife. 'Come to breakfast,' he orders carelessly. 'We will leave for Russia tonight.' Smiling grimly, he hurries her away to his ancestral palace, Hotel Zouroff, in St. Petersburg.

The house was grand, gorgeous, brilliant; adorned in the taste of the Second Empire to which it belonged; glittering and over-laden, superb yet meretricious. The lines of servants were bowing low; the gilded gaseliers were glowing with light, there were masses of camelias and azaleas,

beautiful and scentless, and heavy odours of burnt pas-
tilles on the heated air.

But in the glittering world of St. Petersburg, Vere is not
happy either. 'The girl who had gone to bed with the sun
and risen with it, who'd thought it simple pleasure to find
her first primrose was now Princess Vera, and was for ever in
the glare, the unrest, and the splendour of a great society.'
Ouida was obviously very pleased with her analogy of the
moths, for de Corrèze keeps on worrying about them:

> The moths will corrupt her ... the moths will eat all that
> fine and delicate feeling away, little by little; the moths
> of the world will eat the unselfishness first, and then the
> innocence, and then the honesty, and then the decency;
> no one will see them eating, no one will see the havoc
> being wrought; but little by little the fine fabric will go,
> and in its place will be dust. Ah, the pity of it! The pity
> of it! The webs come out of the great weaver's loom lovely
> enough, but the moths of the world eat them all.

Presumably de Corrèze could have prevented Vere's corruption by marrying her himself, but then there would have
been no story worth telling.
Vere gives birth to a baby, but it soon dies and she feels
once again that her life has been crushed out by her husband
as white roses are crushed by a hand. With meaningful symbolism (and alliteration) she proceeds to cruelly crush a cluster of white roses on the terrace of her palace. Ouida is not
unaware of the terrible plight she had put her heroine in. It
is her opportunity to give her readers some home-spun philosophy about the cruel nature of life:

> Young lives are tossed upon the stream of the world, like
> rose-leaves on a fast-running river, and the rose-leaves are
> blamed if the river be too strong and too swift for them,
> and they perish. It is the fault of the rose-leaves. When she
> (Vere) thought that this life must endure all her life, she

felt a despair that numbed her, as frost kills a flower. To the very young, life looks so long.

The love between Vere and de Corrèze continues spasmodically. They meet every so often briefly, to yearn and long and suffer the agony of unconsummated passion. But though there can be no physical consummation, they do share spiritual communion through music—when she hears him sing either in an opera house, or at a fashionable soireé when he sings a love song directly to her, and she is the only person in the assembly who understands its full implications. Ouida does not depict these lovers as totally smug in their sexual continence. Their chastity would be worthless as a symbol if they were not tempted as others are. They *do* feel sexual desires, but Vere thrusts the temptation from her with a phallic simile, 'as though it were a coiling snake', and begs him to leave her.

'If you love me indeed, leave me; there is sin enough, shame enough, spare me more. If indeed you love me, be my good angel—not my tempter!'

He was pierced to the heart; he, the lover of so many women, knew well that moment in the lives of all women who love, and are loved, when they sink in a trance of ecstasy and pain, and yield scarce knowing that they yield, and are as easily drawn downward to their doom as a boat into the whirlpool. He saw that this moment had come to her, as it comes to every woman into whose life has entered love. He saw that he might be the master of her fate and her.

For an instant the temptation seized him, like a flame that wrapped him in its fire from head to foot. But the appeal to his strength and to his pity called to him from out that mist and heat of passion and desire. All that was generous, that was chivalrous, that was heroic, in him, answered to the cry. All at once it seemed to him base— base, with the lowest sort of cowardice—to try and drag the pure and soft spirit to earth, to try and make her one

Ouida, from a photograph taken about 1870

Shadowed Lives by Annie S. Swan. Left, the frontispiece to the 1888 edition; right, the jacket picture of Oliphants Castle Series.

with the women she abhorred. He took her hands, and
pressed them close against his aching heart.

'Better angels than I should be with you,' he murmured;
'but at least I will try and save you from devils. No man's
love is fit for you. I will go, and I will never return.'

Prince Zouroff, still smiling grimly and crushing roses, has
long since stopped behaving like Vere's husband and is enjoying himself at the great gambling-tables of Europe, with a
couple of tarts—a half-mulatto girl called Casse-une-Croute
and Aimée Pincée, an ex-circus rider from the Hippodrome,
who both sound more lively than the 'white rose Vere', who
retreats to a self-imposed exile in Poland. The thoughtless
recklessness of Prince Zouroff is shown by his excessive brandy
drinking and his sport of shooting glass drops off chandeliers.

Zouroff and de Corrèze engage in a duel over Vere's
honour; de Corrèze nobly, and rather stupidly, shoots deliberately up into the air, but Zouroff cunningly shoots
de Corrèze through the throat, without killing him. 'All the
fame of his life and its splendour were snapped asunder in
their prime and perfection as a flower is broken off in full
blossom.'

'I have shot your nightingale through the throat. He will
sing no more!' Zouroff writes to Vere. By destroying de
Corrèze's singing voice—that symbol of purity and beauty—
Zouroff has ultimately proved himself unworthy of Vere's
marital fidelity. She takes off her wedding-ring and tramples
it underfoot, leaps into a sledge and at dead of night 'with
the stars burning in the steel-hued sky', and alone except for
her dog, she speeds across the frozen steppes of Poland, with
the wolves howling all around, to Corrèze's bedside in Paris.
Although it might have seemed up to now as though she only
loved him for his exquisite voice and the ecstasies it caused
in her ears, this is not the case. Even though he is now dumb,
she still loves him. She leaves the barbarous Prince Zouroff
(who rapidly has the marriage annulled and marries Duchesse
de Somaz), and flees with de Corrèze to the heart of the Alps
where the air is 'pure and clear as crystal, strong as wine'.

Strengthened, if not inebriated by this heady air, de Corrèze makes good his losses and starts to write music instead. The couple settle down to a quiet life of illicit, but musical, bliss. Vere is nearly as lovely as before, but not quite, for the corruption of moths is not reversible.

> From her memory the pollution of her marriage never can pass away, and to her purity, her life is for ever defiled by those dead years, which are like millstones hung about her neck ... she was innocent always, and yet ... When the moths have gnawed the ermine, no power in heaven or earth can make it ever again altogether what once it was.

The last word, as the first, is with Lady Dolly, who sits miserable with self-pity in her fan-lined boudoir in Hyde Park, being comforted by her lady friends:

> 'Everything is so dreadful ... Only to think that I cannot know my own daughter! And then to have to wear one's hair flat, and the bonnets are so stupid, not becoming, say what they like, and the season is so stupid.'

While she was writing *Moths* Ouida imagined herself into the role of Princess Vere. 'She would receive her guests arrayed from top to toe in white satin, seated in a red-satin upholstered armchair with an air of languid artificiality that was exasperating for her friends to bear.' But Ouida herself did not have the beautiful end of her heroine Vere in the alcoholic mountain air. Despite her enormous popularity, as she grew older she became increasingly eccentric and cantankerous towards her publishers, and finally died in squalor and total poverty. Her well-wishers erected to her memory a memorial drinking fountain for horses and dogs, in Bury St. Edmunds, with this inscription:

> Here may God's creatures whom she loved assuage
> her tender soul as they drink.

7

Ah! Love, my Hope is Swooning in my Heart or the Death of the Three-Decker Novel

'MAKE 'EM LAUGH, make 'em cry, make 'em *wait*,' was Wilkie Collins's maxim for successful popular writing. The three main ingredients of a good novel, he claimed, were an intricate plot, some humour, and a bit of a love-story thrown in. Victorian readers also required some sensational element that would make them gape with wonder and gasp with horror. It could be of a macabre, or supernatural or sexual nature. But Wilkie Collins tended on the whole to avoid sexual sensation. Although he did not attempt to convert readers to any religious persuasion, or even exhibit any strong religious inclinations in any direction, he still held a straightforward code of right and wrong, and his fiction was clean and wholesome. His novels are often criticised today as being little more than mechanical contrivances of suspense, thrills and plot written solely to satisfy word-hungry audiences. While no one can claim that his work is highly sophisticated, it is considerably preferable to much of today's equivalent, but amoral, thriller-violence fiction.

His recipe for successful formula-writing was adapted for her own use by one of the most popular writers of romance of the seventies and eighties, Mary Elizabeth Braddon, who was cited by her publishers as 'The Queen of the Circulating Libraries'.

No one can be dull [they claimed] who has a novel by Miss

Braddon in hand. The most tiresome journey is beguiled, and the most wearisome illness is brightened, by any one of her books. Miss Braddon is the Queen of the circulating libraries.

Her well-known titles include *Henry Dunbar, Strangers and Pilgrims, Sir Jasper's Tenant, Eleanor's Victory*, but she will be remembered best for her novel *Lady Audley's Secret* (1862) about a beautiful, angel-faced lady who murders her husband by pushing him down a well. Three editions of this novel sold out within ten days of its publication, and there went on to be another five editions within the first three months. It owed something of its success to the impact made two years earlier by Wilkie Collins's *The Woman in White* (1860), which has been called the first-ever detective novel. The public had thus been prepared for the new kind of writing, the mystery-thriller or mystery-romance.

Miss Braddon was an efficient, intelligent and self-controlled writer. Certainly she exercised more control over her plots than either Ouida or Rhoda Broughton ever showed themselves capable of. But although Miss Braddon was never carried away, Ouida-style, by the emotions of her characters, she was wary enough of the requirements of her readers to include a proportion of passionate intrigue in her novels. But the emphasis is on intrigue rather than physical passion; amorous scenes are always restrained and there are few heaving breasts or breathless kisses. The 'sensational' matter tended to rely instead on violent death, madhouses, deceit, treachery, suicide, arson and mislaid corpses. Despite this, she always hung on to a strong, simplistic moral tone: virtue triumphs, and wrong-doing is punished, in some retributory way, although not usually till the end of the story. In *Charlotte's Inheritance* the villain of the story dies, in the last chapter, of exposure one wintry night and is discovered in the morning, lying on the heroine's doorstep covered in snow and frozen solid.

This mixture of mystery plus violence plus passion plus the ultimate triumph of goodness proved extremely palatable to her readers and, besides sixty-odd novels, Miss Braddon also wrote numerous stories and serials for the monthly magazines. But her ingenuity was not necessarily stretched to its limits. Permutations of the same plots and characters turn up repeatedly. One theme of which she seemed particularly fond was that of the young girl whose beauty and apparent innocence bely her true nature which is conniving and evil. This is the theme of the best-seller *Lady Audley's Secret*, and reappears in a slightly altered form in *Taken at the Flood* (1875).

The moral of *Taken at the Flood* points out the sin, and the foolishness, of marrying, not for love, but for material gain. The lovely heroine, although she does not actually resort to murder like the heroine of *Lady Audley's Secret*, spurns her humble but honest lover, and pursues instead the sixty-year-old lord-of-the-manor; having married him she has him shut up in a madhouse. Possibly Miss Braddon had a personal dislike of attractive young girls; more likely, she knew that her older female readers could draw comfort from stories which showed that all that glitters is not gold.

For all its worthlessness, the glitter of the girls is nonetheless described meticulously. Lavish descriptions of a heroine's attire had not yet become a traditional part of romantic fiction as they did later, particularly in historical romance where detailed and accurate accounts of 'period' costume are an integral feature. In some romantic fiction of the 1950s and 1960s the account of the heroine's outward appearance is developed to such an extent that one is given a peepshow of her entire toilette, rather in the nature of a Louis XIV *levée*, including a description of her bath, the putting on of her underclothes as well as her outer ones, the application of her make-up, and the combing out of her hair. But some indication, however slight, of the heroine's physical attributes has always been an important part of the romantic novel, and Miss Braddon indulged herself as much in detailed descriptions of the wicked heroines as in the innocent.

Sylvia Carew, heroine of *Taken at the Flood*, was quite

amazingly lovely, strictly according to the style of the time:

> Perhaps the greatest attraction of her beauty lies in its rarity. She follows no common type of loveliness; her placid beauty recalls the form and colouring of an old Venetian picture. The features are classic in their delicate regularity. The nose, straight and finely chiselled, the upper lip short, the mouth a cupid's bow, but the lips somewhat—the veriest trifle—thinner than they should be for perfection; the chin short, round and dimpled, the forehead low and broad, the shape of the face an oval.
>
> The colouring is more striking. Sylvia is exquisitely fair —that alabaster fairness—with no more bloom than the heart of a blush rose—which is in itself almost sufficient for beauty. But this complexion, which by itself might be an insipid loveliness, is relieved by eyes of darkest, deepest hazel; that liquid brown which the Venetian masters knew so well how to paint; eyes of surpassing softness, of incomparable beauty.

The first hint that beneath Sylvia's 'old Venetian picture loveliness' lurks something sinister lies in the fact that those lips are the veriest trifle thinner than they should be. Thin lips, whether they are on a man or a woman, are a sign of a mean nature. Another hint for the discerning reader that Sylvia's heart does not match her beauty comes in a further discussion of her hair.

> The rich warm brown has a tinge of reddish gold, and female critics aver that Sylvia has red hair. They do not deny her beauty. That is beyond criticism. They merely allege the fact. Sylvia's hair is red.

And red hair, in romantic fiction, is very significant. In real life one may know of quiet mousy redheads, or gentle, helpful ones. But in romantic fiction it indicates at the very least a fiery temperament, but generally something far worse.

Descriptions of the hero's and heroine's hair, its colour,

quality and quantity, have always been important in romance. In 1867 Mrs. Oliphant noted with some distaste the frequent references to hair in Ouida's novels:

> We note, in glancing here and there through the luscious pages, that there is always either a mass of glorious hair lying across a man's breast, or a lady's white and jewelled fingers are twined in a gentleman's chestnut or raven curls —preferably chestnut ... The amount of use got out of ... (this) ... powerful agent in *Strathmore* and *Idalia*, seems something remarkable. Hair, indeed, in general, has become one of the leading properties in fiction.
>
> (*Blackwoods*, 1867)

Today, it is still one of the leading properties, and a heroine's hair never seems to get lank or greasy but remains like 'gold silk' or 'pure gold'.

In Miss Braddon's *Taken at the Flood* (1875) the red-haired Sylvia's true nature remains latent at first. To begin with, Sylvia is delightfully, naturally in love with Edmund, a good-looking, humble, but pure-hearted man with an honest face, clear grey eyes and a suntanned 'country gentleman's complexion'. Their relationship follows the standard course with secret meetings at dusk beneath the trysting tree, wild-rose blushes brightening the young girl's face, and an angry father who complains that Sylvia goes out a-walking in the lanes too late and too often. Undeterred, she meets her up-right Edmund, and as they stand beneath the boughs of a spreading chestnut tree, he 'plights his troth'. At any rate, he says with great feeling, ' "My Sylvia!" ' as if a world of meaning were shut within the compass of those two words'. But once Sylvia's cunning ambitions to marry the rich old squire, Sir Aubrey, have begun to show themselves, the story moves rapidly forward under such interest-arousing chapter-headings as: 'Sylvia Writes a Letter', 'Sir Aubrey is Interested', 'His Interest Deepens'. The plot, like Sir Aubrey's interest, continues to deepen and the chapter-headings become increasingly histrionic: 'Passion's Passing Bell', 'Alas! Our Lips

are held so far apart', 'Love, Thou Art Leading me from
Wintry Cold', 'A Useless Life is an Early Grave', 'Ah! Love,
my hope is swooning in my heart', 'Who said "Let Death
come now! 'Tis Right to Die!"?' and 'The Purple Light of
Love'.

The title, *Taken at the Flood*, refers to the line in *Julius
Caesar*, 'There is a tide in the affairs of men, Which taken
at the flood leads on to fortune'. Sylvia wishes to do just that,
to lead herself on to Sir Aubrey's fortune. Having successfully
married him, she then has to get rid of him. Conveniently,
Sir Aubrey's lunatic paralytic brother, Mordred, has died in
a madhouse. Before anyone discovers the death Sylvia dresses
up Mordred's corpse to look like Sir Aubrey; she then has Sir
Aubrey disguised as his brother and shut up in his place in
the madhouse. Why he does not protest at this indignity is
not fully explained. Meanwhile, in all her schemings, Sylvia
has the assistance of an old housekeeper who turns out to be
her own, presumed dead, mother. This summary may seem
complicated. The original plot is even more so. Miss Braddon's plots, although not flamboyantly extravagant like those
of Ouida, are always involved; in another of her novels, *Only
a Clod*, the plot is so complicated that not only the reader,
but also one of the characters in the book finds himself confused by events. ' "Is this the plot of a French novel?" he
asks of one of the other characters. "If it is you had better
tell us the title of the book, and let us read it in the original.
There may be some chance of our thinking it interesting
then." '

With Sir Aubrey safely and unprotestingly locked away in
a darkened room, Sylvia is free to marry her original suitor,
young Edmund. But the marriage ceremony is dramatically
interrupted by the arrival of a sly Jew, Shadrach Bain, who
slides in and out of the narrative whenever the reader's interest
may be flagging. ' "What can you have to say?" asked Sylvia,
looking up at him. Great heaven, what a blanched, death-like
face she lifted from the shelter of her lover's breast; from
brow to lip white as her wedding veil!' Shadrach Bain, who
has himself always been in love with this heartless heroine

but has been thwarted, ultimately gets his revenge by revealing all Sylvia's misdeeds and thus bringing about the conclusion of the story. Sylvia duly gets her punishment by being struck down with the plague. As she lies on her deathbed, she reflects on her sins and concludes that the search for material richness does not bring happiness after all.

> She lifted her eyes to that glad summer sky, and thought how the sunlight and summer of her life had passed away for ever.
> 'I have tried to be fortunate as well as happy—tried to have all good things,' she reflected, 'and in trying for too much have lost all.'

So that there might be a final reconciliation-scene, Sylvia's first suitor, Edmund, comes and sits with her during her last hours. Their deathbed embrace is not unlike the last deathbed kiss in Rhoda Broughton's *Red As a Rose Is She*, except that for that dying heroine, the innocent Esther, there was a last-minute reprieve from expiry and she recovered. For the corrupt sinner Sylvia death is irreversible.

> Once, very near the end, there came a gleam of light. The lips, which had been voiceless for many hours, moved faintly, and Edmund, leaning down to catch the feeble whisper, heard Sylvia's last words, 'Kiss me once again before I go —as you kissed me in the churchyard—before I betrayed you...'
> Living and dying lips met in the last kiss that had been fatal.

With Sylvia out of the way, upstanding Edmund is able to become an M.P., marry a worthy, domesticated girl and settle into a quiet life of connubial bliss in Berkeley Square. And the story, overcoming the wickedness and treachery of the earlier part, ends on the required note of moral optimism: 'Thus the peaceful domestic life flows on—happy and not unuseful—not that empty and unprofitable life which Goethe has called worse than an early grave.' In this sentence, which may seem out of context and virtually meaningless, Miss Braddon manages to convey exactly the right sentiment of middle-class respectability and wholesome uplift.

Romantic novelists are often embarrassingly prolific. Miss Braddon is no exception to this. But though at first her sixty novels may seem to be solely preoccupied with feminine treacheries and lovely-faced murderesses, she does not always portray this disillusioned view of young women. There are heroines who are perfectly pure, even despite their ever-so-slightly red hair. *Vixen* (1879) is a romance about a thoroughly likeable girl. Instead of being the sinner, she herself is the innocent victim of the trespasses of others. For no heroine, however pure, is truly a heroine unless a number of dreadful things happen to her, in order to prolong by complication, misunderstanding, chance, death and the evil machinations of others, the blissful moment when she is united with her true love. 'You were certainly destined from your cradle, Evelina, to be a heroine, and no heroine can expect to pass through life without many sharp trials.' (C. Pardoe, *The Confessions of a Pretty Woman*, a nineteenth-century railway novel.)

In present-day romances there is increasing reliance on fate or natural disaster (avalanches, runaway buses, air crashes) to complicate the life of the heroine, for the concept of evil as a real and destructive force is no longer so acceptable, and the out-and-out villain, too, is a dying breed (with the exception of some of the romances of Barbara Cartland, where sin is the synonym for illicit sexual intercourse, and a villain is a seducer). Where there *are* characters who have clearly done wrong, their wrong-doings are frequently excused or explained away by some home-spun, or vaguely-defined, popular psychological disorder such as schizophrenia brought about by an unhappy childhood. Today's readers are presumably more soft-hearted than those of the last century, and would rather see villains carted off in a padded van to the mental hospital than led to the executioner's chamber.

But at the time when Miss Braddon was writing *Vixen*,

psycho-analytical study was still in its infancy; so villains were still a possibility, and evil a living force.

> The purple veins stood out darkly upon his pale forehead, his eyes had a haggard look; he was like a man consumed inwardly by some evil passion that was stronger than himself—like a man possessed by devils.

It is interesting to compare Miss Braddon's description of the physical attributes of a virtuous heroine with a bad one. Both the virtuous Vixen (whose name is really Violet, anyway), and the sinful Sylvia in *Taken at the Flood*, are beautiful. Whatever the state of a romantic heroine's soul it is a convention that she does not have a limp, spots or double chins. Curiously, both Vixen and Sylvia have red hair, but it is a very different sort of red. While Sylvia's striking colouring was quite *clearly* red, Vixen's reddish-auburn masses, which tumbled down her back, were not, Miss Braddon assures us firmly, really red at all. 'The rippling hair was too warm an auburn to escape an occasional unfriendly remark from captious critics; but it was not red hair for all that.' Also, where shameless Sylvia had lovely, but thin, lips, the praiseworthy Vixen has thick ones:

> The mouth was a thought too wide; but it was a lovely mouth notwithstanding. The lips were full and firmly moulded—lips that could mean anything, from melting tenderness to sternest resolve ... the throat was full and round also, a white column supporting the tawny head, and indicated that Vixen was meant to be a powerful woman.

Vixen's lips were sometimes 'a little parted to show the whitest, evenest teeth in Hampshire', and she had a chin which was full and round and dimpled. In all, Miss Braddon concludes, she was 'lovely enough to meet the most critical connoisseur of feminine beauty'. Considering that Vixen was only meant to be fourteen years old at the time of this description, she was clearly quite a mature girl for her age.

The love-interest between her and her childhood
playfellow, titled Rorie, is played out against a background
of Hampshire county life. Their trials and tribulations in
love are intermingled with family retainers, stables, grooms,
lawn meets, balls and several good days in the hunting-field.
Vixen also has to contend with some natural deaths, a case of
suspected arson, her mother's near-incestuous marriage, her
own banishment to Jersey, and a jilting at the altar.

Miss Braddon was less willing than many romantic novelists to sacrifice everything to the love interest. Her heroine's
responses are as hypersensitive and over-written as any of
Rhoda Broughton's, but they are more often shown reacting
to violence or death than to the encircling arms of an adoring
suitor. Vixen's emotional behaviour when her dear old father
has a seizure in mid-saddle after a long day's hunting would
make any parent proud. The old man falls off his horse into
the mud. Vixen is off her mount in a flash and by her father's
side.

> He lay like a log, face downwards upon the sodden leaves
> just inside the gate. The farmer had dismounted and was
> stooping over him, bridle in hand, with a frightened face.
> 'Oh, what is it?' cried Violet frantically. 'Did the horse
> throw him—Bullfinch, his favourite horse? Is he much
> hurt? Oh, help me lift him up—help me, help me!'
> 'It wasn't the horse, miss,' said the farmer. 'I'm afraid
> it's a seizure.'
> 'A fit!' cried Vixen. —'Oh papa, papa—darling—dar-
> ling—'
> She was sobbing, clinging to him, trembling like a leaf,
> and turning a white stricken face up towards Roderick.
> 'Do something to help him, for God's sake—do some-
> thing!' she cried; 'you won't let him lie there and die for
> want of help.'

In fact, it is too late to do anything as the Squire is already
thoroughly dead of his sudden fit, but Vixen refuses to leave
him.

Miss Braddon draws the full melodramatic possibilities from the situation as, night falling, Vixen lies alone in the muddy wood, clinging on to her father's corpse in a thoroughly distraught way.

> She bent her face down to his lips.
> O God! not a flutter stirred upon her soft cheek as she laid it against those pallid lips. The lower jaw had fallen in an awful-looking way ... The crescent moon shone silver pale above that dim gray wood. The barked trunks gleamed white and spectral in the gathering dark. Owls began to hoot in the distance; frogs were awaking near at hand; belated rabbits flitted ghost-like across the track. All nature seemed of one gray shadowy hue, silvery where the moonbeams fell.

Even after her father has been decently buried, Vixen continues to grieve in a most unnaturally enthusiastic manner, persuading her mother that the Squire's study and indeed the whole house are to remain exactly as they were in his lifetime. The excesses of Vixen's mourning are as extravagant as Queen Victoria's for Prince Albert, except that in his case it is a daughter mourning her father, and not a wife her husband. Such is Vixen's reverence for her late father, one begins to suspect that she is in love with *him*, not Rorie. In fact, she is in love with her horse.

It is on Titmouse that she lavishes all her kisses and endearments and whom she calls her 'dear, darling precious treasure of a ponykins'. At times of deep distress, it is dear Titmouse who is the only friend she has left in the world, though she is quite fond of Rorie's dear horse, Blue Peter, and her father's dear horse, Bullfinch, too. In one rather half-hearted attempt at a romantic scene, when the lovers Vixen and Rorie are walking through the moonlit pine forests, their two horses accompany them, and the scene is coyly observed more from the horse's point of view than Vixen's.

Miss Braddon is much more in her element when writing of the impediments to true love than when writing of its smooth-running raptures, and she puts much passion into the writing of Vixen's moments of distress and thwarted love. There is always some twist in the tale, some excuse or mis-understanding which postpones a kiss. On the rare occasion when the lovers do seem to be making some headway (Rorie's lips are close to her pale cheek, and his arm feels every beat of her passionate heart), she ruins the romantic mood by sharply reminding him of a dreadful promise he made to his mother on her deathbed, to marry the local duke's daughter. Rorie pushes on with his declaration of love but the tone seems to have become hysterical rather than passionate:

'I will break the toils that bind me. I will be yours, and yours only. I have never truly loved any one but you, and I have loved you all my life—I never knew how dearly till of late. No, dearest love, never did I know how utterly I loved you till these last summer days which we have lived together, alone and supremely happy, in the forest that is our native land. My Violet, I will break with Mabel tomorrow. She and I were never made for one another. You and I were. Yes, love, yes; we have grown up together side by side, like the primroses and violets in the woods.'

It was acceptable for the Victorian hero to be far more sensitive, highly-strung, and histrionic than those of today. Certainly no modern hero would allow himself to make such an emotionally uncontrolled speech, nor would today's heroine find such a frank display of feeling attractive.

Lest Vixen should be carried away by Rorie's repetitious protestations of love and thus bring the story to a conclusion, a certain roguish cad, Captain Winstanley, is introduced to stir up trouble. He manages to come between not only Vixen and Rorie, but also between Vixen and her horse. He is a man with nothing but evil intent, determined to get at her inheritance in some way. Having failed to woo *her* (she is too mixed up with her horse to notice), he, in a rather sensational change of affection, not unlike the situation in Ouida's *Moths* where Prince Zouroff marries his lover's daughter, marries her

mother instead. He then sacks all the stable-hands and servants, cuts down Vixen's mother's dress allowance to £1,700,
sells Vixen's father's horse, and has Vixen banished to Jersey
where she is once more overcome with grief.

The high-society background of this story is, like that of
many of Miss Braddon's novels, sketched in with her own
special brand of affectionate irony; there is just enough mock-
ery in her descriptions to please those of her readers who
were not a part of high society.

Miss Braddon describes Vixen's mother as being so obsessed by the world of fashion that, not only is she given to
wearing extraordinary, Paris-made dresses—'Theodore's last
invention was a kind of skirt that necessitated a peculiar
gliding motion in the wearer, and was built upon the lines
of a mermaid's tail'—but also, even as she lies dying, she has
her maid read aloud to her from the *Court Journal* a detailed
account of an aristocratic lady's wedding dress:

> The bride was exquisitely attired in ivory satin, with
> flounces of old Duchesse lace, the skirt covered with tulle,
> bouilloné, and looped with garlands of orange-blossom—
>   'Pauline,' murmured the invalid feebly, 'will you never
> learn to read with expression? You are giving me the
> vaguest idea of Lady Evelyn Fitzdamer's appearance.'

Even readings from the *Court Journal* cannot keep this
woman of fashion alive for ever; and her death is just one
more of those 'many sharp trials' that Vixen, as a romantic
heroine, must pass through before her situation is resolved.
With her mother dead, the cad Captain Winstanley disappears
to South America; the deceased Squire's old horse, Bullfinch,
is given back to her, Rorie's fiancée Lady Mabel jilts him for a
lord on the eve of her wedding, and so the childhood sweethearts, Rorie and Vixen, 'the veriest boy and girl husband
and wife who had ever trodden the forest glades' are at last
united. Miss Braddon finally allows herself a bit of bucolic
sentimentality as she describes the quiet springtime wedding
in the village church, decorated 'with only the wild flowers

which the school children could gather—primroses, violets, the firstlings of the fern tribes, cowslips, and all the tribe of innocent forest blossoms, with their quaint rustic names, most of them as old as Shakespeare'. The couple, united in 'simple and unalloyed delight' set off on their six-months honeymoon to Switzerland with a promise to the servants that they will be 'back in time for the hunting'.

It was significant that Violet and Rorie of *Vixen* should choose Switzerland for their honeymoon; it reflects the growing trend, not just for the adventurous or very rich, but among the fashionable bourgeoisie too, to use Europe as their holiday playground. Rhoda Broughton observed in a novel of 1899 that 'everybody is steaming and yachting and training over the face of Europe'. In fact, in the actual context of the novel *Vixen*, the couple's choice of Switzerland seems out of character, for Rorie had earlier complained of the dullness of that country:

> 'There's a family resemblance in Swiss mountains, don't you know? They're all white—and they're all peaky. There's a likeness in Swiss lakes, too, if you come to think of it. They're all blue, and they're all wet. And Swiss villages, now, don't you think they are rather disappointing?— such a cruel plagiarism of those plaster chalets the image-men carry about the London streets, and no candle-ends burning inside to make 'em look pretty.'

But with the maturity of marriage he obviously had a change of heart and was ready to conform to the current fashion.

As the English became more widely travelled, there was an increasing craving by readers of popular fiction for foreign escapism. By the end of the century, the moral uplift of the triumph of good over evil, or the happily-ending love-story, was no longer enough. Readers wanted the added interest of some local colour. While straight romances favoured the more familiar countries of Europe, especially Switzerland and Italy, there was also the development of the thriller-

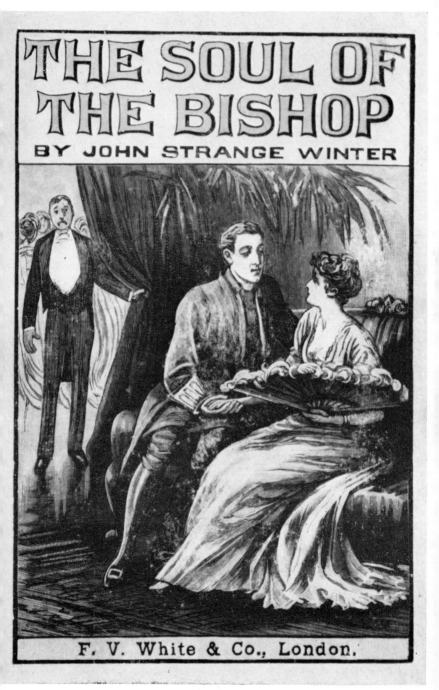

The Soul of the Bishop by John Strange Winter. Jacket picture of Fifth Edition, 1895

Florence Barclay at the time *The Rosary* was written, 1905 from *The Life of Florence Barclay by one of her daughters* (Putnam)

romance, which used the whole world for its background.

The later novels of Miss Braddon were concerned increasingly with adventure and mystery; her characters, caught up in webs of intrigue, dash recklessly from one far-flung corner of the world to another, so that they can be viewed against an ever-changing variety of background settings—Tasmania, Alaska and the Klondyke Rivers, down the South African diamond mines and then back to Mayfair and the West End.

Although she included the obligatory love interest in these thriller-romances, the plots really revolved around huge sums of money—dowries, inheritances—for which unscrupulous characters gambled, murdered and risked their honour.

Charlotte's Inheritance (1868), is the story of how all her relatives scheme to appropriate orphaned Charlotte's legacy; but there is a twist and a cloying moral to the tale, for it transpires that Charlotte's inheritance from her parents is not money at all but 'a sunny disposition and tender, unselfish nature'. Any expectations the reader may have of reading about ill-gotten financial gain are firmly replaced by a description of the exemplary Charlotte's heart 'whose innocence and affection made home a kind of earthly paradise, and gave to life's commonest things a charm that all the gold ever found in California could not have imported them'.

Another of Miss Braddon's highly moral and very curious tales is *Only a Clod*, a thriller-romance with undertones about the crumbling of the social classes, about a rich man's valet—'tall, broad-shouldered and muscular in build as a modern Hercules'—who, although he *is* only a working-class clod, turns out to be both more intelligent and more virtuous than his employer. The employer, a gentleman-villain, is a prison warden in Tasmania and his unscrupulous nature is illustrated by the fact that when he is supposed to be guarding the convicts, he sits on his balcony hopefully dreaming up means by which they could all commit suicide; they could, he reflects, eat poison, or drive rusty nails into their veins. The clod-valet finds many opportunities to 'better' himself and, as a reward for his unfailing virtue, is enabled to both woo and win the beautiful heiress that his erring employer was after. The gentleman-villain not unnaturally tries to murder him for this, leaping at him 'in a sudden rage, like a wounded tiger'. But in the end it is he who dies, of madness in a Swiss hotel, and the clod lives happily ever after with the heiress.

The standard background for the writings of Mrs. Radcliffe and other romantic novelists of the eighteenth century had been ivy-clad ruins, dark forests and fast-falling twilights; but by the end of the nineteenth century the Alps took over. The key setting was replaced by snowy mountains, frozen streams, and bright sunlight. Today, snowy mountainous districts—Switzerland, the Dolomites, Austria, the Pyrenees—still provide the archetypal romantic spectacle. Situations involving private tubercular sanatoria, skiing championships, and handsome Alpine botanists are contrived in order that the heroine can have the chance to thrill to the majestic beauty of the mountains and be invigorated by the cold wine-like air, at the same time as being involved in some worthwhile cause.

The nineteenth-century popularity of foreign settings, with a tendency towards snowy peaks in the background, is well illustrated by the fact that the best-selling, most widely read book of 1893 was *Ships That Pass in the Night*, a novel set in the sparkling winter wonderland of a German winter resort at Petersdorf. It is a story of extreme pathos and sentimentality, and its action, or rather non-action, for absolutely nothing whatsoever happens, takes place in the depressing situation of a hospital for consumptive patients, many of whom—this being 1893—had little chance of surviving their illness. The author, Beatrice Harraden, was a protégée of Mrs. Lynn Linton, which perhaps accounts for the sombre theme and the metaphors throughout, about 'The Mountains of Life', and 'The Temple of Knowledge'. The narrative is filled with self-important truisms of a vaguely philosophic, wholly banal nature, such as this: 'We start life thinking we shall build a great cathedral, a crowning glory to architecture, and we end by contriving a mud hut.' The story of *Ships That Pass in the Night*, which so captured the imagination of the public, is about a young tubercular girl, Bernadine, who goes to Petersdorf to recover or die. There she meets a man enigmatically called The Disagreeable Man, and she and the reader learn about Life.

The details of interesting local colour are provided by decriptions of frozen waterfalls, 'snow-girt' streams, great firs of the forest 'patient beneath their snow-burden', Alpine flowers 'nestling in their white nursery', 'vast plains of untouched snow, whiter than any dream of whiteness, jewelled by the sunshine with priceless diamonds, numberless as the sands of the sea'. Quaint local characters liven up the scene, too, such as 'Wärli, the little hunchback postman, a cheery soul', and a little Parisian *danseuse* who says, with touching courage which is meant to cut to the heart of one's soul:

> 'I do so want to get better, chérie. Life is so bright. Death: ah, how the very thought makes one shiver! That horrid doctor says I must not skate; it is not wise. When was I wise? Wise people don't enjoy themselves. And I have enjoyed myself and I will still.'

All human life—and death—are here; platitudes about life and death were uttered by the living and dying guests against a magical background of sparkling snow, and that was the book's appeal.

There is perhaps some link here between this kind of popular reading-matter and the Sunday colour magazines of today which present appalling facts about the brutality of the world illustrated by attractive top-quality, beautifully coloured photographic material.

Another highly popular romance of that decade was Mrs. Hoare's *A Faulty Courtship*, subtitled *A Tyrolean Romance* (1899). Its approach is similar, and about as self-important, as that of *Ships That Pass in the Night*, the difference being that it has slightly more emphasis on love than on death.

The love-story of Heinrich and Gretchen is set amongst

the Tyrolean mountains, and Mrs. Hoare thus gives herself unlimited freedom to discuss the many changing moods of the snow-capped mountains which 'reared themselves up against the sky in calm majestic beauty'. She describes too the charming chalets, the rushing torrents, the lowing cows, the mountain cascades, 'the cruel Winter when the voice of Nature is silent' and, above all, the flowers. Even at a climactic moment when Gretchen has fallen down a mountain-side (but is luckily saved from a swift and horrible death by her skirt catching in an overhanging branch), the author notes in passing which of the charming colourful Alpine flowers were in bloom at the time: 'the well-known gentian, deep-blue campanula, and bright yellow arnica'. There are also un-gainly anthropological notes on the local people. 'The Tyro-lese are hard-working and frugal, their tastes are simple, and their wants but few. They are also intensely pious, as is known wherever the traveller wanders.' The Tyrolese, as revealed by Mrs. Hoare, talk a curiously stilted language which is no doubt her way of showing that they were humble peasants, and foreigners at that.

'I like it not,' said the Frau, referring to the subject of Gretchen's absence.

'Folly wife! Where is your sense?' asked Forbach laughing. 'Gretchen is as steady as old Time.'

'The path which she has to take is slippery with the rains of last winter,' faltered the mother; 'let me go and see what has happened to our child.'

In fact, Gretchen was quite safe on the slippery paths; but her simple frugal Tyrolean parents meet a nasty end. They are crushed to death by an avalanche almost in front of Gret-chen's eyes.

'Do help me; I am nearly in despair, and no one will attend me,' she cries, flinging herself down on the snow when she has discovered they are dead. The reader is often dis-tracted from the story of the lovers by the many natural and unnatural disasters which occur abroad. The 'foreignness' of this kind of story to some extent paved the way for Elinor Glyn's *Three Weeks* in 1907, with its invented mid-European country. But although readers may have been acclimatised by *A Faulty Courtship* to taking an interest in the love-lives of foreigners, the simple pious behaviour of people like Gretchen and Heinrich can in no way have prepared the public for Elinor Glyn's new heroine, the free-thinking, free-loving princess whose liberated cosmopolitan ways were to cause such a furore in 1907.

Before the turn of the century though, another furore in the literary world, which had been boiling up for some years, finally came to a crisis. It concerned the question of the three-volume novel. Until the 1870s novels were not published in single volumes; they were always published in anything from two to seven volumes, with three volumes being the number that Mudie had chosen as most appropriate for his library. But by the mid-1870s there were murmurs and noises that this somewhat uneconomical form of novel was doomed. Publishers became aware of the advantages of by-passing the lending libraries and selling novels, at a lower price, directly to the public. But as the future well-being of the novel, in whatever form, would have repercussions both economic and literary on so many people in the literary world, publishers were not able merely to cease issuing novels in multiple volumes. Everybody in any way connected had to have their say; the whole question caused heated discussion, growing alarm, mounting suspense, indignation, and fierce correspondence. Literary societies, libraries, publishers, booksellers and, not least, authors, were all involved; all had their say. There was one angry letter in the *Pall Mall Gazette* mysteriously signed by the anonymous 'X'. The decline and death of the three-decker was in its complications and intrigue not unlike the plot of one of Miss Braddon's mystery romances.

One point, however, is quite clear: the extreme length of the three-decker novel allowed the author to digress into usually irrelevant reflections, meditations and moralisations.

But in spite of the liberty for verbosity offered by the old three-decker, most popular authors were in favour of the new one-volume form. Hall Caine, the Isle of Man novelist, said:

> I believe greatly in the single-volume form of publication for popular fiction, and since the circular (from Mudie's), I have not published any novels in three volumes ... Six shilling volumes of fiction are selling remarkably well.

And Rider Haggard, author of *King Solomon's Mines* and the Alan Quatermain stories, also approved the new form, as well he might; for *She*, his adventure story involving black and white magic, cannibalism, and the most beautiful woman in the world, aged 2,000 years, was one of the first novels ever to be issued in one volume. It was published in 1886 and sold 25,000 copies within the first three months. Even by today's standards of sales this is remarkable, but in 1886 it was especially so when one considers that for readers accustomed to borrowing from the circulating library it was quite a new step actually to buy a novel, even at the reasonable price of six shillings.

Ouida had a half-hearted inclination to preserve the old three-decker form, but Miss Braddon was one of the very few authors who actively tried to defend it. Her novel, *Sons of Fire*, was one of the last novels to be published in three volumes; this was done in 1895, almost with an air of defiance. But it was a last-ditch stand, for in that same year, the three-decker can be said to have finally died; and two years later, in 1897, only four three-volume novels were published. The gradual expiry of the circulating libraries followed soon after. Mudie's, which had caused a revolution in the reading habits of a nation during the nineteenth century, went into a steady decline in the early years of the twentieth, and was finally swallowed up by Harrods in the 1930s.

8

High Passions in Big Houses

VIEWED RETROSPECTIVELY, THE Edwardian period is a Golden Age of Romance. It is the ideal period for the nostalgic treatment of the historical romance, and its popularity with romantic novelists comes second only to the life and times of Mary, Queen of Scots; it offers all the advantages for the kind of background which transports readers from the drudgery of real life to the heady luxury and glamour of a historical past. Certainly, the popular image of Edwardian England, as many social historians have pointed out, is of a time of gaiety, extravagance, luxury and flamboyant wealth.

> From a variety of popular media the simplest among us has at least a crude impression of an aristocracy and a plutocracy whose gay and often gaudy glitter was maintained by hierarchies of submissive servants, of homes adorned—as George, Duke of York, wrote to his wife in 1901 —'with all that Art and Science can afford', the backgrounds for gargantuan dinner parties and gorgeous balls in the metropolis, and for weekend parties of near-feudal splendour in the country.
> Marghanita Laski, *Domestic Life in Edwardian England*

The picture that is found in popular fiction of the Edwardian age as one long house-party was doubtless true for a very small minority. One explanation for the wealth of this minority is given by J. B. Priestley:

> It was an era when the new wealth of the financiers was added to the old wealth of the great families of landowners. Direct taxation was still so low it could almost be ignored. The cost of living had not yet risen. Masses of domestic servants, on whom this society depended, were willing to be hired for absurdly small wages and what is more important, considered it a privilege to serve such grand people, the nobility and gentry ... The Edwardian was never a golden age, but seen across the dark years afterwards (World War I) it could easily be mistaken for one.

But the appeal of *La Belle Epoque* to today's romantic novelists is more than just the wealth. It was also a time, in the romantic myth, of feminity, a time when 'women really knew how to be women', or, more accurately, when 'ladies knew how to be ladies', for these quasi-historical romances are seldom about anybody but the rich, the reason being, presumably, that today's readers find it easier to identify with a rich, lazy (though amiable) aristocrat than with one of the overworked, under-paid, greasy kitchen-maids. Writers like Barbara Cartland are attracted, too, by the 'elegance', 'beauty', 'glamour' and 'sophistication' of the period, which can be recaptured in an 'enthralling love-story' set in 'the elegant Edwardian era', or 'a dramatic tale of the golden world of Edwardian Society'. There is, moreover, a belief that people who are wearing old-fashioned clothes are more interested in the preservation of chastity. As Barbara Cartland said recently:

> Of course, it's so much easier, let's be frank, to write a romantic book set in an old-fashioned era than today, because then virginity counts. You can write a whole book on somebody protecting their virginity as long as they're in costume—it's very difficult in a permissive society.

In fact, the society of that golden world is quite as much

remarkable for its sexual laxity and religious hypocrisy shel-
tering behind a screen of false propriety and morality, as it is
for its elegance.

As Viola, Lady Roehampton's daughter in V. Sackville-
West's *The Edwardians,* says accusingly of the society she is
obliged to mix in:

> The society you live in is composed of people who are both
> dissolute and prudent. They want to have their fun, and
> they want to keep their position. They glitter on the sur-
> face, but underneath the surface they are stupid—too
> stupid to recognise their own motives.

An important feature of best-selling writing is 'dependence
on nostalgia, the feeling that past things are moving and significant simply because they are past ... the popular novelists
can depend on this distancing of events, by itself, to create
pathos' (P. N. Furbank in *The Twentieth Century Best-
Seller, The Modern Age.*) The Edwardian period is long
enough ago for heroines to be dressed in what is considered
to be a feminine, romantic style of costume—that is to say,
wide decorated hats, long skirts, frills, leg-of-mutton sleeves
—and to enjoy the 'period' quaintness of oil lamps and horse-
drawn carriages. But, combined with the attraction of these
period accessories, is the fact that the Edwardian era, although
in the past—and thus endowed with a kind of soft glow, both
gentle and glorious—is nonetheless part of the *present*
century; it is not so lost in history as to present any serious
problems about the characters' perspective on life; there is no
difficulty of coping with a heroine's 'old-fashioned' outlook.
With an Edwardian heroine, an author can combine the advantages of a twentieth-century mind with a long skirt and a
lady's maid. The fact that there were plenty of servants in
large households is also beneficial to the atmosphere. In order
that a romantic heroine, from any period past or present,
can have the necessary free time to fall in love in the complicated way that romance demands, she must not be burdened
with the time-consuming tasks of ironing her own petticoats,

making her bed, or even just clearing the breakfast table. Today, romantic novelists are a bit pushed by the fact that servants and lady's maids aren't exactly dropping off the trees (though there is available in the world of romantic fiction a far higher proportion per household of wise, servile, loyal dailies and housekeepers than one finds in real life). The elegant Edwardian era was not an age of social conscience. There was no political unrest. God was in a convenient place —in church on Sundays. The servants were undemanding. Indeed, they appear to have enjoyed enough vicarious thrills from the ups and downs of their mistresses' love-lives not to complain about bad conditions or overwork. And, altogether, life was admirably organised for a gay time of pleasure and love.

Although today's romantic novelists view the Edwardian age through a glamorous perspective, the romantic fiction of the time was neither glamorous, elegant, feminine nor particularly golden. Until the publication of Elinor Glyn's *Three Weeks* in 1907 there were no new trends, no outstanding ideas, no new ways of falling in love: in fact, no new departures of either a religious or a sexual nature.

Although there were no new approaches to love, there were plenty of the old, for, by the beginning of the new century, the reading habits of the nation had undergone yet another revolution. The Education Act of 1870 had made elementary education available to all, and the Education Act of 1876 had made it compulsory for all, up to twelve years old.

By the turn of the century the reduction in the price of a novel from 31/6d. to 6/- had gone lower still, so that book buying and owning ceased to be the prerogative of the rich. The start of the twentieth century saw the beginning of an era when really cheap books were available to everybody. The circulating libraries, which anyway had been patronised mainly by the middle classes, were replaced by publishers' own 'libraries'. Every publishing house had at least one, and sometimes several, cheap series. Chatto and Windus offered the Piccadilly Novels at 3/6d. each, the Mayfair Library at

2/6d., the Pocket Library at 2/-, the Handy Novels at 1/6d., and finally the Popular Sixpenny Novels. Hurst and Blackett, Newnes, and Hodder and Stoughton all had Sevenpenny Libraries (Hodder and Stoughton's sevenpenny novels had a coloured frontispiece); Macmillan's had a sevenpenny and a shilling library. From Hutchinson's a reader could buy, for one shilling, a novel in 'Cloth Gilt with a Wrapper in Colours', and for sevenpence a novel printed 'in clear type on good paper, and tastefully bound in art cloth, with a designed title page, and a frontispiece on art paper'. The issuing of Collins's sevenpenny series, Collins' Handy Modern Fiction, marked, in their own words, 'the greatest revolution the world of books has ever witnessed. It is now possible to obtain for a small sum a real library of the best books by the best authors of modern times.' The volumes were, they went on, well printed, and the covers 'dainty and attractive'. These libraries consisted mainly of adventure novels, popular romantic fiction and re-issues of the popular classics. (The 'classics' now included not only George Eliot and Trollope, but also Wilkie Collins, Mrs. Henry Wood, and Miss Braddon.) Among the popular novelists who benefited from this boom in publishing were Baroness Von Hutten, Eden Phillpotts, Katherine Cecil Thurston, Kathlyn Rhodes, Mrs. Baillie-Reynolds, Mabel Barnes Grundy, May Sinclair, Mrs. Baillie-Saunders, Emma Jane Worboise, Florence Maryat, Rosa N. Carey, Mary Cholmondeley, Amelia Barr, Katharine Haviland Taylor, Mrs. Lovett Cameron, Violet Tweedale.

The romances of this period are marked for their preoccupation with material rather than spiritual values. They are endlessly about the upper classes, London society, and the rich aristocracy. There had been a period of romantic puritanism when the rich were generally wicked and self-indulgent, while animals and the poor were virtuous and sensitive. But any such Victorian sentiment had now gone. The poor had vanished from popular fiction, or at any rate had been conveniently forgotten. Thus, with no social conscience or difficult spiritual problems hanging over her, the heroine was free to enjoy or suffer the exquisite pangs of love against the background of tennis parties, tea parties, croquet parties, balls and operas, and frequent sociable weekends (known as Saturday-to-Monday visits). These stories about young women's intense feelings in big houses fulfilled an urgent need among their middle-class readers who, with their own rigid caste-system and codes of etiquette and gentility, longed to imitate the aristocracy and plutocracy whose glamorous lives they followed avidly in the picture magazines. Readers of *A Sore Temptation* by Adeline Sergeant, or *Out of the Night* by Mrs. Baillie-Saunders, *The Expensive Miss Du Cane* by S. Macnaughton, *Lady Elverton's Emeralds* by Dorothea Conyers, or *The Making of a Marchioness* by Mrs. Frances Hodgson Burnett, could have dukes and duchesses, butlers, footmen and stable hands brought into the comfort of their own front parlours without ever discovering what a sham it was. But even if any of the gaudy rich had had time to read a romance they would have been unlikely to draw attention to the inaccuracies of high life as portrayed in it for, 'The code was rigid. Within the closed circle of their own set, anybody might do as they pleased, but no scandal must leak out to the uninitiated. Appearances must be respected, though morals neglected.'—V. Sackville-West, *The Edwardians*.

'Love was one thing; middle-class virtue another' observed Sebastian, the languid aristocratic seducer in *The Edwardians*. But for the upper classes as portrayed in *fiction*, love and middle-class virtue were synonymous. A heroine's sexual purity was never in question, nor did she ever seem to experience any sensations of physical desire, but this was probably because, with all the intrigues and mistaken identities, there was never time for physical contact between lovers. The desperate adherence to morality and reputation seems quite hysterical, especially when compared to, say, the careless way some of Ouida's characters tossed aside their lovers.

Religious problems still featured in some romances of the time. *The Secret Citadel* (1913), by Isobel Clarke, tells of the marriage of a woman to a man 'not of her faith' and how she is torn between loyalty to her church and love of her husband.

But the obsessive religious preoccupations and evangelical fervours of earlier heroines were more often replaced now with occasional feelings of respectful recognition of the Church, brought on by candle-light and sweet singing.

The Edwardians' concern with physical comforts and material values is particularly well illustrated by the romance *Temptation* by Effie Adelaide Rowlands, published in 1907. Mary, a young orphan, destitute, starving and on the brink of suicide, is offered by a mysterious titled lady a life of ease and luxury and wealth if she will impersonate a missing heiress (whom she luckily resembles). Mary succumbs to the temptation and accepts a life of luxury amongst the gentry. She is immediately whisked off in a cab to become mistress of a large country house, and to have liveried servants wait on her, blazing log fires to keep her warm, an abundance of Paris-designed clothes, rooms filled with soft lights, velvet carpets, hothouse flowers and tropical palms—a house furnished, in fact, with 'all the luxury of appointment that is so necessary and so very ordinary to the very rich'.

Although the heroine's heart is temporarily 'agonised and darkened by shame', she manages to overcome this. She does not pay any penalty for succumbing to temptation, nor does she have to forfeit any of the riches that have come her way by dint of her deception. She undergoes the various difficulties and hindrances to true love that are necessitated by her position as heroine, but none of them is permanent. The past temporarily catches up with her in the form of an embittered old servant from her former life who recognises her and denounces her (proving again the Edwardian romantic tenet that the well-bred are agreeable and the poor are not). But even this predicament is overcome, and Mary is reinstated in her position of mistress of the big house. She is wooed by the local squire, Sir George, whom the other local lovelies are after but who, it conveniently turns out, is Mary's cousin, thus giving her prior claim to his heart. She marries him and thus secures for ever her position as lady of the manor.

The moral, far from suggesting that love brings its own rewards or that girls who sell their souls for material gain will endure a fate worse than death, seems to suggest quite the reverse: that ill-gotten gains bring the reward of true love, that if girls are sensible enough to sell their souls for wealth, they will probably get a title, a house, a place in society, and a good loving husband as well.

Admittedly, at the opening of *Temptation* Miss Rowlands, with lavish use of exclamation marks and repetition of 'alone', makes it clear that her young heroine is *so* destitute, her plight *so* ghastly (and she is so unused to life on a park bench) that when she made her decision she really had no alternative but to accept the offer:

> Alone in the world!
> Alone! With only seventeen years of life behind her!
> Why, she was but a child!
> Many and many a girl of her age in this rich, cruel, splendid city of London, was still guarded and protected with the care lavished on a beloved child.
> And she, poor little soul, was alone! Quite—quite alone!
> How many times had she said that over to herself, as she had sat shivering in the raw wind of this wintry November?
> She was faint with hunger, weak with the fatigue of acute mental thought, weary with much walking. How many, many miles she had walked, poor child, in her vain search for work: for the means to provide herself with food and shelter!

In an earlier novel, when authors were more concerned with the state of their heroines' souls, Mary would probably have been made nobly to face death by starvation rather than enjoy something that was not hers by right. But in this novel her temptation and submission to temptation are not presented as sin but as the outcome of fate. It is clear that she is a virtuous heroine, a sweet and lovely girl adored by her new household of servants. 'It was impossible not to like Miss Verney. She was so gentle; she had always a kind word.'

Not only a likeable girl, but a well-bred one, too. Though they might temporarily fall on hard times, heroines are invariably refined. Middle- or working-class girls did not have the manners, gentle ways and delicate faces that would encourage readers to identify with them. Blue-blooded girls have about them, even beneath sometimes shabby exteriors, a certain noble air, or a marble white skin, a finely chiselled nose, or a gracious manner of speaking which other aristocratic characters instantly recognise. Mary's good breeding is recognised by the mysterious lady who first tempted her:

> 'Your destitution cannot hide the fact that you are refined, that you are what the world calls a lady.'
> The girl's white face flushed for an instant.
> 'My father was a gentleman and a scholar.'

That she is the daughter of a scholarly gentleman is very important for two reasons. Firstly, it somehow *justifies* her behaviour; it makes her deception and impersonation of the heiress understandable and excusable: a girl brought up in society and used to a comfortable life is naturally expected to do all she can to get back there. And secondly, from the point of view of the workings of the plot, it makes it all much easier for her to slip into a place in society without anybody becoming suspicious. Only her maid, while she brushes and coils Miss Mary's lovely hair, notices something in those large sad eyes.

> 'And for all her riches,' the maid said to herself, 'she do make me sad. She has got a look in her eyes that touches me somehow. Well, if there's anybody in the world as ought to be happy, surely it's her. She's got everything in the world that she can want. I'd like to see her a little bit brighter; but perhaps that will come, for one like her there's sure to be the best of futures.'

Temptation is one of the earliest romances of Effie Adelaide Rowlands. During the thirty-odd years of her writing career, which went on until the mid-thirties, she produced over two hundred novels, all variations on the theme of love with complications, but with no marked religious, political or moral note. There is the suggestion that the state of being in love brings not only spiritual happiness but material good fortune as well. If a girl's love is true, she will marry the right man and be happy and rich for the rest of her life. Most of Effie Adelaide Rowlands' two hundred titles make her subject matter abundantly clear: *Beneath a Spell* (1910), *Brave Heart* (1911), *Love's Harvest* (1922), *Love for Love* (1922), *Brave Love* (1926), *The Love of His Life* (1927), *A Loyal Man's Love* (1907). Although the amorous ring of some of these titles may indicate a rich harvest of searing passion and tight clinches, they don't live up to their promise. Many of her heroines avoid having to kiss by fainting, 'She gave a low cry, and stretched out her hands ... she reeled forward, struggled a little, and then, catching impotently at a chair as she fell, she sank huddled and unconscious.'

The romantic novelists writing in this period at the beginning of the century had to overcome the Victorian ideal of the goodness and worthiness of the middle-classes and to reinstate members of a rich fast set as amiable characters. This attempt to raise the prestige of the aristocracy was made particularly well in some of the forty romances by Bettina, Baroness von Hutten, written between the early 1900s and the 1930s. Her lords, dukes, peers, earls, marchionesses, are friendly, lovable, human, often slightly eccentric characters. One of her noblemen, the Earl of Kingsmead, brother of the heroine of *The Halo* (1907), is a charming grubby little chap of twelve years old, on whose tousled head the coronet is unwillingly worn. Thus, the pathos of a child bearing adult responsibilities is added to aristocracy appeal.

At a time when real life lords were said to be eloping with chorus-girls, and duchesses with wandering violinists, Baroness von Hutten produced her own version of a society scandal, *Pam* (1902), her most successful romance. An aristocratic, beautiful, but wayward lady elopes with a handsome mellifluous-voiced Italian tenor, and settles in glorious but illicit love in Italy. The realism of the setting does not go far. The emphasis is on the lyrical beauty of the lovers' landscape.

Behind the villa a gentle, olive-covered slope led to the sea, and through the trees, as though they had just risen from the blue water, came Pauline Yeoland and 'the man'.

Over the softly stirring lights and shadows cast by the trees on the coarse grass, one of his arms lying across her shoulders, moving slowly, as if from pleasant fatigue, their movements harmonising like the voices in an often-sung duet, they emerged from the trees, passed up a little flight of stone steps, and came towards the house, not talking, yet evidently in closest companionship of mind and feeling.

Baroness von Hutten again gets the added value of infant pathos by blessing their union with a dewy, innocent child called Pam, who, when asked her name, replies with what is intended to be engaging frankness and touching gravity, 'Pamela, just Pamela. It appears that children whose parents are not married have only one name.'

As usual, there is a loyal servant in the background who is ill-paid for her devotion to her mistress:

Whatever one's position and station may be, one has but one life, and Jane Pilgrim had sacrificed hers that night twelve years ago, when she had accompanied her young mistress to Dover, where Sacheverel, the tenor, was awaiting them.

And while the mistress, wrapt in the perfect warmth of her great love, felt no cold, the maid, standing alone and bereft of her old garment of self-respect, shivered and ached under the bitter winds that shook her as they blew unheeded by the woman for whose sake she had denuded herself.

The joy was all Pauline Yeoland's; the shame all Jane Pilgrim's. And the natural consequence of it was that while Pauline in her happiness grew sweeter and gentler, losing the carelessness and flightiness of former days, Jane, all unrewarded, became bitterer and sharper as time went on. All of which is as things should not be, but as they sometimes are.

The tragic, innocent figure that the Baroness made out of the illegitimate girl-woman Pam was so successful that she pushed on with the pathos, and in 1906 produced *What Became of Pam*; and then in 1923 *Pam at Fifty*, and ten years after that, in 1933, *Pam's Own Story*.

Mrs. Baillie-Saunders was another popular and prolific romance-writer of the period who produced the right mixture of 'insight' into high society, popular psychology, materialism, sentimentality, and a dash of love. *London Lovers* (1906), as its title suggests, is set in sophisticated London society. The characters are fearfully occupied in dashing around in motor cars, 'talking ceaselessly in high-pitched voices', from one large country houseparty to another, and then on to the theatre, opera, race-meetings, smart restaurants, and St. Moritz. Besides the excitement of this way of life, an impression of the confusion and exhaustion of being in society comes over. Only the hero and heroine ever have time to stop and reflect about love.

It goes without saying that all heroines are waiting for love, for the supreme moment of falling in love, for the state of being in love. Some heroines are quite unaware of this impending inevitability and are caught unexpectedly by it. Other, possibly less ingenuous, heroines are fully aware of the fact that waiting for love is the whole reason for their existence. Winnie is one of these. Having been kissed in a cab by a cad, she hurries up to her room and, after scrubbing the unwanted kiss from her cheek with a handkerchief, moons into the night, dreaming of that supreme experience that lies ahead of her:

> She went and sat with her bare arms resting on the dressing-table gazing intently at the dim lovely ghost of herself that loomed out of the shadowy mirror, and again lost herself in that dream of love to be that had been awaked by the kiss of an idle wretch in an idler moment; that vision of the great-to-be, the coming, crowning glory, that she was woman enough to yearn for, and girl enough to make wholly selfish.

The man who kissed her sinned not against morals but against Love. He is seen to be a cad for kissing her when he wasn't under the influence of an irresistible passion.

The heroine, Winnie, is from a hard-up but very old family; the hero, Mordecai Levison, 'a mysterious determined-looking person with a fire in his eyes' is a Jew. The novel is, daringly, about the problems of Jews entering London society. But, as one of the gentile characters points out, 'They are everywhere now, you must admit. There are so many Jews in the best circles you can't count them. And, unfortunately, you *can* count the Christians, on one hand.'

Mrs. Baillie-Saunders' intended championship of the Jews takes the form of a patronising reverence of all that is Jewish. She is continually referring to the Levisons' 'Eastern-ness'—their eastern ways, eastern gestures, eastern appearance—and she reverently refers to the hero's mother as 'This Mother of Israel'. However, for all his eastern ways, Mordecai falls in love just as any gentile gentleman might have done in 1907:

His glance rested unhesitatingly on Winnie, while the slow blood rose to his face and temples, and a sort of jerk seemed to shatter all his habitual and subconscious notions. Winnie's face under the cherry-blossom tree suddenly caught him as something deathless, as eternity itself, eternal youth, eternal woman, eternal May. That character of Winnie's face that made it seem to partake of May mornings went into the soul of Levison, and, for the first time in his dull life, he saw a May morning; for the first time in his life he was consciously aware of cherry-blossoms; suddenly the dim secret of a blue wistaria seemed to hover into his consciousness. Winnie was chattering to a woman friend, telling her some amusing story, and her deep-set eyes were sparkling and dancing, and her whole piquant face dimpling with fun, and flecked softly with the pearly shadows of the foaming blossoms over and around her gracious head. It was a poem of motion as well as line— the lovely woman's face, the dancing blossoms, the tossing leaves, the May sunshine. It was a thing, a moment, never to be forgotten. Shakespeare might have caught and kept it for us in a sonnet. It was a second's flash of absolute beauty, a beauty expressive of the divinity of first love. To him it was the vision of the first woman in the first garden. They were the first of all cherry-flowers, and the first of all wistarias; there never had been any others. Love suddenly flung aside the petals of his prison and stepped forth, dew-blown and laughing into the first of all possible worlds.

In the view of Mrs. Baillie-Saunders, it is not so much the racial aspect of Mordecai's Jewishness which makes him an unsuitable partner for the lovely Winnie, as the religious part. As a Jew, he is apparently a heathen. He therefore undergoes a wonderful conversion during a harvest festival evensong, brought about partly by the effects of candlelight, incense, the vestments of the clergy, the ritual of the service, the old-world music, and partly by Winnie's 'stately, pure-browed beauty':

> The tune was a most haunting and melodious Gregorian, weird, and hushed, and swaying to a solemn march time. As its deep and sonorous chords came floating through the clouds of incense, it seemed to him to be a holy song to the woman of his vision. 'Bride of Christ'—the use of the word 'bride' came not in its ecclesiastical sense, but as a glorifying title to the vision of perfect beauty and purity he had conceived, the still, white woman with Winnie's face ... She was to him, in that darling moment, the beckoning of an angel to the things that are afar. Slowly the grand strains died away; the choir was departing by way of the cloisters, and their distant voices echoed softly fainter and fainter in the monotonously recurring melody, to and fro, surging, sighing, sobbing, fainting.

This ceremony is not so much a conversion to Christianity as a confirmation of his conversion to the religion of heroine worship, which had been revealed to him once and for all beneath the cherry blossoms.

Besides the preoccupations with the upper classes, there was also a growing interest in matters of the mind. The development of psychoanalytical ideas spread even into popular fiction to produce, for instance, *The Devil's Garden* (1913) by W. B. Maxwell, 'a study of elemental passions and penetrating psychology', or *The Dominant Passion* (1913) by Marguerite Bryant, a story of 'passionate hatred, enthralling characters, insight into the recesses of the human mind'.

Two other curiosities of the period were 'garden romances' and passionless romances about young girls and their jolly capers. By their vigour and sporting cheerfulness, these seem to be in many ways close to the Angela Brazil type of school story, except that they are not set in schools and that procuring a husband rather than being in the First XI is the ultimate goal of these hearty ladies. Evelyn Everett-Green wrote a number of them, including *Priscilla* (1900), *The Deerhurst Girls or a Triple Alliance* (1907), *Netta, Two boys and a Bird* (1907), and *The Romance of Miss Hilary* (1901). Many of these were published by the Society for the Promotion of Christian Knowledge and the Religious Tract Society, and were clearly aimed at young girls on the threshold of life, which perhaps accounts for the absence of passion, desire or any strong emotion. Desire in romantic fiction has always been a thing of the spirit rather than the body. Although the heroine's state of mind may be exposed, there can never be graphic descriptions of physical encounters, for romantic heroes and heroines, even those of the present day, do not have erogenous zones.

In *Priscilla* it is patriotism more than anything else which triggers off matrimony. Priscilla, while in trouble on an Austrian mountain, is greatly relieved to see the hero turn 'a square, British face up towards her'.

Among other exponents of this form were 'Rita' (*Peg, the Rake* (1894) and *Kitty, the Rag* (1896), Ethel Hueston (*Prudence Says So* (1916), and *Prudence of the Parsonage* (1915)), and Mabel Barnes Grundy (*Two in a Tent—and Jane* (1913) and *Candytuft—I mean Veronica* (1914)).

The Edwardian 'garden romances' were initially sparked

off by the successful *Elizabeth and her German Garden* (1898), by Lady Elizabeth Russell, (Countess von Arnim). It is not strictly a romance but it uses the same blend of sentimentality, quasi-poetic prose and a vague reverence for life in general, but instead of being about a lady's relationship with a man, it is about the well-bred author's own relationship with her garden, and how the changing seasons, the flowers, the birds and the beauty of the bright green whortleberry refresh her spirit. The necessary religious note is there in that the pleasant lady narrator sends grateful, admiring prayers to God every so often for creating such a world.

The tone of genteel pantheism with undertones of the gardening expert, Percy Thrower, was caught by other writers of the time, too. Even a professional bee-keeper, Edward Tickner Edwardes, turned his hand to it with *Honey-Star* (1913), 'a charming romance steeped in the fragrant atmosphere of old bee-gardens'. He was later dubbed 'the Thomas Hardy of Sussex'.

Hands of Healing (1914), by Theodore Flower Mills, was a garden story which succeeded very well in combining the love-interest with the gardening notes. A refined but poor lady, Miss Leonare, retires to an overgrown country cottage to wait for death. From the description of her, she seems at first to be about eighty, but it transpires that she is really only twenty-nine but has been jilted by a scoundrel called Henry, with whom she was once much in love. She cuts herself off from the world but finds that growing things in her garden and the delights of the countryside gradually bring her back to life.

It is spring in my life as well as in my dear, gracious garden, but here there is a constant struggle. I try to fight down the rising sap ... this pulsation of a woman's heart, which I had thought never to feel again—I cannot afford to let this make itself felt unchecked ...

My crocuses are in full glory, bands of gold, with a cluster of purple and white here and there, like a jewel or pearl and amethyst strung on a gold chain.

The narrative and the suspense are all centred around her horticultural life. Will the tulip bulbs she put in in November really come up in the spring?

> Today a barrow-load of good earth piled on the top of my new garden bed transformed a wretched poverty-stricken-looking waste plot of ground into a really respectable bed which could not disgrace any lady's property.
> Meanwhile, my green friends flourish. The young foxgloves are running up their great fat buds ever taller and taller.

A delight in gardening also helps the sap to rise again in the local squire whose wife has died. His speciality is fruit-growing, but in shared thoughts on the quality of the local earth and the possibility of planting gooseberries, love between him and Miss Leonare blossoms like their gardens.

The night before their marriage, to add a touch of melodrama, Leonare's former scoundrel lover, Henry, reappears, his wife also having died. He begs forgiveness. Leonare sticks by her gardening squire but together they agree to adopt Henry's child, Hope. And two years later 'to Hope was added a little Joy'.

Novels like this were mild, insipid and totally harmless.

9

The Spur of Religion

AT A TIME when the mainstream was moribund in themes of materialism and social intrigue, Elinor Glyn and Florence Barclay breathed a new zest back into romantic fiction.

With the publication in 1907 of Elinor Glyn's *Three Weeks*, physical passion, which hitherto had been superseded by either the more ephemeral aspects of love or by the more prosaic business of inheritances, dowries and titles, returned. Once again, as in the time of Ouida or Rhoda Broughton, romantic fiction became something controversial, shocking, and deliciously readable. But it was more than just the ardour of the kisses of *Three Weeks* that caused a stir. For the first time the hero and heroine consummated their love. It was Elinor Glyn who coined the word 'it' for 'the strange magnetism that attracts both sexes, and that is found in tigers and cats'. What is more, the lovers enjoyed their 'it', and gloried in it; and most unusual of all, they were not married to each other.

During the Edwardian period, not only was extreme importance attached to a woman's reputation, but also it was generally believed that women, well-bred ones that is, could not, or did not, enjoy sexual intercourse. In his biography, *An Edwardian Youth*, Sir Lawrence Jones relates how one of his fellow undergraduates studying medicine, asked a doctor whether women enjoyed sexual intercourse. They were told: 'Speaking as a doctor, I can tell you that nine out of

ten women are indifferent or actively dislike it; the tenth, who
enjoys it, will always be a harlot.' When there was a prevailing
current of opinion such as this, a popular heroine's obvious
enjoyment of carnal knowledge was bound to cause interest.

Florence Barclay's heart-stopper, *The Rosary*, was published in 1909. It was said to have been read and wept over
by every housemaid in the British Isles. What Florence Barclay put back into romantic fiction was deep religion. From
The Rosary onwards, heroines began once again to be
troubled by the state of their souls and their lovers' souls;
once again began to experience deep and fervent relationships
with the Lord. Mrs. Glyn's preoccupations with sex, and Mrs.
Barclay's with God may, on the face of it, seem to have little
in common, but they were both, in their different ways, ardent
revivalists of the erotic-divine message, that message which
attempts to prove, through mortal love, the existence of God
and his divine love. 'Those who enjoy passionate love-making,
tempered by religion ... will not fail to find pleasure in Mrs.
Barclay's story,' said the *Scotsman* of *The Rosary*, while Mrs.
Glyn said of her own work, 'Of all the emotions which Human
beings feel, Love is the most divine. It is the vital spark which
makes Life, it is the expression of the soul.'

Elinor Glyn explained that the purpose of love in the Creator's scheme is 'to bring a touch of heavenly happiness into
human existence and to uplift and glorify the soul of man'. So
the joyous adulterous rompings in *Three Weeks*, far from
weakening her religious message, are intended to intensify it,
for the more intense is earthly love shown to be, the more
intense is God's love thus proved to be.

Elinor Glyn had red hair and green eyes; during her honeymoon she swam naked and alone up and down the Brighton
public baths, which her new husband had hired for two days
for the specific purpose of being able to admire his bride
with her red hair trailing behind her in the water. But after
this propitious start to married life, the husband gradually
proved to be less interested in the 'divine expression of his
soul' than in the shooting of pheasants. 'I missed the romantic
love-making that I had dreamed of, but I was very much

attracted by his merry blue eyes and perfect teeth,' wrote Elinor Glyn of her husband. Many critics have suggested that the torrid passions and erotic parables she wrote were no more than the day-dreams of a frustrated wife; and she herself admitted that *Three Weeks* was written to satisfy 'the unsatisfied longings for a sympathetic companion'. But there was more to it than this. She had her earnest motives as well.

In a preface to one of the numerous editions of the notorious *Three Weeks*, she stated somewhat plaintively her two primary aims in writing the novel:

> I personally meant it very simply when I wrote it. I wanted to show the tremendous force of a great love for elevation of character, and the inevitable result of the breaking of any law, whether of God or of Man.

The elevation of character that she wished to show is clear enough; she states at intervals that her hero, having been in love, is now seeing things with different eyes, is at last appreciating the natural beauties of the world. But the message of the 'inevitable result of the breaking of any law' is harder to unearth beneath the rosy bowers she creates for illicit love.

The story of *Three Weeks* is, at its base, the far from original tale of the mature 'older woman' who befriends a young Adonis and initiates him in the arts of love—a situation with obvious advantages to both parties. In this novel, it is given an unusual twist by the fact that this 'older woman' is the fabulously beautiful, madly sexy, reigning princess of a mysterious mid-European kingdom. This country has curious, though unexplained, political difficulties (and was to some extent based on the 'Ruritania' invented by Anthony Hope in *The Prisoner of Zenda*, which had been published a few years before). The hero, Paul, aged twenty-three, a member of the English ruling classes, is 'tall, straight, fair and strong' (the variations on this include 'young, fresh and foolish' and 'young, fair and strong'); he possesses a supple lithe body, and is generally on the threshold of life, ready to be instructed in its delights. Paul is doing the Grand Tour of Europe somewhat listlessly, when he is picked up in his hotel by a mysterious lady. At least, she doesn't actually pick him up, but she makes eyes at him the whole time he is eating his dinner, and follows him up a mountain-side in a funicular railway. Paul has never seen anything like her before. It is doubtful whether the majority of readers had either. Her face is 'startlingly white, like a magnolia bloom', her throat is 'rounded and intensely white', her hands 'slender and white with that transparent whiteness of mother of pearl', and her mouth is 'straight and chiselled, and red, red, red'. To crown it all, she moves with a 'gliding, feline movement, infinitely sinuous and attractive'.

> What a figure she had! Sinuous, supple, rounded, and yet very slight.
> 'She must have the smallest possible bones,' Paul said to himself, 'because she looks all curvy and soft, and yet she is as slender as a gazelle.'

This mysterious person manages to make Paul fall in love with her, without laying a finger on him. It is all done with the power of her eyes, 'weird chameleon eyes', which seem to penetrate into his very soul. The effect is so wonderful that sometimes his heart seems to stop beating. 'They seemed to draw him—draw something out of him—intoxicate him —paralyse him.'

Having tantalised him almost beyond endurance, the lady then takes Paul under her wing and offers to teach him about love and life. They go off to spend three immortal weeks together. She lives in luxurious Slavic splendour; her hotel room is perpetually filled with eastern perfumes and an abundance of exotic hot-house flowers; she has a couch draped with a tiger-skin (a symbol in popular mythology for a particular kind of animalish sexual abandon), and piled with pillows made of expensive fabrics or embroidered in silk and gold. She has a propensity to dress in gauzy diaphanous garments, to wear quantities of priceless jewellery and often a coronet as well. Her worldliness, her sensitivity, and her many winsome ways, such as suggesting that they both drink their wine from the same glass, soon have Paul absolutely captivated. 'To say he was intoxicated with pleasure and love is to put it as it was. It seemed as if he had arrived at a zenith, and yet he knew there would be more to come.'

Sure enough, there is.

A madness of tender caressing seized her. She purred as a tiger might have done, while she undulated like a snake. She touched him with her finger-tips, she kissed his throat, his wrists, the palms of his hands, his eyelids, his hair. Strange subtle kisses, unlike the kisses of women. And often, between her purrings, she murmured love-words in some fierce language of her own, brushing his ears and his eyes with her lips the while. And through it all, Paul slept on, the Eastern perfume in the air drugging his senses.

The loving goes on and on. They travel from Lucerne, up to the mountains, then on to Venice, growing daily more in love.

Throughout the repast his lady bewildered him with her wild fascination. Never before had she seemed to collect all her moods into one subtle whole, cemented together by passionate love. It truly was a night of the gods, and the exultation of Paul's spirit had reached its zenith.

'My Paul,' she said, when at last only the rare fruits and the golden wine remained, and they were quite alone—even the musicians had retired, and their airs floated up from a gondola below. 'My Paul, I want you never to forget this night—never to think of me but as gloriously happy, clasped in your arms amid the roses. And see, we must drink once more together of our wedding wine, and complete our souls' delight.'

An eloquence seemed to come to Paul and loosen his tongue, so that he whispered back paeans of worship in language as fine as her own. And the moon flooded the loggia with her light, and the roses gave forth their scent. It was the supreme effort of art and nature to cover them with glorious joy.

'My darling one,' the lady whispered in his ear, as she lay in his arms on the couch of roses, crushed deep and half buried in their velvet leaves. 'This is our souls' wedding. In life and in death they can never part more.'

The story is lifted up from its intrinsically sordid level by being voluptuously written and by the supposedly 'noble' motives of the lovers. Elinor Glyn's own conception of the lady was:

A deep study, the analysis of a strange Slav nature, who from circumstance and education and her general view of life was beyond the ordinary laws of morality. If I were making a study of a tiger, I would not give it the attributes of a spaniel; I would still seek to portray accurately every minute instinct of that tiger to make a living picture.

The princess's motive in seducing Paul is not primarily lust, though this must come into it, but political expediency. She needs to conceive an heir of fair Aryan descent for her mid-European kingdom and she sees in Paul not just his virility, fertility and lithe supple body but also 'something straight and true in manhood'. She has, in fact, already got a husband but he is a drunken, unfaithful, evil-living hound of hell, and infertile into the bargain. This does not exonerate her from the sin of adultery, but in Elinor Glyn's view it justifies it to some extent.

Paul does not actually have any noble motives about anything, but his devoted love for the princess is shown, despite its adulterous nature, to be rather splendid, as is the fact that by fathering her child, he is to be instrumental in saving a kingdom. (The laws governing small mysterious European kingdoms are rather different from our own; apparently illegitimate infants, conceived during torrid Venetian nights, can ascend to the throne.)

While 'frenzied kissing' and 'fiercely uttered love-words'
are described with thrilling realism, the actual act of love,
necessary as it is to the plot, occurs with more discretion between paragraphs and is indicated by a line of dots, thus:
................., or else between chapters. 'Oh, glorious youth!
And still more glorious love!' ends one chapter, and the
next begins 'Who can tell the joy of their awakening?' And if
dots or the passing of time between chapters do not make it
clear that sexual intercourse has taken place, Paul's exhaustion
the following morning should.

Readers may feel cheated of a description of coition after
all the big build-up, but, as Mrs. Glyn repeatedly points out,
her aim was not to try to be as shocking as possible but to
show the 'elevation of character' which can be precipitated by
love. In Paul, the Princess had perceived 'the soul sleeping
there' and, after a night or two of love under her guidance,
that soul begins to stir. Paul's imagination is expanded. He
learns to look at and admire God's world in a new and wonderful way.

> For the first time in his life Paul saw with different eyes—
> just the beauty of things—and forgot to gauge their sport-
> ing possibilities. An infinite joy was flooding his being,
> some sensation he had not dreamed about even, of happiness
> and fulfilment.

To encourage this elevation of character, the princess edu-
cates Paul in many ways apart from love; for instance,
as they sit together in her exotic barbaric rooms, she reads
aloud to him in Latin.

The exultation of Paul's mad passion is soon followed by
sentimentality, to be followed by grief, then bitterness, and
finally tenderness mixed with joy, reverence, thankfulness
and praise; in fact, the full range of basic human emotions
is here.

At the end of the three weeks, Paul returns to England and
the lady to her Balkan kingdom where her child is born. She
sends a lock of its fine gold hair to Paul. He kisses it and cries

and two more of the fringe benefits of lust are pointed out: the birth of his own son reminds Paul of his love of God, and it also makes him realise how much *his* own mother must have loved *him*. The joy of paternity is short-lived, however, for he rapidly hears that his lover-princess had been brutally murdered by her husband. (After Elinor Glyn's portrayal of this wicked king, there was a glut of drunken, mad, devilish husbands in romantic fiction, beating their dogs, horses, servants, and occasionally their wives.) The princess's violent death was, Elinor Glyn said, 'inspired' by the real-life assassination in 1903 of Queen Draya of Servia which had caught her imagination.

With the death of his lover, Paul is overcome by a terrible grief which lasts for five years. But finally his emotion changes to glorying and praising when his child is crowned boy-king. Paul attends the coronation of the son he has never met, and finds all other feelings are swept away in the 'onsurge of tenderness'.

It was in a shaft of sunlight from the great altar window that Paul first saw his son. The tiny upright figure, in its blue velvet suit, heavily trimmed with sable, standing there proudly. A fairy, rosy-cheeked, golden-haired English child—the living reality of that miniature painted on ivory and framed in fine pearls which made the holy of holies of the Lady Henrietta's writing-table.

And as he gazed at his little son, while the organ pealed out a *Te Deum* and the sweet choir sang, a great rush of tenderness filled Paul's heart, and melted for ever the icebergs of grief and pain.

And as he knelt there, watching their child, it seemed as if his darling stood beside him, telling him that he must look up and thank God too—for in her spirit's constant love, and this glory of their son, he would one day find rest and consolation.

'The book meant everything to me; it was the outpouring of my whole nature, romantic, proud, and passionate,' Mrs. Glyn

said. She also explained, many, many times, exactly what it
was all about.

> The underlying moral of the story is made plain in the
> gradual regeneration of Paul, the full development of whose
> character is achieved only when, through loss and suffering,
> all debts are paid at last.

What strikes the reader today as being more immoral than
the couple's wholesome lust in this novel is their total dependence on luxurious aphrodisiac props to help along
their nights of bliss. Their love for one another seems,
on its own, to be not strong enough to ensure sexual content-
ment; elaborate preparations are made in each of the various
hotels they stay in. The boudoirs are turned into 'bowers of
roses', tables are heaped up with 'tuberoses, stephanotis, lilies
of the valley'; a 'cupid fountain of perfume' plays. Elaborate meals are eaten, and rare wines drunk. The princess's
own particular tipple is Tokay, the choice Hungarian grape
liqueur. On the lovers' last and most glorious night of love,
the princess even goes so far as to send to Paris (they are in
Venice) for a cook, an artist, and 'a boy with a plaintive singing voice'. She also hires violinists to play to them all evening from behind 'falling trellises of roses' (the reader may
well wonder who they were intended to fall on).

Three Weeks was, on Elinor Glyn's own admission, read
and praised by 'crowned heads, Australian bushmen, bishops,
Klondyke miners, mothers and priests of the Church'. By
1916 it had sold two million copies; by 1933 over five million.
But however well the bishops and Klondyke miners had received it, there were many others, particularly the English
press, who found it immoral and distasteful. It was even
banned in one American state. A few years after its original
publication Mrs. Glyn wrote, somewhat plaintively, that some
people had obviously misunderstood her intention and failed
to appreciate the 'deep inner meaning' of the 'thrilling story'.

> The minds of some human beings are as moles, grubbing
> in the earth for worms. They have no eyes to see God's

sky with the stars in it. To such *Three Weeks* will be but a sensual record of passion. But those who do look up beyond the material will understand the deep, pure love, and the Soul in it all, and they will realise that to such a nature as 'the Lady's', passion would never have run riot until it was sated—she would have daily grown nobler in her desire to make her Loved One's son a splendid man.

Undeterred by the criticisms of mole-like minds, she went on producing dozens of romances well into the thirties, with such titles as *Glorious Flames* (1932), *The Great Moment* (1923), but, possibly owing to later acute financial problems which compelled her to support her mother, husband and daughters by her writings, messages of divine love gave way increasingly to the 'sensual record of passion'. The heroes are men with 'wild earthy passions' and splendid eyes which 'blaze with the passions of wild beasts'; the heroines are proud re-fined girls whose nostrils quiver at intervals. There are many moonlit nights, superbly uniformed army officers, Arab stal-lions, ballets and balls, and kissing which goes on and on.

In one second he had bent and kissed her neck. It was done with such incredible swiftness and audacity that even had they been observed, it must only have looked as though he bent to pick up something she had dropped. But the kiss burnt into Tamara's flesh;

and

The magnetic personality of the man was so strong. As he spoke his lips touched her ear. A wild thrill ran through her, she almost trembled, so violent was the emotion the little seemingly accidental caress caused her. A feeling she had never realised in the whole of her life before;

and

Stealthily the Prince drew nearer, and with a spring, seized her and clasped her in his arms.

'Now, now you shall belong to me,' he cried. 'You are mine at last, and you shall pay for the hours of pain you have made me suffer!' and he rained mad kisses on her trembling lips.

Although many of the later heroes, audacious, fiery-blooded animals though they are, kiss swiftly and hotly, they never quite manage to get their heroines into bed. On one occasion a Russian prince, with sleepy oriental eyes, a chiselled mouth and a firm jaw, simply loses heart at the last moment. He drives the heroine in a troika through a snowstorm to an isolated chalet, with the explicit intention of raping—and thus 'taming'—her. But when she conveniently faints, his wild-beast passion melts into compassion.

With a bound Gritzko leaped up, and seizing her in his arms carried her into the middle of the room. Then he paused a moment to exalt in his triumph.

Her little head, with its soft brown hair from which the fur cap had fallen, lay helpless on his breast. The pathetic white face, with its childish curves and the long eyelashes resting on her cheek, made no movement. The faint, sweet scent of a great bunch of violets crushed in her belt came up to him.

And as he fiercely bent to kiss her white unconscious lips, suddenly he drew back, and all the savage exultation went out of him.

He gazed at her for a moment, and then carried her tenderly to the couch and laid her down. She never stirred. Was she dead? Oh, God!

In frightful anguish he put his ear to her heart; it did not seem to beat.

In wild fear he tore open her blouse, the better to listen. Yes, now he heard a faint sound. Ah! saints in heaven! She was not dead.

Instead of raping her, he weeps and kisses her cold unconscious feet.

Florence Barclay's *The Rosary* was published two years after *Three Weeks,* in 1909. She wrote it after she had strained her heart during a bicycle ride and was forced to spend several months lying down. Her characters behave as histrionically, love as ardently, suffer as fervently, and are in general just as confused by their emotional lives as Mrs. Glyn's, but it is all done on a pure and spiritual plane; '...St. Paul has laid it down as an inspired rule for the human mind: "Whatsover things are pure, whatsoever things are lovely, whatsoever things are of good report, think on these things."'

To many romantic novelists the things that are purest, loveliest and of best report are young girls falling in love, and for these writers erotic and divine love become extremely confused; their profound loving is all carried on without the inconvenience of sex. Florence Barclay's characters gain as much mounting pleasure from a knowledge of the love of the Lord as Mrs. Glyn's do from days and nights of sin; their elevating passions are expressed, not in a rain of rapid kisses, but in outpourings of troubled spirits. Their nights are spent not in bed, but in reading the Bible and praying.

My aim is: Never to write a line which could introduce the taint of sin or the shadow of shame into any home. Never to draw a character which should tend to lower the ideals of those who, by means of my pen, make intimate acquaintance with a man or a woman of my own creating.

There is enough sin in the world without an author's powers of imagination being used in order to add even fictitious sin to the amount. Too many bad, mean, morbid characters already, alas! walk this earth. Why should writers add to their numbers and risk introducing them into beautiful homes, where such people in actual life would never for one moment be tolerated. A great French writer and savant has said: 'The only excuse for fiction is that it should be more beautiful than fact.'

The result of her writing only on subjects which are 'more beautiful than fact' is that there are no villains in her novels.

Foolish people, misguided people, or people who are in need of conversion fill her pages, but never anybody who might do or think anything which would sully her readers' minds.

But although this approach is different from Elinor Glyn's, the message is the same. All love is a divine expression.

The background settings of *The Rosary*, as with most romantic fiction of the Edwardian period, include lavish descriptions of the upper crust of life. Florence Barclay's gentry are charmingly eccentric or endearingly rich, and the heroine, Jane, is an orphaned Honourable. She is a plain but big-hearted girl of thirty, on the shelf. Then she discovers that a famous society painter called Garth has fallen in love with her, having heard her wonderful singing voice. She is in love with him but, because she knows that physical beauty is very important to him, she feels she must sacrifice her own love and not allow him to saddle himself with a plain-faced girl like herself.

Later she hears that he has been blinded in a shooting accident. (By an unfortunate stroke of fate, bits of shot bounce off the trunk of a tree to pierce the retina of both of Garth's eyes.) Jane longs to rush to his side but is afraid that he will think she has only come out of pity and will spurn her love. So she pretends to be a hired nurse and when she has won Garth's confidence, and listened to him, in his blind delirium, saying enough complimentary things about her, she finally reveals, by singing his favourite song, who she really is.

Luckily, his talents are many. Though he can never paint again, he turns his hand to music and becomes a composer, inspired by her lovely voice.

The 'masquerade device', the trick whereby the heroine gets herself into a situation, usually by pretending to be someone else, where she can hear admiring things said about herself, is common to many romances of the upper-class cult, as it enables the 'poor little rich girl' heroine to prove, by having a taste of life among the lower classes, that she is not a snob. In *The Princess Priscilla's Fortnight* (1905), by Lady Elizabeth Russell (Countess von Arnim), a German princess, bored with her regal life, masquerades as an impoverished (though genteel) lady and lives uncomfortably with one loyal maid, in a damp cottage in a small English village. After she has performed some good deeds in the locality, she grows bored. One of the villagers runs off with her money, so she is forced to return to her palace and to the prince who wants to marry her. The moral appears to be that everybody should be grateful for their lot, be it high or low, but that princesses should be especially grateful because they may find themselves quite unsuited to a rough life. Another example of the masquerade theme is *The Parish Nurse* (1905), by Mary E. Mann, in which the well-bred daughter of an English general discovers that the man she was about to marry has a wife still living, so she is forced to go and be a parish nurse in a country district. Luckily, the local squire (recognising the refined person beneath the nurse's uniform) falls in love with her, and by curious coincidence, his ex-lover is the very same woman that the nurse's ex-fiancé was married to. The squire and the nurse marry, and the nurse is reinstated among people of her own class.

In *The Rosary*, Jane continues to pose as blind Garth's nurse, encouraging him to talk freely about the girl (herself) he loves so deeply long after it would seem logical to reveal who she really is. But the longer she can masquerade as Nurse Gray, the more tributes she can elicit to herself.

Self-centred as this may appear, it is presented in the novel as a great sacrifice. Under her assumed identity, Jane does not merely nurse her love back to health; she is able to convince him of *her* love, and restore his will to live, thus proving the vital and restorative powers of the state of being in love.

Garth's love for her is originally sparked off, like the love of so many romantic heroes, by music. The actual moment he falls in love is when he hears Jane sing for the first time, at her aunt's musical soirée. Jane, agreeing at very short notice to replace a famous opera singer who has appendicitis, is greeted by an unenthusiastic and disappointed audience.

Jane smiled at them good-naturedly; sat down at the piano, a Bechstein grand; then, without further preliminaries, struck the opening chord and commenced to sing.

The deep perfect voice thrilled through the room.

A sudden breathless hush fell upon the audience.

Each syllable penetrated the silence, borne on a tone so tender and so amazingly sweet, that casual hearts stood still and marvelled at their own emotion; and those who felt deeply already, responded with a yet deeper thrill to the magic of that music.

> 'The hours I spent with thee, dear heart,
>   Are as a string of pearls to me;
> I count them over, ev'ry one apart,
>   My rosary,—my rosary.'

Softly, thoughtfully, tenderly, the last two words were breathed into the silence, holding a world of reminiscence —a large-hearted woman's faithful remembrance of tender moments in the past.

The listening crowd held its breath. This was not a song. This was the throbbing of a heart; and it throbbed in tones of such sweetness, that tears started unbidden.

Garth is so moved by this that all he can do is to utter 'in a low voice, vibrant with emotion, "My God! Oh, My God!"'; an understandable reaction.

'The Rosary' was a popular song of the period suggested to Mrs. Barclay by one of her daughters while she was writing the book and asked them what the heroine should sing. It must soon have become one of Mrs. Barclay's favourites, too, for the full words of the three verses are printed out twice over on each occasion that Jane sings, and in some editions the music is also included in the text so that readers could not merely identify with the heroine but could impersonate her thrilling voice. Linking a romantic novel with a sentimental song of the time was, in fact, quite common, as, for instance, in *Song of a Single Note* (1904), by Amelia Barr (author of *Was It Right to Forgive?*), where the 'Song of a Single Note', which actually has several, is included in the text.

In *Elizabeth and Her German Garden* Lady Elizabeth Russell goes even further and includes in her narrative the musical notation of bird song.

According to her daughter's biography—*The Life of Florence Barclay*, by one of her daughters—music was as important to Florence Barclay in real life as it was in fiction, 'Music to my mother was not a hobby, not an accomplishment, not even, one is tempted to say, a gift—it was more like a faculty, inborn, insistently demanding to be used, providing for her the very purest joy.' Florence Barclay doubtless shared Ouida's belief that 'the ear has its ecstasy as have other senses'. The intensity of her heroine's musical experience was rivalled only by the intensity of her own:

> Music was to her what the faculties of sight or hearing are to others—necessary adjuncts to consciousness—only supplying, too, an objective wealth of glory and joy and revelation, so that it was hopeless to expect anyone fully to understand.

Like her heroine Jane, she had a good singing voice herself, and composed a little. In *The Following of the Star*, one of her own settings to a hymn is included in the text and attributed to the young missionary hero. She believed in the purifying, glorifying and even converting powers of music.

Like Elinor Glyn, Florence Barclay uses the metaphor of the tiger to describe a state of passion. But while Mrs. Glyn's feline simile denotes the *female* lover, for Mrs. Barclay it is the male who plays tiger, though halfway through she brings in a symbolic lion as well:

> Garth, tonight, was like a royal tiger who had tasted blood. It seemed a queer simile, as she thought of him in his conventional evening clothes, correct in every line, well-groomed, smart almost to a fault. But out on the terrace with him she had realised, for the first time, the primal elements which go to the making of a man—a forceful, determined, ruling man—creation's king. The echo of

primeval forests. The roar of the lion is in them, the fierceness of the tiger; the instinct of dominant possession, which says: 'Mine to have and hold, to fight and enjoy; and I slay all comers!' She had felt it, and her own brave soul had understood it and responded to it, unafraid; and been ready to mate with it, if only—ah! if only—

In this passage Jane is wistfully wishing, 'Ah, if only the *situation* were different'. Then she could be different, and love could be different. There is no suggestion that she should react differently to any of the trying situations she finds herself in.

Romantic fiction is not a literature of character-development, nor a literature for conveying profound ideas, but a literature for building up, tirelessly time after time, to dramatic, histrionic, emotional set-pieces, while the characters' responses to these situations remain constant. Here, for example, is the description of the moment—which has had an inordinately long build-up—when Jane finally decides to reveal to the blind Garth, by singing 'The Rosary', who she really is:

'The Rosary' has but one opening chord. She struck it; her eyes upon his face. She saw him sit up, instantly; a look of surprise, expectation, bewilderment, gathering there.

Then she began to sing. The deep rich voice, low and vibrant as the softest tone of 'cello, thrilled into the startled silence.

'The hours I spent with thee, dear heart,
  Are as a string of pearls to me;
I count them over, every one apart,
  My rosary; my rosary.
Each hour a pearl—'

Jane got no further.

Garth had risen. He spoke no word; but he was coming blindly over to the piano. She turned on the music-stool, her arms held out to receive him. Now he had found the woodwork. His hand crashed down upon the bass. Now he had found her. He was on his knees, his arms round her. Hers enveloped him—yearning, tender, hungry with the repressed longing of all those hard weeks.

He lifted his sightless face to hers, for one moment.
'You?' he said. '*You?* You—all the time?'
Then he hid his face in the soft lace at her breast.

While Florence Barclay did not perhaps go so far as to imagine that her writings were divinely inspired, she did sincerely believe that, in the troubled passions of her characters, she was offering people a positive, wholesome view of divine perfection:

She was out to supply her fellow men with joy, refreshment, inspiration. She was not out to make art for art's sake, or to perform a literary *tour de force*, or to rival the makers of fiction of the past. The busy men and women who form the majority of the reading public, and who read fiction by way of relaxation, do not desire to have productions of literary 'art' supplied to them, that their critical faculties may be exercised and their minds educated to a precise valuation of dramatic form, powerful realism, high tragedy. They ask merely to be pleased, rested, interested, amused, inspired to a more living faith in the beauty of human affection and the goodness of God.
The Life of Florence Barclay by one of her daughters

10

On the Threshold of Holy Sanctuaries

FLORENCE BARCLAY WAS a parson's wife with a great deal to do in the parish besides writing, and she was not nearly so prolific as most other romantic novelists. Apart from some short stories, (including *The Wheels of Time*, a 'novella' on which *The Rosary* was based) and devotional papers, she wrote less than a dozen novels. Her first, *Guy Mervyn*, published in 1891 some sixteen years before Elinor Glyn's *Three Weeks*, took the same daring theme: that of a young man's noble love for an older married woman; but *Guy Mervyn* failed to make a great impact on the reading public, as the firm publishing it went bankrupt and only a few copies were distributed.

The plots of all her novels are highly improbable but, as befits a parson's wife, the recurrent theme is of the Christian conversion of one or other of the partners in love. Earthly love cannot be wholly real until he or she has also found the love of God, come home to the Father's House, had his broken halo restored or, if a woman, until 'her heart beats in unison with the heart of the Virgin Mother in Bethlehem's starlit stable'. The revelation of true earthly love and of true heavenly love is often simultaneous, the one acting as a catalyst on the other.

In *The Rosary* it is Garth who is the semi-heathen partner; but the sufferings of going blind and the power of Jane's love bring him back into the fold. On their wedding night Jane is able to point out that it was the Lord who led them safely through the darkness and brought them blissfully to each other.

In *The Broken Halo* (1913), a brilliant and ambitious doctor called Dick is shown to be more interested in saving lives than souls. He marries a rich old lady whose money will enable him to buy a smart London practice but it is not till she helps him to have 'the spirit of prayer awoken in him' that he learns of the 'true wonder and preciousness' of his love for her.

> He had not yet allowed himself to realise all it meant— this strange sweet glow and glory in his heart. But he knew his Little White Lady loved him, with a love altogether above his comprehension, altogether beyond his experience. Yet the depths of his nature responded, just as, tonight, his soul had responded to spiritual truths which were as yet mysteries, but which he accepted in simple faith, and knew he would, day by day, go on to fully apprehend.
>
> Earthly and heavenly love, in the fullness of their perfection, had been revealed to him together; and his heart stood still on the threshold of these holy sanctuaries; his wondering mind believed and accepted, but postponed full understanding, until the first bewilderment should be past.

A religious atmosphere, a tone of spiritual reverence is conveyed by enthusiastic use of capital letters, not only for the personal pronouns of members of the Trinity, but also for anything which sounds vaguely religious—Unseen, The Great Chance, Love, Life, The Little White Lady—and by frequent repetition of emotive words like thrill, throb, tender, soul, gentle, strange and sweet; and by quoting large chunks of the better-known scriptures.

It is a religion of nostalgia for the reader as well as for the characters. Christmas carols and well-known hymns (often quoted in full) bring on strange emotional feelings in characters, and thoughts about lost childhood often result in instant conversion.

It is in the shared emotional-cum-religious experiences of

this sort that the lovers find their true togetherness, rather
than in sexual experiences. Whenever possible, even if the
lovers are married, physical desire is postponed, killed off altogether, or in some way made impossible by the intricacies
of the plot. In *The Broken Halo* the wife, who is anyway,
owing to another aspect of the plot, meant to be in her late
seventies, has a weak heart so she and her youthful husband,
Doctor Dick, have separate rooms; on the very night that he
discovers his deep burning love for her, she dies of a heart
attack, thus putting off till the Great Forever consummation
of their marriage.

The loss of his ancient wife is presented as a reward for the
young doctor's conversion, as she leaves him all her money
and he is free to marry someone younger.

In *The Following of the Star* (1911), the alliance between a
rich heiress and a poor missionary is entirely a *mariage de
convenance* which enables her to give him money for his
missionary work. He leaves for Central Africa immediately
the marriage has been performed.

Unknown to one another though clear to the reader, who is
a sort of impotent god seeing into everyone's souls, the couple
are desperately in love with each other, and carry on a heart-
breaking love-affair by letter between her stately home and
his typhoid-ridden swamp. When all the misunderstandings
of crossed letters have been sorted out, and she has been converted and a normal relationship would at last seem possible,
they do not go about it in anything like the normal way. Instead, they have a curious life-giving intercourse through the
arms. The missionary, who is temporarily dying, lies in bed,
while the heiress kneels by his side in what she admits is a
very uncomfortable position, clutching her husband's head
against her breast. Her arms enfold him and he gives a re-
sponsive thrill. As it also happens to be Christmas Eve, she
sings 'Hark the Herald Angels sing'. The doctor in charge
persuades her to remain in this position all night, as it is the
only thing that can save her husband's life:

'Keep up heart, Mrs. Rivers. Remember that every moment

of contact with your vital force is vitalising him. It is like pouring blood into empty veins; only a more subtle and mysterious process, and more wonderful in its results. Let your muscles relax, as much as possible. We can prop you with pillows, presently.'

The doctor went softly out.

'All night, if necessary,' repeated Diana's happy heart, in an ecstasy of hope and thankfulness. 'A bundle of myrrh is my well-beloved unto me; he shall lie all night—all night —Oh, God, send me strength to kneel on, and hold him!'

She could feel the intense life and love which filled her, enveloping him, in his deathly weakness. She bent her whole mind upon imparting to him the outflow of her vitality.

As a parson's wife, Florence Barclay ran Sunday school and prayer meetings. She also gave birth to numerous children and her interests were in the most simple things in life: in animals, 'especially little birds, robins and thrushes, common sparrows', and in friendship and 'the joy of helping humble people along the road to Heaven'. It is not possible to judge how many of her millions of readers she actually assisted along the road to Heaven, but it is clear that, in the mystical euphoria of her novels, many people found spiritual comfort. As the *Publishers' Circular* had announced in 1897, 'Of all forms of fiction, the semi-religious is the most popular'.

After the initial impact of Elinor Glyn's *Three Weeks* and Florence Barclay's *The Rosary*, the way was open for the subsequent 'semi-religious' romances of Ethel M. Dell. Such gripping stories as *The Way of An Eagle* (1912), *The Lamp in the Desert*, *The Hundredth Chance* (1917), *The Black Knight* (1926), *The Knave of Diamonds* (1913) are a highly readable mixture which combines the spiritual, quasi-religious themes of Florence Barclay with the drama, the action, the full-blooded adventures and dashing officer heroes of Ouida's style.

Many of Ethel M. Dell's innocent, but strong, heroines are, like so many of Mrs. Barclay's characters, tormented by spiritual doubt. Anne Carfax in *The Knave of Diamonds* knows in her darkest hour the need for prayer, but cannot pray:

> Powerless, she sank upon her knees by the open window, striving painfully, piteously, vainly, to pray. But no words came to her, no prayer rose from her wrung heart. It was as though she knelt in outer darkness before a locked door.
>
> In that hour Anne Carfax went down into that Place of Desolation which some call hell and some the bitter school of sorrow—that place in which each soul is alone with its agony and its sin, that place where no light shines and no voice is heard, where, groping along the edge of destruction, the wanderer seeks his Maker and finds Him not, where even the Son of God once lost His faith.

Similarly, Stella in *The Way of an Eagle* is beset by doubts and fears, though in her case they are not specifically religious doubts but intense emotional 'feelings'; there is nonetheless the implication that even these 'feelings' are in some way spiritually worthy. 'And again very deep down in her soul there stirred that blind, unconscious entity, of the existence of which she herself had so vague a knowledge, feeling upwards, groping outwards, to the light.'

Although heroines may doubt and grope for a couple of hundred pages, there is always, at the end, a satisfactory conversion or discovery of some symbol representing renewed faith. In *The Lamp in the Desert* the symbolism is clear enough; Christ is a Lamp which lights up the Desert of the world:

> The Lamp that God had lighted to guide her halting feet...
>
> Was it by this that she would come at last into the Presence of God Himself, and realise that the wanderers in the wilderness are ever His especial care?

In *The Way of an Eagle*, the symbolism often appears to be sexual rather than religious. Muriel frequently has visions and dreams of the man she fears (and ultimately learns to love) as an eagle who is going to carry her off into the mountains.

> As the sunset glory deepened, and the crags of the mountains above glittered golden as the peaks of Paradise, Muriel saw a vision of her lover as an Eagle and the mountains full of horses and chariots of fire!

and

> Tired out at last she slept, and dreamed that an eagle had caught her and was bearing her swiftly, swiftly, through wide spaces to his eyrie in the mountains.

E. M. Dell's sensitive and virginal heroines tend, like so many of Florence Barclay's, to be powered by passions and doubts that are simultaneously of an earthly and a heavenly nature. The trail of the heroine's religious doubts runs a parallel course to her difficulties and sufferings of mortal love. In *The Lamp in the Desert*, Stella's ultimate acceptance of her Creator, the Lamp, after a prolonged period of muttering and confusions in the heart, occurs at the same time and in the same mystical way as her rediscovery of her love for Everard.

In *The Way of an Eagle*, too, Muriel and her eagle-hero, Nick, finally discover each other while communing with nature from the top of a mountain.

Dell heroes are men of decision:

> 'Do you know what we are going to do as soon as we are married, sweetheart? We are going to climb the highest mountain in the world, to see the sun rise, and to thank God.'
> She turned her face upwards with a quivering smile.
> 'Let us be married soon then, Nick.'
> 'At once,' said Nick promptly.

. . .

There was a faint quiver in the air as of something coming from afar, a hushed expectancy of something great. A chill breath came off the snows, hovering secretly above the ice-cold water. The stars glittered like loose-hung jewels upon a sable robe.

Ah, that flash as of a sword across the sky! A meteor had fallen among the mountains. It was almost like a signal in the heavens—herald of the coming wonder of the dawn.

. . .

The morning found them high up the mountainside with their faces to the east.

Sudden and splendid, the sun flashed up over the edge of the world, and the snow of the mountain crests shone in rose-lit glory for a few magic seconds, then shimmered to gold—glittering as the peaks of Paradise.

They did not speak at all, for the ground beneath their feet was holy, and all things that called for speech were left behind. Only as dawn became day—as the sun-god mounted triumphant above the waiting earth—the man's arm tightened about the woman, and his flickering eyes grew steadfast and reverent as the eyes of one who sees a vision . . .

'Prophet and priestess we came—back from the dawning,' quoted Nick, under his breath.

Despite their 'religious' content, there was considerably more blood and thunder to E. M. Dell's novels than Florence Barclay, writing only what was 'of good report', was able to include in hers. There are tempests, infant deaths, runaway horses, wife-beating, men going violently mad, fine young men crippled for life. The heroes are always aware of the necessity of risking their lives to protect the honour of the heroine. This bravery often results in a number of hand to hand fights to the death. 'So long as his heart should beat he would defend that one precious possession that yet remained—the honour of the woman who loved him and whom he loved as only the few knew how to love'.

But by far the most dramatic situation for virgin protection she devises is the opening scene, set on the North-west frontier, of *The Way of an Eagle*. The natives are attacking the garrison at Pashawar. Only four white men and a seventeen-year-old girl (the Brigadier's motherless daughter) are left alive. They have not a hope of holding on till reinforcements arrive. While the battle rages, the girl is locked into her bedroom for safety, where she is taking opium to steady her nerves. The blood-curdling shrieks of the natives, the jungle noises, and the dying cries of soldiers are heard all around. The Brigadier—'there was tragedy, hopeless and absolute in every line of him'—calls together the other three white men and asks which of them is strong enough to kill his daughter:

'I have to think of my child. She will be in your hands. I know you will defend her to the last ounce of your strength; but which of you'—a terrible gasping checked his utterance for many labouring seconds; he put his hand over his eyes— 'which of you,' he whispered at last, his words barely audible, 'will have the strength to—shoot her before your own last moment comes?'

The Indian army provides the background to a number of the romances. E. M. Dell was herself the wife of an army officer, Lt. Col. G. T. Savage, D.S.O., and the accounts of life in an army community are based, loosely, on experience. Clearly, there were both the delights and the dangers of being a young white woman living in India in the 1900s; and many of the heroines have, like Stella in *The Lamp in the Desert*, as much of a love-hate relationship with that country as they have with their lovers.

She went to the window to gaze wistfully out across the verandah. That secret whispering—the stirring of a thousand unseen things—was abroad in the night. The air was soft and scented with a fragrance intangible but wholly sweet. India, stretched out beneath the glittering stars, stirred with half-opened eyes, and smiled. Stella thought she heard the flutter of her robe.

Then again the mystery of the night was rent by a cry of some beast of prey, and in a second the magic was gone. The shadows were full of evil. She drew back with swift, involuntary shrinking, and as she did so she heard the dreadful answering cry of the prey that had been seized.

India again! India the ruthless! India the bloodthirsty! India the vampire!

The plot of *The Lamp in the Desert* is quite extraordinarily improbable. Orphaned Stella Denvers is sent out to be with her brother Tommy Denvers in India. The other women in the English community will not accept her. A marriage is arranged between Stella and Ralph Dacre but Tommy is downright sick about it. 'How would you feel, I wonder, if you knew your one and only sister was going to marry a rotter?' he confides in his superior officer, Everard Monck, who is himself secretly and desperately in love with Stella.

The marriage goes ahead. No sooner have the bridal couple departed for their honeymoon than Everard receives a letter from his brother in England happening to mention that a Ralph Dacre already has a wife living, an ex-music hall actress who is serving a prison sentence. This means that Dacre's marriage to Stella is invalid. Worse, it means that Stella's honour is already blemished. Everard, pretending to his Mess that he is returning to England, dresses up as a crippled beggar and catches up with the false honeymooners. At night while Stella sleeps in her tent, Everard reveals himself to Dacre and says that either Dacre must run away and pretend to be dead, or else Everard will reveal to everybody the truth of his bigamy. He does not wish to do this, however, as it would also publicise the dishonour to Stella of the invalid marriage, of which consummation has taken place. Dacre flees with an oath on his lips.

Stella settles back into the English community as the widow of Ralph. Everard goes slightly mad, suffering from a combination of fever and desperate love of Stella. He tries to attack her. Then he kisses her 'fiercely, blindly, even violently'. She agrees to marry him, but is still unhappy as she feels that her life is 'pursued by a remorseless fate' and that flaming swords bar her path whichever way she turns.

Everard's brother turns up with the news that Ralph Dacre's music-hall wife, in fact, died three days before the marriage to Stella; therefore that was not a bigamous marriage, whereas Everard's to Stella now is. Everard resigns his commission, disappears into the jungle, once more disguised as a beggar, and keeps watch over Stella wherever she goes. Ralph returns to claim Stella, but is inadvertently shot by brother Tommy.

Stella gives birth to a child by Everard, who dresses up as an Indian ayah (nurse) and is employed by Stella to care for their child, who is sick. The baby dies.

The house is attacked by natives. Everard, still disguised as an ayah, carries unconscious Stella to safety and reveals all. Stella, having suffered so much, learns to love him for his true worth.

In this novel there is so much action, and the hero Everard is so frequently occupied with disguising himself that there is little time for sexual encounters between anybody. But this is not to say that E. M. Dell was not capable of describing the kiss. In *The Knave of Diamonds*—the title itself is a euphemism for the hero—Nap Errol, a half-Red Indian bastard, who lures the heroine to an isolated inn with the express intention of seducing her:

His quick breath scorched her face, and in a moment almost before she knew what was happening, his lips were on her own. He kissed her as she had never been kissed before—a single fiery kiss that sent all the blood in tumult to her heart. She shrank and quivered under it, but she was powerless to escape. There was sheer unshackled savagery in the holding of his arms, and dismay thrilled her through and through.

Yet, as his lips left hers, she managed to speak, though

her voice was no more than a gasping whisper. 'Nap, are you mad? Let me go!'

But he only held her faster, faster still.

'Yes, I am mad,' he said, and the words came quick and passionate, the lips that uttered them still close to her own. 'I am mad for you, Anne. I worship you. And swear that while I live no other man shall ever hold you in his arms again. Anne—goddess—queen woman—you are mine—you are mine—you are mine!'

Again his lips pressed hers, and again from head to foot she felt as if a flame had scorched her. Desperately she began to resist him, though terribly conscious that he had her at his mercy. But he quelled her resistance, instantly with a mastery that made her know more thoroughly her utter impotence.

He then tries to violate her, but a freak electric storm blows up. He is struck by lightning through the window and disappears. She faints. But in the end she marries him.

E. M. Dell's novels are well-written of their kind—with that 'luxuriant vitality' that Q. D. Leavis wrote of—but E. M. Dell did not have the literary pretensions of some other popular romantic novelists. She was not seeking for literary glories in the way that Marie Corelli or Elinor Glyn did. Nor did she claim, as Elinor Glyn did, that the intentions of her work were misunderstood. The loyalty of her readers was enough for her. Indeed, one of her novels, more or less a pot-boiler, which tells the love-story of two characters, Noel and Peggy, who had already featured in the earlier romance, *The Keeper of the Door*, was actually written at the request of and dedicated to some of her readers, and entitled *By Request* (1927):

I dedicate this book to the Public who will read it, and especially to those among them by whose request it is written, as a very humble token of my deep gratitude for their kind and sympathetic appreciation of my work, of the real worth of which none holds fewer illusions than I, who would make it worthier if I could both for their sakes and my own.

In 1933 Ray Smith's Twopenny Library reported that the three women authors most in demand were still Ethel M. Dell, Elinor Glyn and Marie Corelli—in that order.

II

Marie Corelli: Some Unknown Form of Energy

No SURVEY OF popular romantic fiction would be complete without Marie Corelli. In all her attitudes to life and writing she is an archetypal romantic novelist: her supreme arrogance, her lack of education in thinking or feeling, her themes of God and love (a love not just sexual but universal), her passion, vitality and enthusiasm, her sentimentality, extended specially to cover 'flowers, nature and music', her enormous popular appeal—these are the hallmarks of the first-class romantic novelist.

But though she is a prototype romance-writer, it is very difficult to categorise her work with that of any other group of romantic novelists. She was a law unto herself, and the subjects she chose to write about did not stick to any of the general trends. Marie Corelli wrote about everything, all subjects treated with the same crusading and evangelising zeal. No subject was too big or too small for her to take on. Whether denouncing female smoking and low-cut dresses, expounding on world politics, or introducing God Almighty as one of the key characters in a novel, she put her heart into the job.

Suddenly the red and glowing chaos of fire above him changed into soft skies tinged with the exquisite pearl-grey hues of twilight, and he became conscious of the approach of a great invisible Presence, whose awful unseen beauty overwhelmed him with its sublimity and majesty, causing him to forget altogether that he himself existed. And Someone spoke,—in grave sweet accents, so soft and close to him that the words seemed almost whispered in his ears,—

> 'Thy prayer is heard,—and once again
> the silence shall be broken. Nevertheless
> remember that "the light shineth in darkness
> and the darkness comprehendeth it not".'

Deep silence followed. The mysterious Presence melted as it were into space . . .

The Master Christian (1900)

Although her novels are quite unlike either the mid-Victorian moralising romances from the Religious Tract Society, which put forward patterns of behaviour for young wives, they are equally unlike the later erotico-spiritual religious revivalism of Elinor Glyn or Florence Barclay. Her themes are more doctrinally daring than the former, but less amorous than the latter. By her own definition, she wrote three types of novel: religious novels, novels of the imagination, and novels with a purpose, but she insisted that 'all are religious in their fervent re-iteration of the gospel message'. Her interpretation of that gospel message, though, is unorthodox and unlike most people's. But, although a heretic, she was quite sincere in her attempts to solve all the problems of the universe, from the creation of the world to the final overthrowing of Satan, and in her efforts to bring about a conversion of the whole world to her 'better' way of thinking. This very high-minded ambition is something she shares with all the popular romantic novelists, as Q. D. Leavis pointed out:

What these highly popular novelists have won their reputation by, in fact, is this terrific vitality set to turn the machinery of morality. In a novel by Marie Corelli, Hall Caine, Florence Barclay, Gene Stratton Porter, the author is genuinely preoccupied with ethical problems, whatever side attractions there may be in the way of unconscious pornography and excuses for day-dreaming.

But it goes further than this. Writers like Marie Corelli are not just *attempting* to 'turn the machinery of morality'. They really do believe that they have it in their literary (and God-given) power to succeed.

The lack of a sense of proportion is paradoxically the biggest limitation of many romantic novelists. Most writers, as Graham Greene pointed out in *The Dark Backward: A Foot-note* (1935), get to a point where they realise that there is something that they *cannot* do. Bad writers do not have this limitation.

> The consciousness of what he cannot do—and it is some-times something so apparently simple that a more popular writer never gives it a thought—is the mark of the good novelist. The second-rate novelists never know; nothing is beyond their sublimely foolish confidence as they turn out their great epics.

The common denominator of popular romantic novelists is not primarily their beliefs in the boy-meets-girl story, but in the powers of falling in love. Their shared objective is their genuine desire to improve the world, which combines with an unswerving belief that they *are* doing so.

That the world is not being radically altered is explained, not by the fact that this message may be the wrong one, or badly expressed, but by the fact that most people are such blind fools, or else so sinful or permissive, that they refuse to listen to it. Marie Corelli described herself as a 'Voice in the Wilderness', a prophet who understood the Truth, and was willing to impart it, but to whom few were willing to listen. 'I could not teach you the Divine transfiguring charm,—un-less you, equally with all your hearts and all your love, reso-lutely and irrevocably WILLED to learn.' Preface to *The Life Everlasting* (1911).

But for those who willed to learn she had various revelations of the Truth. One of them goes like this:

There is only One Way of Attainment, and the clue to that Way is in the Soul of each individual. Each one must find it and follow it, regardless of all 'influences'—which may be brought to bear on his or her actions,—each one must discover the Centre-poise of Life's movement, and firmly abide by it. It is the Immortal Creature in each one of us whose destiny is to make eternal progress and advancement through endless phases of life, love and beauty; and when once we know and admit the actual existence of this Immortal Centre we shall realise that with it all things are possible, save Death. Radiating outward from itself, it can preserve the health and youth of the body it inhabits indefinitely, till of its own desire it seeks a higher plane of action,—radiating inwardly, it is an irresistible attractive force drawing to itself the powers and virtues of the planet on which it dwells, and making all the forces of visible and invisible Nature subject to its will and command. This is one of those great Truths which the world denies, but which it is destined to learn within the next two thousand years.

The Life Everlasting

In this stream of effusive confusion one idea stands out clearly, which is that the Truth is only now being revealed (through Miss Corelli) to the world, a theme which crops up fairly often in her works. 'Only in these latter days has the world become faintly conscious of the real Force working behind and through all things—the soul of the Divine, or the Psychic element, animating and inspiring all visible and invisible Nature.'

The emphasis of her religious teaching is seldom on Biblical events, but is nearly always about a divine or mysterious 'something' which is happening in the present day, or going to happen in the future. The difference between this and the supernatural adventures of, say, a Rider Haggard novel is that for him it was a work of imaginative fiction, whereas

Marie Corelli believed everything she wrote.

Marie Corelli was born in 1854. She was illegitimate and became, by adoption, the daughter of a Scottish doctor, Charles Mackay, whom her mother married. She was to have had a musical career; in fact she began training as a pianist but various domestic problems prevented her finishing her tuition, so she took up her pen. She never married (she is said to have been a 'confirmed man-hater'), but eventually settled with a lady companion, Bertha Vyer, a minor poet, in Stratford-on-Avon, where she was a well-known eccentric.

As a child she had various meetings and 'relationships with angels' which led her to believe she was divinely inspired. Later, as a young girl, she went to a convent school where she became so 'absorbed in the mysteries of religious life' that she considered founding a new religious Order of her own, an entirely original community of Christian workers, of which she, of course, would be the leader. When she grew up she continued to hear voices and see visions and it was these 'singular psychical experiences' which formed the basis of her first book, *A Romance of Two Worlds*, published in 1886. It is a semi-autobiographical, semi-fictional account of a divine experience, combined with vague theories of electricity, and the useful purpose of the novel was to clear up, once and for all, the knotty points on the subject of the Creation and 'to prove the actual existence of God and Heaven'.

The heroine of the story, suffering from apathy and nervous irritation, goes to Paris to consult a 'physical electrician', who, besides being a sort of doctor, also happens to be a direct descendant of one of the three wise men of the east. The consultation takes place in his hotel off the Champs Elysées and, after he has cured her by means of electricity, he offers to let her see what no mortal has been before. He sends her spirit out of her body, and she is lifted up to inspect the planets, and see the workings of the universe.

The centre of the universe is revealed as being a huge electric circle, around a globe of opal-tinted light where God lives. God Himself is a shape of pure electric radiance, and He implants an electric germ into every living soul. Unfortunately, this germ of electricity doesn't always turn into the radiant burning light it should. So God laid Christ as an 'electric cable' between mortals and Heaven.

During this spiritual experience, the heroine is unable to see the moon, which is only a 'chimerical electrograph', but she *is* given a glimpse of the electric cable, Christ:

> And when the Redeemer stepped out of the Inner Circle, the angels drooped their radiant heads like flowers in hot sunshine. I alone, daringly, yet with an inexpressible affection welling up within me, watched with unshrinking gaze the swift advance of that supreme Figure.

A Romance of Two Worlds was published in 1886, and during the seventies and eighties the wonders of electric light were gradually coming into more general use. Paris was one of the first cities to use electric street lighting; in 1878 the Avenue de l'Opéra was lit by sixty-two arc lamps. London followed suit, and a year later a mile and a quarter of road between Westminster and Waterloo was lit up. Marie Corelli was obviously very impressed by this, and the wealth of other scientific discoveries and advances which were taking place during her lifetime, to such an extent that she confused them, at the most naïve level, with spiritual advancement.

Most of her scientific 'facts' are based on tiny snippets of misinformation which she then embellished with an instinctive *feeling* about them, whenever possible finding some link-up between the physical and the spiritual world. In this novel, *A Romance of Two Worlds*, it is between electricity and God; in a later novel, perhaps after she had heard of antisepsis, between germs and good and evil forces:

> Everything in the Universe is engaged in some sort of fight, so it seems to me. The tiniest insects are for ever combating each other. In the very channels of our own blood the poisonous and the non-poisonous germs are constantly striving for the mastery.

Some twenty years after *A Romance of Two Worlds* was first published, she changed her views about electricity and moved on to radio-activity. She explained, with scientific 'proof', that what she had really meant when she said that God was electricity was that He was radio-activity:

> 'Radio-activity' is perhaps the better, because the truer term to employ in seeking to describe the Germ or Embryo of the Soul, for—as scientists have proved—'Radium is capable of absorbing from surrounding bodies *some unknown form of energy* which it can render evident as heat and light.' This is precisely what the radio-activity in each individual soul of each individual human being is ordained to do,—to absorb an 'unknown form of energy which it can render evident as heat and light'. Heat and Light are the composition of Life;—and the Life which this radio-activity of Soul generates *in* itself and *of* itself can never die.

This idea that radio-activity is the secret of life cropped up again in her last novel, *The Secret Power* (1921).

What Marie Corelli was offering the public in *A Romance of Two Worlds* and later novels was the best of both worlds —science plus religion. At a period of growing scepticism, she was giving a reassurance of immortality, a proof of God, but with a modern scientific 'explanation'. The book went into numerous editions and was translated into many languages, and one Church of England clergyman wrote to the author to say that the book's 'revelations' had saved him from suicide.

In *A Romance of Two Worlds*, as in most of her novels, the story, characters and plot are quite secondary to her opinions on spiritual matters. Her heroines, though, are usually based on an idealised version of herself, the most extreme example of which is Mavis Clare (sharing the same initials as Marie Corelli), heroine of *The Sorrows of Satan* (1895), who is a lady writer. This 'woman of genius with a thinker's brain and an angel's soul' is victimised by the Press who are jealous of her 'mental superiority', her success, and her moral purity; but her real followers, the public, admire and appreciate 'the intellectual power and grasp and power of her novels'; throughout the heroine's trials she preserves 'a child's heart and a child's faith'.

Marie Corelli did not see herself as an entertainer at all, and her novels are filled out with sermons and lectures on life and soul:

> Every great truth has at first been no more than a dream,— that is to say, a thought, or an instinctive perception of the Soul reaching after its own immortal heritage. And what the Soul demands it receives.
>
> Every bodily sense we possess is simply an imperfect outcome of its original and existent faculty in the Soul,— that our bodily ears are only the material expressions of that spiritual hearing which is fine enough to catch the lightest angel whisper,—that our eyes are but the outward semblance of those brilliant inner orbs of vision which are made to look upon the supernal glories of Heaven itself without fear or flinching.

There is little amorous intrigue in Marie Corelli's romances; love-affairs between characters do sometimes occur but she was clearly not very interested in or impressed by Eros. The worthiest of her heroines fall in love with God or religion, and it is accounts of a divine, mystical and universal love that fill her books. An Angel comes to one of her heroines and explains:

> 'In Life's great choral symphony, the keynote of the dominant melody is Love! Without the keynote there can be no music,—there is dumbness where there should be sound, —there is discord where there should be harmony. Love! the one vibrant tone to which the whole universe moves in tune,—Love, the breath of God, the pulsation of His Being, the glory of His work, the fulfilment of His Eternal Joy.'

In direct contradiction to her own assertion that the dominant melody in life should be Love, she was for ever delivering bitter attacks on people and ideas. The causes in contemporary life that met with her disapproval were many and varied. *The Sorrows of Satan* (1895) is an indictment against the Press, sexual novels and Swinburne; *Jane* (1897) is a protest against the vulgarity of 'swagger' society; *The Mighty Atom* (1896) is a protest against atheism and is dedicated to

> 'those self-styled Progressivists who, by precept and example, assist the infamous cause of education without religion, and who, by promoting the idea, borrowed from French atheism, of denying to the children in Board schools and elsewhere the knowledge and love of God as the true foundation of noble living, are guilty of a worse crime than murder'.

In *Boy* (1900) she attacks drunken fathers and in *The Master Christian* (1900) all forms of religious hypocrisy. She was quite democratic in her attacks and all issues, great and small, received the same weight of enthusiasm.

One of the earliest of her many good causes was to show up the evils of absinthe addiction. Although this was a very real and terrifying problem in France during the late nineteenth century, it was not something the English were particularly prone to. So why Marie Corelli (who was of Scottish descent, though she sometimes claimed to be half Italian) wanted to champion this particular foreign cause is not really clear. Possibly it was because it enabled her to express the universality of her mind by means of some bright Parisian scenes, including a description of the daring novelty, the cancan.

Wormwood (1890), subtitled *A Drama of Paris*, is the tragic tale of a well-to-do Frenchman and all the ruin—social, financial and, above all, moral—that comes to him because of his addiction. He loses both the rich girl he loves and the virtuous girl who loves him; he murders his fiancée's priest-lover and, worse still, he loses his sense of national honour.

He finally goes mad. (Wormwood is the English name for the bitter herb from which absinthe is made; it is used in making vermouth and certain medicines, but when turned into the liqueur it is extremely poisonous.)

The story has, not unnaturally, an extremely pessimistic tone to it; the epigraph she chooses is a quotation from the Book of Revelations which, though not particularly meaningful taken out of the context of the whole passage, has a certain horror-laden prophetic ring to it, 'And the name of the star is called Wormwood: and the third part of the waters became wormwood; and many men died of the waters, because they were made bitter.'

The story is narrated in the first person, by the absinthe drinker himself while he is in the process of going mad. The manufacture in France of absinthe was finally made illegal in 1909, but whether *Wormwood* was in any way instrumental in bringing about the change of law is uncertain.

Among Marie Corelli's other dramatic novels of the imagination are *Vendetta* (1886), about an Italian nobleman who is buried alive during a cholera epidemic in Naples, and escapes only to learn of the infidelity of his wife; *Thelma* (1887), about a Norwegian princess; *The Soul of Lilith* (1892), about a child's soul which is stopped in its heavenward flight by a man who, with the soul's help, wants to discover the Unknown; *Ziska* (1897), about another girl's soul which returns to earth many years after her death to exact vengeance on her murderer; *Barabbas, a Dream of the World's Tragedy* (1893). None of these books was well received by the critics. And after the publication and poor reception of *Barabbas* in 1893 she refused to allow the critics to review her books unless they bought them themselves. She later amended this and allowed free review copies to be applied for, but only by bona fide reviewers who wished 'to consider it beyond the extent of a mere paragraph or quotation without context'.

Most popular romantic novelists have been mocked by the Press, though today the trend seems to be more towards a note of tolerance and playful teasing. But Marie Corelli seems to have received more than her share of harsh criticism. This was partly her own fault, for having classed herself as highly literary, she is too often judged by literary standards, instead of by some other standard more suitable to this form of popular reading-matter. Strangely, it was not just her contemporaries who felt drawn to criticise her; today, she is still a target for abuse. Her name is often brought up in serious literary surveys, only in order to dismiss it, 'Of "Marie Corelli" (Minnie Mackay) no more need be said than that the pretentious treatment of lofty themes by the illiterate for the illiterate was in itself a sidelight of the period.' (George Sampson.)

Her books have also been said 'to appeal only to mass sentiment' and to be 'mainly vulgar sensationalism', all of which is, of course, quite true. But when a note of bitter resentment creeps in, it is clear that the severity of criticism is less in proportion to a romantic novelist's silliness than to her success, and it is galling that writers like Marie Corelli should manage to draw an enthusiastic and demonstrative response from their readers, while more serious writers often do not. The fact is that Marie Corelli's readers came back for more because in her books they heard what they wanted to hear. An Oxford undergraduate wrote to her:

> Your immense popularity is the result, as it seems to me, of your originality and sincerity, your passionate appeals to the people's feelings (which, often unlike their opinions, have always truth in them) combined with dramatic power, are directed on the points which at present most nearly touch the hearts as, for instance, the vague impression that science is overthrowing religion and the best hopes of man.

Her themes and ideas, outrageous and new as they seemed on first sight, were established ideas, dressed up in a new sugar-coating which gave the reader the impression that he was expanding his mind, exploring exciting new horizons while at the same time she was merely reinstating all his reactionary ideas.

An example is the attack on atheism in *The Mighty Atom*, which was hardly a new theme. Many writers had dealt with the subject before 1896, but in her story Marie Corelli gives the problem a melodramatic sentimental presentation. She makes the issue seem not intellectual but 'a thing of the heart'. Briefly, the story is of a young boy of eleven whose tutor teaches him that souls are not immortal, that God doesn't really exist, and that human beings are all atoms. The consequence is that young Lionel Valliscourt commits suicide. The scene where his teacher and his father find him hanging from the beams by a blue silk sash is enough to make even an atheist weep:

> 'My god! My God!' cried the Professor, wildly invoking the Deity whose existence he denied—'Valliscourt—go—go! Don't look—don't look! The boy has killed himself!'
> But Mr. Valliscourt pushed past him into the room, and there stood, ... rigid and dumb, ... staring, ... staring upward, at a strange and awful thing,—a piteous sight to make God's angels weep, ... a child-suicide! A child's dead body swinging heavily from the oaken rafters,—a child, hung by a length of soft blue sash-ribbon, which though shining from tender hues in the morning sunlight, and daintily patterned with an innocent daisy-chain, yet held the little throat fast in an inexorable death-grip!

Despite the hostility of the Press and the intellectuals towards Marie Corelli, there is no denying her phenomenal success. By 1911 Marie Corelli's first novel, *A Romance of Two Worlds*, was into its thirtieth edition and still selling. In that same year her other novels had been issued in the following number of editions:

Vendetta: 28th edition
Thelma, a Norwegian Princess: 41st edition
Ardath, the Story of a Dead Self: 20th edition
The Soul of Lilith: 17th edition

Wormwood: A Drama of Paris: 17th edition
Barabbas, A Dream of the World's Tragedy: 45th edition
The Sorrows of Satan: 56th edition
The Master Christian: 12th edition (177th thousand)
Temporary Power, a Study of Supremacy: 2nd edition
    (150th thousand)
God's Good Man; A Simple Love Story: 14th edition
    (152nd thousand)
Holy Orders; The Tragedy of a Quiet Life: 2nd edition
    (120th thousand)
The Mighty Atom: 29th edition

Even more important than the sales figures of her books was
the fierce loyalty of her readers. One of her fan letters was
from a colour-sergeant in the 1st Battalion of the Gloucester-
shire Regiment, fighting in the Boer War, who sent her a
spent cartridge he had made into a useful pencil holder, and
revealed that her books were enjoyed by both his fellow
soldiers and the enemy. Besides the Church of England clergyman who was saved from suicide by her first novel, she was
read and admired (to her huge satisfaction) by other literate
people, including (according to one of her contemporary bio-
graphers, Kent Carr) Tennyson, Gladstone, the Dean of
Gloucester, Dean Wilberforce, Ella Wheeler Wilcox, many
undergraduates at Oxford, the Dowager Duchess of Roxburgh,
the Empress of Austria and other crowned heads of Europe,
the Prince of Wales and Queen Victoria. It was the patronage
of royalty that Marie Corelli particularly enjoyed.

While she was on one hand being mocked and lampooned
by her critics, she became for her admirers almost a cult
figure, everything she said or did being recorded and her
books being read like holy writ. There was also the *Marie
Corelli Birthday Book* (published in 1897) with illustrations of
her best-known heroines; the *Marie Corelli Calendar* (1913)
with a different quotation from her works for each day of the
year; and the following list of her thirty dislikes was published at the turn of the century, with an air of reverence
and respect for her every whim, in a magazine, *Ladies' Realm;*

it is a curiously unbalanced collection, featuring such serious, if somewhat vaguely-defined dislikes as 'lack of enthusiasm in a great cause' as well as the more clearly-defined 'American millionaires'. But despite its self-importance and the way it shows up her own hypocrisies and prejudices, it does give a good indication of the high ideals she set herself and the rest of the world:

The man who is his own God Almighty;
The woman who cannot consecrate her life purely and faithfully to one great love-passion;
The priest who preaches and does not practise;
The 'new poet' who curls his hair with tongs and writes his own reviews;
The modern marriage market;
Women bicyclists and he-females generally;
Tuft-hunters and worshippers of Royalty;
American millionaires;
Fuss, hurry and lack of courtesy;
The man who thinks that every pretty woman he sees is, or ought to be, in love with him;
The woman who finds charm in every man except her own husband;
Pretended 'friends' who are secret foes;
Music—when it isn't wanted;
William Archer and his god Ibsen;
Society noodles;
Ladies of title who allow their portraits to be on sale in the shops for any cad to buy;
The Woman who Did;
Low conduct in high places;
Cynics and pessimists;
Want of sympathy with little children;
Lack of enthusiasm in a great cause;
Sneerers at faith and aspiration;
Materialists;
The man or woman who has outlived romance;

    The hostess who interrupts conversation between two
       friends merely to introduce a bore;
    The 'funny man' at a party;
    Being taken in to dinner by an uncongenial partner as old
       as Methuselah;
    The health-faddist and consumer of tabloids;
    And last and greatest dislike of all—moral cowardice.

Miss Corelli must be admired for the way she stuck to what
she believed to be important, even at the risk of making
a fool of herself. The real sadness is that such fanaticism
was not directed towards a more useful or productive
cause.

For all her high-minded homilies on the importance of
spiritual matters over worldly, she was quite partial to a bit of
sumptuous luxury, in her imaginative prose if nowhere else.
Sometimes she gets round this one by endowing her celestial
palaces and heavenly halls with luxurious comforts, but at
other times she describes lavishly appointed rooms for their
own sake.

In *The Life Everlasting*, her heroine, who is a hard-working,
gentle, smiling, intelligent, good-natured young woman, endowed with unusual psychic powers and the secret of abound-
ing vitality (and who is, of course, modelled on the author
herself), is invited to go on a cruise around the Scottish highlands on an American millionaire's yacht:

    I was shown the cabin, or rather the state-room, which was
    to be mine during the cruise. It was a luxurious double
    apartment, bedroom and sitting-room together, divided
    only by the hanging folds of a rich crimson silk curtain,
    and exquisitely fitted with white enamelled furniture orna-
    mented with hand-wrought silver. The bed had no resem-
    blance whatever to a ship's berth, but was an elaborate full-
    sized affair, canopied in white silk embroidered with roses;
    the carpet was of a thick softness into which my feet sank
    as though it were moss, and a tall silver and crystal vase,
    full of gorgeous roses, was placed at the foot of a standing

mirror framed in silver, so that the blossoms were reflected double. The sitting-room was provided with easy chairs, a writing-table, and a small piano, and here, too, masses of roses showed their fair faces from every corner. It was all so charming that I could not help uttering an exclamation of delight, and the maid who was unpacking my things smiled sympathetically.

Miss Corelli's sumptuous choice in interior decoration enhances the escapist qualities of such a description.

Marie Corelli had such verbal diarrhoea that she wrote about and described the most trite occurrences with pseudo-poetic effusiveness. Thus, this heroine, when she goes to bed, does not just drop off into silent unconsciousness like ordinary people, but gives a running commentary about it:

I lay down in my luxurious bed, and slipped away into the land of sleep.

Ah, what a land it is, that magic land of Sleep!—a land 'shadowing with wings', where amid many shifting and shimmering wonders of darkness and light, the Palace of Vision stands uplifted, stately and beautiful, with golden doors set open to the wanderer! I made my entrance there that night;—often and often as I had been within its enchanted precincts before, there were a million halls of marvel as yet unvisited,—among these I found myself,—under a dome which seemed of purest crystal lit with fire,—listening to One invisible, who,—speaking as from a great height, —discoursed to me of Love.

Marie Corelli's pseudo-poetic, pseudo-biblical descriptive style sweeps one effortlessly along on what seems to be a spiritual plane. But the real urge behind her most purple passages is clearly sexual. Her mystical effusions are filled with the most powerful erotic symbols, which luckily she herself did not understand. Her intensest writing is frequently reserved for the ultimate confrontations between herself and Jesus

Christ, presented in a style which can only be described as orgasmic. In the following passage from *The Life Everlasting* the heroine, having been lifted up to an extra-terrestial place amongst the angels, now has to walk through a hall of living fire in order to return to Earth:

I found myself surrounded on all sides by darting points of light which instead of scorching and withering me like a blown leaf in a storm, were like cool and fragrant showers playing all over me! Amazed, I went on—and as I went I grew bolder. At one step I was bathed in a rain of delicate rays like sparkling diamond and topaz—at another a lovely violet light shrouded me in its rich hues—at another I walked in melting azure, like the hues of a summer sky— and the farther in I went the deeper and more glowing was the light about me. I felt it penetrating every pore of my skin—I held my hands out to it, and saw them look transparent in the fine luminance,—and presently, gaining courage, I threw back my veil and breathed in the radiance, as one breathes the air! My whole body grew light, and moved as though it floated rather than walked—I looked with unfatigued, undazzled eyes at the glittering flames sparkling harmlessly about me which changed to lovely shapes of flowers and leaves beneath my feet, and arched themselves over my head like branches of shading trees—and then all at once, down the long vista I caught sight of a Shape like that of an Angel!—an Angel that waited for me with watchful eyes and outstretched arms!—it was but a moment that I saw this vision, and yet I knew what it meant, and I pressed on and on with all my Soul rising in me as it were, to go forth and reach that Companion of Itself which stood waiting with such tender patience! The light around me now changed to waves of intense luminance which swept upon me like waves of the sea—and I allowed myself to be borne along with them, I knew not whither. All at once I saw a vast Pillar of Fire which seemed to block my way,— pausing a moment, I looked and saw it break asunder and form the Cross and Star!—I gazed upward, wondering—

its rays descending seemed to pierce my eyes, my brain, my very soul!—I sprang forward, dazed and dazzled, murmuring, 'Let this be the end!'

12

Hall Caine and the Great War

AMONG THE MANY literary enemies made by Marie Corelli was
the Isle of Man writer, Sir Hall Caine. As a publisher's reader
for Bentley's, he recommended the rejection of her first novel,
A Romance of Two Worlds. Though she never really forgave
him for this, it was more the similarities of these two writers
which caused their deadly rivalry. Hall Caine, like Marie
Corelli, had a huge enthusiastic public and was championed
not only by the uneducated masses but by the literate, too.
Among his most enthusiastic admirers was D. G. Rossetti,
with whom he lived for a couple of years. He wrote about big
but simplified ideas, in an emotional presentation and,
although he did not go in for the supernatural and psychical
excursions of Marie Corelli, he, like her, put forward a simple,
quasi-Christian message. Both of them believed themselves to
be the latter-day 'Shakespeare of the prose form'.

Hall Caine lived from 1853 to 1931 and wrote numerous
popular novels and melodramas, many of them centred on the
Isle of Man (the best known are *The Scapegoat* (1891) and
The Eternal City (1901)), but the most romantic of his novels
is *The Woman of Knockaloe* (1923).

Hall Caine was a pacifist for most of his life and this novel,
written shortly after the end of the First World War, is an
impassioned anti-war cry. In telling the story of the forbidden
wartime love-affair between a British girl and a German, its

revealed message is, Isn't war beastly; its evils have repercussions on everybody, even those who think they aren't involved; but true love can purify.

Mona is a tough, proud, God-hating Manxwoman with
'flashing eyes and quivering nostrils', whose farm at Knockaloe
is requisitioned for use as a prisoner-of-war camp:

> She is a splendid girl of about twenty-three or four, dis-
> tinctly good-looking, tall, full-bosomed, strong of limb,
> even muscular, with firm step and upright figure, big brown
> eyes and coal-black hair—a picture of grown-up health.
> Since her mother's death she has become 'the big woman' of
> the farm, managing everything and everybody, the farm-
> servants of both sexes, her brother and even her father.

This tough, almost masculine, anti-heroine is strangely contrasted with the frail German she falls in love with—
the gentle, sensitive, religious Oskar, who is interned in the
prisoner-of-war camp at Knockaloe.

Mona's brother is killed fighting at the front and the
shock of this turns Mona's father, who has hitherto been a
reasonable, devout old man, into a violent, loud-mouthed
religious maniac who lies in bed reading from the Book of Job
and calling on God to drop hot coals of fire on to the Germans.
But, while the old man loses his real faith, thanks to the war,
his daughter, thanks to the love of gentle sensitive Oskar, re-
gains hers. This is a favourite theme in religious romantic
fiction—to contrast the hypocrisies of the orthodox, bible-
reading, church-going Christian with the purer, nobler and
holier beliefs of a more unorthodox believer; this theme is
often extended to the matter of sexual behaviour too, to show
how a selfless illicit love can be purer and more beautiful
than a stale love within matrimony, as in *The Edge O'Beyond*
(1908) by Geraldine Page.

The love between Mona and Oskar is furtive, and dread-
fully pure. They do not kiss. Moreover, as in all classic cases
of romantic love, the affair is doomed from the start; it can
never come to fulfilment, and must end in death.

After 'the war to end wars' is over, and the German prisoners are released, the world is seen to be so full of hate and profiteering that there is no place in it, in Knockaloe, England, or Germany, for the two lovers. They find themselves with no alternative but to tie themselves together with Oskar's coatbelt and jump off a cliff-top into the sea. The failure of the people of Knockaloe to recognise and respect their love is represented as a symbol of the failure of the people of the world to accept the love of God.

Hall Caine's intention with this book, in trying to explain that love is better than hate, peace better than war, is admirable, but he becomes so carried away by his theme of the purity and wonder of Mona's and Oskar's love, that he elevates it to the level of the divine. Their love becomes equated with the love of Christ, endowed with the same mystic powers, capable even of purifying the whole world. The climax of the novel, the lovers' leap to death, however well-meant it was, is, in fact, thoroughly blasphemous. It is represented as a sacrifice 'for the world' on the same scale as Christ's crucifixion. Providing that the world accepts Mona's and Oskar's death, their sacramental death is capable of saving the world from hate and bitterness, and of replacing them with peace and love.

However, the young couple clearly are not divine, for their responses and reactions seem totally inadequate to the enormity and responsibility of the situation. Just before the suicidal jump, Mona hears a hen clucking and, in a moment of regret about leaving the world, observes with shattering banality, 'It seems a pity, doesn't it?' Oskar reminds her that 'it had to be', and she agrees. 'Yes, it had to be. There was no other way, was there?', to which he replies like a clockwork parrot, 'No, there was no other way, Mona.'

Despite their conversational shortcomings, and the blasphemy of their sacramental death, on the purely melodramatic and tear-jerking level their end, going down in a blaze of divine glory, is quite the best end any romantic lovers could aspire to.

At dawn the young couple climb up the heather-clad mountain to make their love leap. 'Tears are in their eyes, but the light of heaven is there also.'

In a few minutes more they are on the cliff head. It over-hangs the sea, which is heaving and singing in its many voices seventy feet blow. The sun is rising, and the sky to the east is flecked with crimson. There is nothing else in sight anywhere and no other sound except the cry of the sea fowl on the rocks beneath.

'This is the place, isn't it?'

'This is the place, Mona.'

'Shall we do as we intended?'

'Yes, let us do as we intended.'

And then these two children of the universal Father, cast out of the company of men, separated in life and about to be united in death, go through the burial service which they have appointed for themselves.

Together, they say the Lord's Prayer, she in English, he in German, symbolising the uniting in God of their two nationalities. Then they sing *Jesu, lover of my soul*, with their heads up and facing out to sea.

Then Oskar unfastens his coat, and taking off the long belt he is wearing he straps it about both of them. They are now eye to eye, breast to breast, heart to heart.

'The time has come, hasn't it, Oskar?'

'Yes, the time has come, Mona.'

'I can kiss you now, can't I?'

He puts his arms tenderly about her and kisses her on the lips. She kisses him. It is their first kiss and their last.

'God bless you for loving me, Oskar.'

'And God bless you, too, Mona. And now good-bye!'

'No, not good-bye. Only—until then.'

'Until then.'

The sun rises above the horizon in a blaze of glory. The broad sea sings her everlasting song. The cliff head is empty.

Like many daring popular novels which run the risk, in the

opinion of their authors, of being misunderstood and misinterpreted, the message is not allowed to speak for itself.
The novel is preceded by fourteen pages of addenda to re-
assure the unwary reader that Sir Hall Caine was not being
unpatriotic in portraying the love between Mona and the
German. Before chapter one there is an emotional epigraph:
'Love is strong as death; jealousy is cruel as the grave ...
Many waters cannot quench love, neither can the floods drown
it.' This is followed by a vague but emotional message of
recommendation from Gladstone saying how much he ad-
mires the author's courage. There is then a twelve-page edi-
torial note by Newman Flowers which says much the same
thing as Gladstone, and goes on to interpret the whole anti-
war meaning of the novel:

> But is the world prepared for it? Is this the hour for such a
> plea? Is the Great War too recent to permit any of the
> nations who engaged in it to forgive their enemies? In this
> new book Hall Caine touches upon wounds that are not
> yet healed and sometimes the touch hurts. If it is an all-
> healing touch the pain may be endured. But is it? What
> will the British people think? What will the Belgians, the
> French and the Americans, who are still suffering from
> bereavements, say to a writer who asks them, in effect, to
> shake hands with the Germans who caused them?

There is also a poem by Coleridge about prayer, followed by
an introduction by the author himself explaining how the
story came to him one night in a dream. (In this he is not
alone, of course, for many religious romances came to their
creators in dreams or psychical experiences.)

The Woman of Knockaloe was published in 1923, some
five years after peace had been declared. But even so Hall
Caine and his publishers were justified in their fears of 'touching wounds that are not yet healed', and in their extreme
sensitivity about being misunderstood. The country had been
emotionally unprepared for all the shocks of the Great War
and it took some time to recover. Claud Cockburn has said

that this war provided some excellent literary food for the popular writers:

> For the novelist seeking mass-appeal in the early 1920s, World War I was a gift, a natural, manna from heaven. It furnished him with a range of fictional and dramatic equipment such as had been ready to hand in the workshops of the Greek classical dramatists.
>
> *Best Seller*

But the potential usefulness of this manna from heaven did not really begin to take effect till a number of years after the war was over, and, even so, popular writers trod very warily at first in dealing with the romanticised 'realities of the cruel trenches' of, say, *Journey's End* (1928), by R. C. Sherriff, or the romanticised post-war disillusionment of *The Green Hat* (1924), or the romanticised facing-up to the realities of a society changed by war of Warwick Deeping's *Sorrell and Son* (1925), for the readership was all the potential relatives of the unknown soldier.

The Great War, the war to end wars, the terrible war, features in very few romantic novels written actually during the war period or immediately after it. In the preceding century, war, soldiering and death had been romantic and glorious, the very meat of romantic fiction. For the mid-Victorian hero, being a Guardsman was a common enough occupation, as with Ouida's Sabretasche and Beauty of the Guards, or Rhoda Broughton's Captain Dare. They looked fine and dashing in their brightly coloured uniforms, and if they had to dash away to fight, leaving bitter-sweet kisses on the lips of their broken-hearted lovers, this had the advantage of prolonging still further the delicious suspense of the story. And for Ouida, even the actual bloodthirsty details of her imaginative battles, with decapitations, and slain corpses piling up, were portrayed as a magnificently colourful spectacle. There was still glory in war—and in death. In the Victorian romances, death marked not the end but the beginning of the ultimate love. Though a tragedy in mortal terms, death could be a triumph in heavenly terms. The glories of war were even used, in metaphor, to raise the prestige of heaven (as in the hymn, 'Onward Christian Soldiers, Marching as to War') in *Red As a Rose Is She*. When the valiant soldier-hero, Robert, dies it is explained that he has 'surrendered his fair soul to his Captain—Christ'.

But with the real mass horrors of the First World War, Christ stopped being a soldier, and war lost this kind of glamour. Too many real heroes were killed, and frequently were not able to die nobly, holding the banner high, with a smile on their faces and Jesus in their hearts. Much of the romantic fiction written during the war years avoids the subject altogether, preferring to take refuge in the old themes of love in society life, or marital complications (e.g. bigamy, as in Florence Ethel Young's *The Bigamist*, 1917).

Among the limited number of romantic novels published during the war years, one of the few which actually mentioned the subject is a sickly-sweet romance by Berta Ruck, *Arabella the Awful* (1918). It is a simple, cheery little tale with some light-hearted satire on the aristocracy, and is designed clearly as a morale raiser.

Arabella, daughter of a common village tradesman, is invited to stay up at the Squire's house as daughter of the family in order to refine her ways. To the family's horror, the eldest son, Eric Cattermole of the Guards, starts to fall in love with 'heather honey brown eyed' Arabella. Luckily for everyone, however, Arabella does not really care for the ways of the rich and prefers her own class of fellow; she falls in love with Sidney Sharpe, the up-and-coming grocer's lad.

On to this jolly little story is attached the propaganda apparatus. The war breaks out and is shown to be a simple case of the Cattermole family and the local lads uniting in a simple fight against the Kaiser. There are jokey references to the Germans' silliness and the English bravery. Valiant Sidney Sharpe volunteers even before he is called up, which causes Arabella to observe that 'If there's a few more like him we shan't have to put up with much more cheek from the Kaiser Bill'. And when Arabella is occasioned to run very fast, she is described as 'chasing up the street as if the German army was fleeing in front of her'. When some young people gather round the drawing-room piano for some ragtime, an out of date hit-song (or 'tune of the moment') is described as being 'as dead as the German boast to eat Christmas dinner in Buckingham Palace'.

In some ways, the war is seen to be mainly no more than a device to shake the girls up into realising how much they love their men. It does not change life much. In fact, Berta Ruck says reassuringly that:

> Life went on as usual at The Grange; the same big staff of servants, the same sumptuous meals, the same routine that seemed as if nothing on earth could ever alter it, from the same cup of tea and slices of wafer bread and (real) butter the first thing in the morning to the same dressing for dinner at night.

Later on, she does hint darkly that at the beginning of the Great War 'the optimists among us were as little prepared for what happened in these years as were the pessimists', but despite this threat of worse to come, she never says what it is. And although she admits that a great many young men *were* killed off, 'poor, splendid, insolent and attractive darlings', all the characters in *her* story survive. Sidney Sharpe comes home, wounded but smiling, to marry Arabella; Eric Cattermole comes back to marry Peggy. And their homecoming to the London hospital where all the girls are working as nurses, is gloriously patriotic:

> At half-past three that same afternoon a crowd lined both sides of the street that led up to St. Hester's Hospital, waiting for the arrival of the expected heroes from the Front.
>
> Presently there was a noise like distant cheering—it was taken up nearer and nearer yet. It broke into a roar of hurrahs, with 'Three cheers for our Tommies!' as they came in a procession of six taxi-cabs, each of which held two men, bareheaded, wrapped about with khaki coats

buttoned on over grey-blue bed-jackets, many of them with slings, all with bright and steady sunburnt faces that grinned a cheery response to the shouts of the crowd, and laughed, and nodded when here and there a flung packet of cigarettes found its mark on the knees of a brave fellow who had been for so long a target for the enemy's bullets.

Berta Ruck justifies her approach to unpleasant realities in the following way:

I belong to the School of Thought (the Non-Thinking School, if you like) that considers 'compensating dream fiction', not as opiate, but as tonic, and prefers to leave the tale on a note definitely gay and hopeful. People condemn the story-teller's cheerfully tidied-up last chapter as the flight from reality. Personally I regard it as the entrance into the original real world...

To the people who ask me why I can't face facts, I would suggest that it takes all kinds of facts to make a world; why should I not describe those I prefer? Why, people ask, do I falsify Life? Why, I ask, do they? I think it is very wrong to give Youth the impression that it is unalterably doomed to disappointment. *'C'est en croyant aux roses'*, says a French proverb, *'qu'on les fait éclorer.'* It is by believing in roses that one brings them into bloom...

It is my creed that the world was created to go merry as a marriage-bell and for the whole human race to be healthy, wealthy and wise enough to be happy on all cylinders.

A Story-Teller Tells The Truth (1935)

After the war, a few romances did try to 'deal with the problems' engendered by war, but the handling of these problems tended to be superficial and sentimental. There was, for instance, *Painted Heaven* (1934) by Netta Musket, which looks at the problem of the 'surplus million' women left over after the war. The heroine, having had the misfortune to lose her fiancé, her brothers and her parents in the war, and with little chance of finding a husband, decides to seek happiness in an

illegitimate child, only to discover that this offers the false
security of no more than a 'painted heaven'. *Complete Surrender* (1931), by Maud Diver, looks at the problem of bereaved mothers, widowed wives and orphaned babies and
shows how love, plus some far-fetched coincidences, can overcome all these misfortunes. An aristocratic lady loses her son
Derek in the war, so to fill her empty life she tries to adopt a
baby boy whose father has been killed and whose mother cannot afford to care for him. By a stroke of fortune, it turns out
that the baby boy is the lady's own grandchild, by her son's
secret wartime marriage. The widowed bride, though virtuous, is not quite of the right class, but it is shown that even
this problem can be overcome by enough love; thus, the
bereaved mother gains a boy grandchild, the widowed wife
gains a rich classy mother-in-law, and the baby boy gurgles his
way through, growing to look more like his dead dad every
day, and bringing sunshine into everybody's life.

In *Strange Roads* (1918) and its companion novel *Strong
Hours* (1919), Maud Diver tries to show the effects of war on
the lives and loves of the Blounts of Avonleigh, 'an ancient
family dating back to the days of Coeur de Lion'. But though
there are some striking metaphors and stirring emotional
passages about the heroism of the valiant young men, and
the ungrudging fortitude of their waiting womenfolk, her
summary of what the war is actually all about, and why they
all keep going off to it is pretty confusing. The novel opens
when the aristocratic officer-hero, who is known to be the
'Brains on the Home Front', is having a few personal thoughts
about war. They are noble but not very elucidating:

To the Honourable Evan Trevanyon Blount, of Avonleigh
Hall, War with a 'great and friendly nation'—War that
had been written down a financial impossibility—had
proved a somewhat disconcerting event. Consequently, he
had been slow to face the full significance and proportions
of a struggle that had shattered his most comforting beliefs;
and, incidentally, a good many other things that could not
be so easily mended.

Even after eight and a half months of Homeric fighting —of muddle and heroism and startling revelations of German psychology—his official atmosphere was scarcely changed, and he himself had shed little of his old faith.

The romantic novelists' handling of political themes has not altered with the passing of time. Many still feel the desire, perhaps to show how broad their scope is, perhaps out of respect and admiration for this powerful thing which is beyond understanding, to put in political references. But too often these turn political issues into crude moral issues, into simple confrontations between evil and virtue, rather than between different ideologies. For instance, in this reference to the Cuba crisis of 1962, from a Caribbean-foreign-setting romance, *Oranges and Lemons* (Isobel Chace), John Kennedy is portrayed as a strong sincere good man, while Castro is no more than a noisy upstart:

> Two years later ... and Cuba was heavy dark headlines in the world's newspapers, with a bearded man shouting defiance from his island, and a grim-faced young man in a white house hurling strength back at him.

The political views of romantic heroes and heroines tend, if anything, to be right-wing and reactionary rather than left. But, ideally, they are apolitical, for in a world where love reigns supreme, politics are not necessary.

In Jennifer Ames's 'political' romance, *Rich Twin, Poor Twin* (1966), in which characters, apropos of nothing, make important-sounding statements like: 'We're plumb in the middle of another crisis, it seems, and the worst one we've had yet by all appearances', the aspiring M.P. hero is prepared, in fact feels it essential, to sacrifice his whole career, all because of his love for the heroine. 'She means more to me than winning this election', he says. Becoming a Member of Parliament and being in love are simply not compatible. In fact, the only character who stays in the political race is the villain, Judson, who becomes 'a rather dull back bencher'.

There is always a suggestion, too, that for a heroine to have political thoughts is in some way unladylike and un-feminine, and spoils her attraction as a lover. In the following passage the heroine is trying to take a reasonable middle-of-the-road attitude towards the suffragette movement, but it is shown that she need not really bother to have any views on it at all because Bertie is so much in love with her that he would give her whatever she wants, anyway:

'Women are making a blasted nuisance of themselves—forgive my language, Gardenia—tying themselves to rail-ings, screaming outside the Houses of Parliament. It makes one quite ashamed of the fair sex!'

'I personally don't want a vote,' Gardenia said, 'but I think women have a very raw deal all round. Look how they are ordered about, first by their parents, and then by their husband. A woman never has a chance to think for herself or do anything she wants to do.'

'I will let you do anything you want to do,' Bertie said in a low voice.

'You are very kind,' Gardenia said lightly.

Barbara Cartland, *A Virgin in Paris* (1966)

13

The Lure of the Desert

THE MAGICAL, TIMELESS and, above all, *indefinable*, qualities of the desert have always been popular in all forms of mass entertainment, hence the success of *The Desert Song*, *Lawrence of Arabia* and frequent television documentaries about the Nile. But the deserts that feature in romantic fiction are of an especially indefinable quality.

> 'The desert is like a woman,' he murmured. 'Seductive and challenging, with depths in which a man may get lost for ever. I have known it in all moods, yet each day its sweeping spaces offer something new. A fresh challenge, a certain torment, and then at night its cool caress, or its crescent moon—the claw of the lover.'
> The wind whispered across the illimitable spaces, and Lorna glanced at the man beside her and saw his profile moulded firm against the glow of the moon.
>
> Violet Winspear, *Blue Jasmin* (1969)

The geographical sitings of romantic deserts are even more indefinable, hovering anywhere between the Spanish Sahara and the Caspian Sea. The desert location evoked by one romantic novelist, Kathlyn Rhodes, author of *The Lure of the Desert* (1916), was described evasively by her publishers as 'the desert, Cairo, the Nile and India'.

In fact, 'the desert' and 'the East' are synonymous. Such phrases as 'nights of Araby', 'shadow and mystery', 'an infinity of space', the deserts 'full of meaning, of variety, of mystery, of terror', 'timelessness of the endless desert sky', or even the use of single words like 'fez', 'arab', or 'sand', summon up hot, palm-tree growing places which could be anywhere east of Calais.

The mixed people who inhabit these far-flung spots know how to live with a savage yet carefree insouciance which we can barely appreciate:

> Down the tiger-striped brilliance of the narrow way surged the men of Casamour; Arabs, Jews, Moors, Negroes, tawny-skinned Berbers with golden eyes; in holiday mood they came, laughing, chattering, spilling over with high-spirits like children newly-released from school. Gay as the figures of some medieval pageantry they moved in their vivid garments, djellabahs of turquoise, of jade green, caftans of violet magenta, cloaks of striped silk, of saffron and indigo. Like skeins of embroidery silk tumbled from some giant work basket the festive draperies glowed.
>
> Elizabeth Hoy, *To Win a Paradise* (1970)

Deserts have cropped up here and there throughout the span of romantic fiction to provide incidental background variations, notably in Ouida's bloody battles fought in Algeria, or in Elinor Glyn's *His Hour* (1910), when the heroine consults the Sphinx to discover a few home truths about herself and her love prospects, and in *The Rosary* when the heroine also consults the Sphinx but discovers nothing she didn't already know.

But it was Robert Hichens, writing in the early 1900s, who first made a romantic speciality out of deserts. His books— *The Garden of Allah* (1904), *The Call of the Blood* (1906), *The Spell of Egypt* (1910), *In the Wilderness* (1917)—though they were called romances, had only a minimal story-line and love interest, usually of a sentimental kind, and the real appeal was his revelation of desert mysteries, and the glimpse he

offered of Egypt's 'sober eternal beauty', and of 'the deep
desires and yearning hunger of the heart and the imagination'
of the desert. In his descriptions of oasis life, of Arab unrest,
of the secrets of sand-diviners, the enigmas of the Sphinx,
and the strong desert men, those 'untamed descendants of
legions of free-born sun-suckled men', there is a total awe and
reverence for any aspect of the Arab way of life, particularly
the Arabs' eating and drinking habits, which is different from
our own.

The Garden of Allah offers all this, plus some spiritual
crises of both the Christian and Muslim religions, and a sweet
and poignant love-story. A line from a Saharan song is the key
text of the story, and when it is not being sung mournfully
by minor characters, it is being repeated meaningfully by the
heroine:

> No one but God and I
> Knows what is in my heart.

She whispers the words to herself. The cool wind of the
night blows over the vast spaces of the Sahara and touches
her cheek, reminding her of the wind that, at Arba, carried
fire towards her as she sat before the tent, reminding her
of the glorious days of liberty, of the passion that came to
her soul like fire in the desert.

The Garden of Allah, published in October 1904, was into
five editions by the end of the year, and another seven the
next year. Twenty-five years later it was into its forty-third
edition and still selling. It was finally filmed in the thirties
with Marlene Dietrich in the main role. But Hichens's readers
were so avid for details of desert life that they were even
prepared to read about it without the incentive of a story-
line. *The Spell of Egypt* (1910), even more successful than
The Garden of Allah, is not a novel at all. It is no more than a
long-winded, emotive, dreamy, romanticised travelogue whose

style is so poetic that it does not actually convey any hard
facts about Egypt at all.

> Why do you come to Egypt? Do you come to gain a dream,
> or to regain lost dreams of old; to gild your life with the
> drowsy gold of romance? To lose a creeping sorrow, to
> forget that too many of your hours are sullen, grey, bereft.
>
> Egypt calls—even across the space of the world; and across
> the space of the world he who knows it is ready to come,
> obedient to its summons, because in thrall to the fascination
> of the 'land of sand, and ruins, and gold'; the land of the
> charmed serpent, the land of the afterglow, that may fade
> away from the sky above the mountains of Libya, but that
> fades never from the memory of one who has seen it from
> the base of some great column, or the top of some mighty
> pylon; the land that has a spell—wonderful, beautiful Egypt.

But the very meaninglessness of this kind of prose cast its
own spell. 'A very high artistic instinct and striking command
of language raise the work far above the ruck', said the *Pall
Mall Gazette*, and *Punch*, too, observed that 'he holds us
always bound by the spell of his artistry'.

Another desert charmer, and contemporary of Robert
Hichens, was Kathlyn Rhodes, popular as a writer of school-
chums stories, who also 'painted with her pen, vivid pictures
of the fire and passion of the East' in such romantic novels as
The Relentless Desert—'a novel set in Egypt which burns
with the passion of the desert', or *The Will of Allah* (1908),
The Desert Dreamers (1909), *The Desert Lovers* (1922), the
erotic content of which have a certain girlish hysteria. She
extracts tremendous mileage from one kiss. One pair of young
Arab lovers manage to experience 'a satisfaction of all their
desires', plus a 'thrilling moment of bliss', plus a 'complete
change in the whole world' all from a single kiss. Her novels
share with Hichens's an idealisation and reverence for all that
is un-European about the Arab way of life. On the whole,
though love in the desert occasionally features in novels of
this period, the emphasis tends to be on the mystical pro-

perties of the desert rather than the physical advantages of love:

> He loved the desert, loved to feel the sand slipping between his horse's hoofs, as they thundered along in the opal dawn, or in the velvety moonlight; loved to sit by the camp fires of the nomads, to listen to their songs, to sleep, later, to the throbbing lullaby of their little drums. He loved the solitude, the complete, unbroken solitude...
>
> Kathyln Rhodes, *A Desert Cain* (1922)

It was E. M. Hull who, with *The Sheik* in 1919, first put the desert on the map as being a good place for sex. The heroine, the beautiful but haughty Diana Mayo, is the first romantic heroine to be sexually assaulted, to learn during three hundred pages of it to enjoy it, and to marry the man who did it.

Diana is a spirited girl who has a strong desire to look at the desert. Against everybody's advice, she sets off like some latterday Lady Hester Stanhope on her expedition:

> She drew a long breath. It was the desert at last, the desert that she felt she had been longing for all her life. She had never known until this moment how intense the longing had been. She felt strangely at home, as if the great, silent emptiness had been waiting for her as she had been waiting for it, and now that she had come it was welcoming her softly with the faint rustle of the whispering sand, the mysterious charm of its billowy, shifting surface that seemed beckoning to her to penetrate further and further into its unknown obscurities.
>
> E. M. Hull, *The Sheik*

However, out of the desert's unknown obscurities rides the Sheik who is so fascinated by her pale English beauty and her obstinate manner that he seizes her off her horse, and takes her to his camp:

> Terror, agonising, soul-shaking terror such as she had never

imagined, took hold of her. The flaming light of desire burning in his eyes turned her sick and faint. Her body throbbed with the consciousness of a knowledge that appalled her. She understood his purpose with a horror that made each separate nerve in her system shrink against the understanding that had come to her under the consuming fire of his ardent gaze, and in the fierce embrace that was drawing her shaking limbs closer and closer against the man's own pulsating body. She writhed in his arms as he crushed her to him in a sudden access of possessive passion. His head bent slowly down to her, his eyes burned deeper, and, held immovable, she endured the first kiss she had ever received. And the touch of his scorching lips, the clasp of his arms, the close union with his warm strong body robbed her of all strength, of all power of resistance.

He keeps her as his unwilling mistress for several months, after which time she realises that she loves him after all, despite—or perhaps because of—all the raping. They marry.

As Claud Cockburn has pointed out in his book *Best Seller* (1972), 'the Mayo-Sheik relationship could, and possibly still can, trigger most interesting medico-erotic discussion', though whether he means about Diana Mayo or her creator, he does not say.

Diana's adventures were possibly a compensation for E. M. Hull's own lack of amorous excitement, for she was married to a dull pig-breeder called Percy and, though her real name was Ethel Maud, she preferred to be called Diana. They lived in Derbyshire and at the time of writing *The Sheik* she had never set foot in a desert. But this is no disadvantage to a romantic novelist.

Quite apart from the excitement of nightly struggles in the Sheik's barbaric yet luxurious tent in the oasis, there are no end of other thrills that E. M. Hull lays on—attacks by rebel Arabs, horse-taming, servant beating and other quaint Arab customs, escapes on horseback into the cruel desert, the threat of death by vultures, the threat of death by sandstorm, attempted suicide, attempted rape by a rival sheik which turns out to be far worse than submission to Diana's own assaulter; and a great many violent deaths of the expendable natives. Erotic passion is strongly linked with fear and pain, and there is a streak of sado-masochism running through the book. The Sheik proves his love for Diana by seizing hold of the rival rapist round the throat:

> With the terrible smile always on his lips, he choked him slowly to death, till the dying man's body arched and writhed in his last agony, till blood burst from his nose and mouth, pouring over the hands that held him like a vice.

The tone of the story appears to justify this murder on the grounds that the victim was about to assault Diana. But as the murderer has himself been doing just this for the past three months, the incident shows him up as a dog in a manger rather than a saviour.

The initial rape is made discreet by being reported in the past historic tense:

> She had fought until the unequal struggle had left her exhausted and helpless in his arms, until her whole body was one agonised ache from the brutal hands that forced her to compliance, until her courageous spirit was crushed by the realisation of her own powerlessness,

and generally the sex is conveyed, not by graphic descriptions of physiological parts but by the constant repetition of crush, kiss, hot, fierce, fire, lips, and by the use of impassioned adverbs. In one dialogue between Diana and the Sheik, E. M. Hull finds no less than eleven different ways for them to speak emotionally. On a single page, Diana 'burst out passionately', and she 'choked furiously'. Then 'she began desperately'. He replied drily. She gasped. He went on evenly. She whispered with dry lips. His answer was given carelessly. She whispered again, but jerkily this time. He continued sarcastically. She murmured faintly. When she has given up gasping desperately and learned to obey and love him, he expresses his love more gently. The pinnacle of tender passion is when he kisses the palms of her hands. This act of devotion had already been performed in previous romances, by blind Garth in *The Rosary* for one. But it was in *The Sheik* that it became an established convention and was a gesture which Rudolph Valentino, who played the Sheik in a film version in the twenties, borrowed from the script to use as his trade-mark of passion in subsequent roles. However, it was Elinor Glyn who claimed to have been personally responsible for teaching Rudolph Valentino how to make this kind of passionate love on the screen. 'Do you know, he had never even thought of kissing the palm, rather than the back of a woman's hand, until I made him do it!'

The story of a white girl, more than that a member of the English aristocracy, loving a man who is very nearly black, might seem to be a liberal anti-racist tract much in advance of its time. But no such luck. Sheik Ahmed Ben Hassan is not really black at all, or even brown. He is really the son of a Scottish earl and a Spanish princess. In fact, from early on Diana had begun to notice various things about him which seemed un-Arab, such as his meticulous cleanliness, his cultured ways, his well-worn French books. But it is the largeness of his hands compared to those of a real Arab that finally gives him away, though according to *The Perfumed Garden* it is not so much the smallness of an Arab's hand as the largeness of another member of his body that is remarkable. But Diana, much raped though she is, appears not to have noticed.

The novel appears, at the outset, to be in favour of the liberation of women. Diana's determination, courage in the hunting field, strength of mind, are praised. But this, like the apparent anti-racist theme, is short-lived, and her early strength of character is shown to be the unfeminine failings of sheer obstinacy and arrogance. But thanks to the power of love, these characteristics are curbed:

> The haughty expression in her eyes had turned to a tender wistfulness, with a curious gleam of expectancy that flickered in them perpetually; the little mutinous mouth had

lost the scornful curve. And with the complete change in her expression she was far more beautiful now than she had ever been.

So this is, ultimately, what love is all about. It makes women want to be submissive to their men, which in turn makes them more beautiful. But does love make Ahmed more beautiful too? Well, yes and no. It makes him more tender, less cruel. Because he loves her, he realises that he can no longer keep her prisoner against her will. Without asking her opinion first, he sends her back where she came from. But this only results in more unhappiness because by now she does not want to leave him. The last part of the book falls into the usual pattern of romantic misunderstandings. But these are, of course, resolved, and the happy lovers, as they turn out to be, fall into each other's arms, and he rains kisses on her shining hair and, 'falling back into the soft French that seemed so much more natural', whispers imploringly to her. At this, she faints, his firm mouth quivers, and he gathers up her soft slim body and tries to revive her:

> Gradually the terrible shuddering passed and the gasping sobs died away, and she lay still, so still and white that he was afraid ... the colour stole back slowly into her face and the little tremulous smile curved her lips. She slid her arm up and down his neck drawing his head down. 'I am not afraid,' she murmured slowly. 'I am not afraid of anything with your arms round me, my desert lover. Ahmed! Monseigneur.'

The Sheik is the most immoral of any of the romances, not because of lewd descriptions of sexual intercourse (the above passage anyway refers to the heroine in a state of unconsciousness, not orgasm), but because of the distorting view Miss Hull presents of the kind of relationship which leads to perfect love, and the totally unprincipled precept that the reward of rapists is a lovely English heiress with a look of misty yearning in her eyes. But the novel could be interpreted as a tract in support of the theory that rape is a physical impossibility, and that any woman who claims to have been attacked in this way was really asking for it. If one accepts unlikely human behaviour, dishonourable motivation, and the theory that what all women really want is to be crushed by a fierce hard, lover, then *The Sheik* makes a lively and entertaining read.

E. M. Hull cashed in on its success with *The Sons of the Sheik* in 1925, but the sons lack their father's strength and the whole thing is sentimental rather than passionately violent. E. M. Hull visited Algeria and produced *Camping in the Sahara* in 1926, and a handful of other eastern/desert novels, but none of them had the same impact as her first.

It was *The Sheik* which firmly established the convention of a desert passion and sparked off a whole train of sandy romances. All of them take E. M. Hull's story as their basic blue-print. Time and again, never seeming to learn from the experience of others, a young girl goes off alone, against everybody's advice, into the desert; is captured by a mysterious, imperious, cruel Arab who rides away with her to his encampment; love eventually blossoms, whereupon it conveniently transpires that he's English, or French, or Spanish, but at any rate not Arab. (One would-be sheik even turns out to be the son of a 'Whitehall official'.)

It is not merely the bare plot outline which is used each time. Various minor details of events in *The Sheik* have also become part of the desert-romance convention. It goes without saying that the Sheik's behaviour is standard. He is hard with a soft centre. He is tall and broad-shouldered, wears a heavy cloak and white flowing robes, and he has hard cruel eyes. This is E. M. Hull's original sheik:

> Diana's eyes passed over him slowly till they rested on his brown, clean-shaven face, surmounted by crisp, close-cut brown hair. It was the handsomest and the cruellest face that she had ever seen. Her gaze was drawn instinctively to his. He was looking at her with fierce burning eyes that swept her until she felt that the boyish clothes that covered

her slender limbs were stripped from her, leaving the beautiful white body bare under his passionate stare.

She shrank back, quivering, dragging the lapels of her riding jacket together over her breast with clutching hands, obeying an impulse that she hardly understood.

'Who are you?' she gasped hoarsely.

'I am the Sheik Ahmed Ben Hassan.'

And here he is in 1969, now called Prince Kasim, in Violet Winspear's *Blue Jasmin*. The descriptive material is much briefer in the more recent variations, owing to increasing printing costs; romantic novels generally are fifty per cent shorter now than they were in the twenties:

Then the tall, cloaked figure turned to Lorna who felt a thrill of fear like no other as she met the man's tawny eyes. Eyes that glittered and commanded and were made extra sparkling by the black lashes that surrounded them and the black level brows that bridged them.

Ann, heroine of *To Win a Paradise* (1970), by Elizabeth Hoy, is brighter than some of her colleagues and realises fairly soon that her desert admirer is no Arab:

Ann caught her breath. The second outrider was bareheaded. That in itself was sufficiently interesting in this galaxy of turbans. But the bare head was blond. Burnedblond the colour of August corn. Berber Arabs could be light-complexioned, Ann knew. But not this colour. No Berber could have that insolently easy square-jawed face, that blunt straight nose, that quietly humorous mouth above a dogged chin. This man looked English! ... He *is* an Englishman, she decided with queer mounting excitement, for only an Englishman would have ridden so spirited a mount without the help of spurs.

The manner in which the Sheik captures the heroine, holding her tightly in his steely embrace, wrapping her head in the suffocating folds of his billowing cloak, is traditional, and the heroine's attire at this time is almost a uniform—a well-cut shirt and riding-breeches, which show off to perfection her boyish figure. A scene showing the Sheik's skill in quietening an untameable stallion (symbolic forewarning of his taming of the heroine) is a standard feature, as is the heroine's habit, during her captivity, of befriending the Arab-lover's pedigree dog and, through love of the dog, learning to love the man.

The thing that *has* to change with the times is the desert itself. In the early twenties it was still possible for it to be a remote and exotic region, cut off from the rest of the world. But now, through the mass media and expanding tourist industry the desert, wherever it is, is accessible to all. In *To Win a Paradise* the heroine seems to treat the whole of the Sahara as though it were merely an extension of her own semi-detached, and remembers even to change into her dressing gown and slippers before kipping down; and another girl in the same novel does not go into the desert without her frilly négligé.

The extreme cruelty and sadism of the original Sheik, and the threats of horrible death, have been replaced by accounts of scenic splendour, descriptions of jewelled palaces, and glamorous harem garments. In fact, sometimes the descriptive material reads like a brochure for a slightly off-beat package-holiday. Evelyn Waugh described in *When the Going was Good* (1946) a pleasure cruise he took round the Mediterranean in 1929:

That assembly of phrases—half poetic, just perceptibly aphrodisiac—which can produce at will in the unsophisticated a state of mild unreality and glamour. 'Mystery, History, Leisure, Pleasure'. There is no directly defined sexual appeal. That rosy sequence of association, desert moon, pyramids, palms, sphinx, camels, oasis, priest in high minaret chanting the evening prayer, Allah, Hichens, Mrs. Sheridan, all delicately point the way to sheik, rape, and harem.

However, though the desert is now as safe as your own front parlour, heroines are aware that with any luck, something nasty *might* still be lurking in all that sand. Lorna in *Blue Jasmin* realises its potentialities and spurns her respectable English boyfriend's warnings:

'You're too attractive to be here on your own, let alone in the desert. I shall come with you!'

'But I don't want you, Rodney.'

'Are you one of those frigid females who gets more fun out of her own company than that of a man?'

'I'm a little bit of a lone wolf,' she admitted. 'I'm sorry, Rodney, but I did warn you that I wasn't here to look for a husband in the tourist season. I am here just to suit myself, and I assure you that I can look after myself. It's kind of you to offer your protection, but I'm not a helpless creature like Dolly Featherton.'

Rodney gazed up at her, taking in her fair hair with its silvery sheen, her large blue eyes, and her slenderness in the blue silk dress. 'If you aren't careful,' he warned, 'you'll meet your match and have some of that haughty coolness kissed out of you. Beware, Lorna! If you're made of ice, then the desert might melt you.'

It is not, of course, the desert that melts her so much as the fire of her own particular sheik, Prince Kasim, although in the matter of sex there's more talk than action. This seems surprising coming from an author, Violet Winspear, who has claimed that her heroes are 'the sort of men who are capable of rape: men it's dangerous to be alone in the room with'. Capable though he may be, Kasim never lives up to the promise.

This is the most apparent difference between *The Sheik* and subsequent desert romances—the absence of sexual violence. The more recent they are, the less sexy. In *Blue Jasmin*, although Lorna frequently feels 'the flick of his tawny eyes' on her, and though he kisses her so that she feels his nearness 'like a flame through her body', and 'his arm like steel about her', Prince Kasim refuses to prove his capabilities. The intimacy of rape is replaced by the intimacy achieved when he replaces her dislocated arm in its socket; in the agony and togetherness of the moment there is a sort of sexuality. She has just tried to escape on one of his best horses, gets caught in a thunderstorm which becomes a sandstorm, is thrown by the horse and dislocates her shoulder; he comes through the fog of swirling sand in search of her. 'Hurt me,' she begs; so he does:

He held her, his face like a bronze mask, and then he took a cigarette-case from his robes and placed one between her lips. A match flared and he put it to the tip. 'A smoke will help the pain ... are you ready?'
She took a deep pull on the cigarette and nodded. Her groan of pain was lost in the howling of the wind as with an expert movement of his hand the Sheikh jerked the dislocated bone back into its socket. She trembled with reaction and a cold sweat broke out on her forehead. A numbness followed the pain, which he said was caused by pressure upon a nerve. With lean, strong fingers he massaged her shoulder and arm until the life seeped back into them.

Eventually they marry and she waits nervously for him on their wedding night. But sex has been forestalled for so long that when he finally appears at the bedroom door, clad in a saffron silk robe, a snowy turban and yellow slippers 'looking as splendid as a prince of the Arabian nights' she faints from shock, which is of course just what her predecessor, Diana Mayo, did whenever things got out of hand.

This swoon provides a fitting climax to the modern refined desert romance. Violet Winspear, whose notion of what is romantic is more genteel than E. M. Hull's, firmly believes in turning out the lights before the action begins. 'We go as far as the bedroom door and then it's good-night ... You don't go into all the acrobatics of a wedding night. It's got to be romantic.'

14

The Greatest Duty of All

DURING THE TWENTIES and thirties a new type of romantic heroine emerged, sophisticated, elegant, languid, but with a certain breathless, questing spirit lurking beneath the glamour. She is less introspective, less philanthropic than her predecessors, but more highly-strung. She smokes cigarettes, drinks cocktails, uses a powder compact, makes frequent use of telephones and taxis, and would not dream of living any-where other than in Town.

The make-believe world that these new girls inhabit is equally sophisticated and glamorous, with an urban and deca-dent lustre. They often live independently, as in *Sally in a Service Flat* (1934), by Mabel Barnes Grundy, in and around Mayfair, as in *A Virgin in Mayfair* (1932) by Barbara Cartland, Soho, Bond Street, and Piccadilly. (There are of course the exceptions; one very avant-garde romance, *Sing for the Moon* (1934) by Mrs. Stanley Wrench, author also of *Love's Fool* and *Burnt Wings*, is set somewhat unprepossessingly 'in and around the Euston Road, the centre of the second-hand car trade'.) By the mid-thirties most heroines had stopped lounging around worrying about their souls, and had gone out to work, with a bias towards jobs which had fashionable, slightly artistic, glamour. Hetty Loring, in *The Flame of Youth* by Mrs. Patrick McGill, is a 'charming assistant in a Bond Street hat shop'. (Selling hats is all right, whereas selling knicker elastic is not.) Jennifer Prudence in *Anything but Love* (1933), by Jennifer Ames, is a successful magazine illustrator. And in *Painted Butterflies* (1931), by Mrs. Patrick McGill, Jennifer Lane (whose body incidentally was 'as supple as an arrow, ready to fly from Life's bow'), climbs the ladder of success as a society dress-designer.

As though full-time careers were not enough, they lead full night lives too. They call their boyfriends by curiously dog-like nicknames like Boy, Man, Doffy, Roddy, Robby, or Plunky. But gone are the days when strolling in the gloaming through the country lanes followed by a quick kiss under the trysting tree could leave the heroine in a state of emotional turmoil for three chapters. Now, all romantic encounters take place in smart restaurants, followed by a show or a visit to a nightclub. Judging by the romantic novels, every eligible girl spent practically every night of the week in a slender slim-cut evening gown, eating at the Savoy, the Berkeley or the Dorchester. But there was no sloping along to the West End just as you were, and letting love do the rest. To ensure full enjoyment, both partners would dress formally for the occasion.

Here are Jennifer and Jason, from Jennifer Ames's *Anything but love* (1933), dining at the Berkeley, to be followed by a show:

> Jason, lean, dark-skinned, was very distinctive in full dress kit. Jenny felt all the other women in the dining-room must be envying her. Or if they weren't they should be! None of their escorts were half as attractive as Jason, she was sure.
>
> Everything was perfectly arranged, even to the orchids that nestled in a bed of maidenhair fern beside her plate. Yet it was all done so quietly you'd never suspect there'd been anything to arrange...
>
> Jason's eyes worshipped her all through that perfectly served meal. And she *did* look lovely tonight. As though her inner glow was reflected on her skin. Her dress was red taffeta. Straight and slinky to the knees, then falling in in-

numerable frills to her toes. It accentuated the gipsy look to her.

Here is Jenny again, this time getting ready to go out to dinner with Jason's brother, Robin, and then on to the Green Dragon Night Club. She has dressed entirely to please her man:

> Jennifer, smiling a welcome from over the top of the bannisters, looked as though she'd had all day to prepare. Such an attractive picture she made in her red crepe dress, neatly tailored. A vivid flame in the dark hallway. Robin loved her in red.

Jennifer is caught between loving Robin, nicknamed Daredevil Rob, a wild chap who test-flies monoplanes and once looped the loop six times in succession, and his more sober brother, Jason. In the end she wisely chooses rich and sober Jason.

Many of the authors of this period—for instance, Berta Ruck, Ruby M. Ayres, Netta Muskett—are still household names today. Romantic novelists are numerous, staggeringly prolific (Annie S. Swan wrote over two hundred and fifty books), and also blessed with extreme longevity. Denise Robins, for instance, who is the 1970s Queen of Romance, was already in the early thirties a thoroughly established romantic novelist, termed by her publishers 'One of our most distinguished novelists'. The names of romantic novelists are further kept alive by the publishers' tendency to re-issue the novels in 'revised' editions, sometimes as many as fifty years after the original publication. The novel is 'updated', the anachronisms removed, and a contemporary dust-jacket or frontispiece added; and since most readers never notice the date of the first edition, there is no obvious indication that the reader is getting a tired old story in modern dress. One of the most outstanding instances of this is the re-issuing of *Shadowed Lives* by Annie S. Swan. It was first published, by Oliphant, Anderson and Ferrier, in 1898; its frontispiece consisted of a demure Victorian etching showing the heroine in high collar, leg-o'-mutton sleeves, and bustle, gazing wistfully out of an open window. The subject of the novel—a burning theme of the 1890s—was the problem of drink. The title refers to the fact that the lives of some of the characters are shadowed with the sin of inebriation. In 1952, fifty-four years later, the book was brought out again. This time the illustrative material consisted of a Technicolored dust-jacket showing the heroine, now dressed in a white satin strapless evening dress, standing on a medieval bridge, gazing into a man's eyes (he is wearing a grey lounge suit), with a castle and a bright sunset in the background. The text is unchanged; the subject is still the problem of drunkenness in the 1890s.

Another, more recent example of a re-issue is *Weekend Woman*, by Ruby M. Ayres, first published in 1939, which reappeared in its revised edition thirty years later. The story is about a girl with an angel's face, called Mariette, who has made a rich but unhappy marriage, and who is forever searching for true love. The blurb on the back of the 1969 edition suggests that the novel is filled with sex: '... Mariette soon discovered that wealth alone could not compensate for a lack of any real affection on her part. And so she turned to other men. One affair followed another in quick succession as she sought vainly for something real to cling to ...' But this is quite misleading. There *are* oblique references to her 'butterfly past', but the heroine is far more preoccupied with what *would* have happened if she *had* slipped up, than in actually slipping up.

When the novel opens, she has just been away for a dirty weekend with a man called Slane, but in fact it didn't come to anything. To Slane's annoyance, Mariette thwarted his passion and would not sleep with him after all:

'Little coward!' he had chided her, not for the first time during the last forty-eight hours; for last night he had almost shouted the words at her in thwarted passion when she had said over and over again, 'I can't—I'm afraid. Yes, of course I love you—but I can't face it—I'm not made that way. I hate scandal—I'm afraid.'

And all the time she hadn't loved him at all, and that seemed a tragedy, because she had risked so much in the mistaken belief that she did love him.

On their way home from the weekend, Slane is killed in a car accident and for the rest of the book Mariette is terrified that her reputation may be irrevocably ruined, and that even though she did not sleep with Slane, her husband may find out about her general gallivanting. Eventually a nice chap called Drummond, a man of the world, a sort of god-figure who knows all, falls in love with her. The husband conveniently dies. In common with many pre-war romances, the novel pretends to be very daring while its principal concern is with upholding the social reputation of the heroine.

Even with the updatings to the text, the novel still does not really come into line with the late 1960s. In the 1939 version, the lover Slane is 'a man on leave from India'. In 1969 he has changed to 'a man on leave from the Middle East oil company in which he had a good job'. In the 1939 version Mariette wears hats when she goes out to lunch; but in the sixties she does not. And in 1939 her rich husband's treatment of restaurant waiters is imperious. 'Here, waiter, keep this stuff hot till I come back,' he orders, and again, 'Where's my dinner?' he demands of the waiter. And to hotel staff he says, 'Come and light the fire some of you fellows—don't stand there gaping.' But by 1969 he knows he is lucky there are any servants left at all, and he says none of these things.

Drummond, the man-of-the-world lover, does not alter over the years. He could come from any romance from the 1880s to the present day:

Not very young, that was her first thought—probably several years older than Slane; good-looking in a manly, rather severe way. Grey eyes, dark brows, dark hair, and a certain ruthlessness about the mouth and chin. But an attractive face, she decided, and suddenly a queer desire arose in her heart to be friends with this man, to arouse his interest, to make him aware of her beauty.

But strangely, his treatment of Mariette changes drastically. In 1939 'he ran his hands over her shoulders and slim body'. But in 1969 he does not touch her at all. As society becomes more permissive, romance becomes more straight-laced; for it is one of the aims of present-day romantic novelists to show the way to a better, purer, more moral way of life.

Other popular writers of the inter-war years included May Christie, Sophie Cole, Alice Eustace, May Edginton, Isobel Clarke, Sophia Cleugh, Maysie Greig (alias Jennifer Ames, alias Ann Barclay, alias Mary D. Warre), Maud Diver, Madame Albanesi (alias Effie Adelaide Rowlands), Margaret Pedler, Phyllis Austin, Bertha M. Clay, Florence Kilpatrick, and Katharine H. Taylor. Many of their romances, as Queenie Leavis pointed out somewhat disparagingly in *Fiction and the Reading Public*, specialise in what she terms 'fantasy-spinning' or 'dream-spinning': *As Long as We're Together, In Search of Each Other, Diamonds and Jasmin, The Make-Believe Lover, The Dream that Happened, Invitation to Love, Song Bird, Wings in the Dusk, Love in Amber, Change Here for Happiness, Runaway Lovers, Half-Past Kissing Time*. But even those more daringly sexy-sounding titles, such as *Cloistered Virtue, The Sin of Eve, Love-Girl, The Vision of Desire*, or *The Waves of Destiny*, seldom hide anything one could term lascivious or immoral.

Despite the new ideas on sexual freedom, free love, and the biological urge which were being advocated in the twenties by writers like H. G. Wells, Aldous Huxley and Bertrand Russell, and the practical advice being offered by Marie Stopes (she gave her first public lecture on contraception in 1922), free love was by no means what the fictional heroine sought. For her, there was still one man for one woman, and chastity was still a virtue; and her virginity was 'something very precious'; more than that, it was:

Something she had kept locked inside her for years. Something which, once broken, could never be repaired. Something he probably didn't know about, couldn't even guess at.

Jennifer Ames, Anything but Love (1933)

The occasional 'bad girl' in romance was 'as modern as a man', 'threw her cap over the windmill', or 'let herself go all the way'; but for most heroines, despite their come-hither behaviour, their warm red lips, and their suggestive orgasmic reaction to kissing, marriage was still the ultimate dream:

He picked her up in his arms and carried her up the narrow stairway to her attic studio.

Jenny lay against him and wished her heart would stop throbbing so violently. It was making her feel queer. Queer fancies, too, drifted through her mind. And hopes, secret hopes she'd cherished from childhood, seemed to line up on each side of the staircase and plead with her ... Of a church, with the sunlight falling in a golden pool on the aisle. Of herself, kneeling there, her hand, cold and timid, in her bridegroom's, while a white-frocked minister read the words of the gospel over their heads. Of her newly-made husband raising her to her feet, tucking her little arm securely and protectingly through his, while the deep organ music swelled and reverberated until it filled the church gaily with Mendelssohn's wedding march. She could feel her own heart swelling too, until she thought it must burst with love, with pride, with a sweet, reassuring sense of *rightness* ... If only she might feel that sense of rightness now!

Jennifer Ames, Anything but Love

The preoccupation with marriage as the ultimate goal, and the final chapter, prompted all manner of nonsensical variations on the kind of situation that might lead up to matrimony. In *The Great Husband Hunt* (1922), by Mabel Barnes Grundy (author of *A Girl for Sale* (1920), *Her Mad Month* (1917), *An Undressed Heroine* (1916)), an eccentric old man

offers a reward of a thousand pounds and a handsome dowry
to the first of his four nice, but unlovely, nieces who manages
to get herself engaged, and 'how the four accept the chal-
lenge and set forth in quest of husbands makes an amusing tale'. Tracing the parallel fortunes on the road to matrimony of several different girls, be they cousins, sisters or
friends, was another well-used theme. *The Road to Anywhere*
(1922), by 'Rita' (still as popular in the late twenties as she
had been in the 1890s), tells the adventures in life and love
of a French girl, a German girl, and an English girl. 'Where
will the Road to Life, the Road to Anywhere, lead them?'
demands the blurb. Or, similarly, *Where Strange Roads Go
Down* (1913) and *Winding Paths* (1911), by Gertrude Page, in
which we follow the love-lives of a pensive girl and a flighty
girl; or *Green Leaf* by Lady Miles, in which Cuckoo, beautiful
but cold and self-sufficient, is contrasted with her cousin Bru-
netta, plain but warm-hearted; or *Her Dancing Partner* (1926),
by Mrs. Patrick McGill, which tells of the 'search for happiness' of two telephone assistants, Coral Wayne, and her 'rather
vulgar little stepsister, Betty Bellamy'.

On and on goes the desperate search along those winding
paths of life for Mr. Right. Somewhat surprisingly, in view
of her supposed emancipation and her career and her inde-
pendence, what the romantic heroine really yearned for was
to feel small, petite even, and cherished and feminine. She
wanted a big strong he-man (with of course a sensitive centre)
literally to sweep her off her feet, hold her tightly in his strong
arms, and sometimes even to maltreat her. 'Frankly, she liked
men and their society. There was, she informed Cyrilla, an
unconscious brutality with most of them, which gave a girl
something to think about.' G. B. Burgin, *Cyrilla* (1922).

Maysie Greig offers her heroine *A Man to Protect You*
(1939). Margaret Pedler had gone further and invented *The
Barbarian Lover* (1923), a hard, strong, arrogant man with a
sun-burned hatchet face and obstinate straight-lipped mouth,
who strides about the wide open spaces of the earth in his
travel-stained khaki-coloured riding-kit, always at hand to
rescue the heroine from whatever dangerous and unlikely

situation she had got herself into. His first act of bravery and chivalry is to save her from a man-eating tiger seconds before it gobbles her up:

> His hand was resting on his hip, and there was a careless arrogance in his whole attitude. Somehow the pose he had unconsciously assumed, together with the great dead beast lying at his feet, seemed to her typical of the man—of his strength and swift, decisive action, and of a certain ruthlessness of character which she sensed in him—the force of which she was subconsciously beginning to fear. It seemed almost to menace her, to threaten the tranquil freedom of spirit which she had always known. She could imagine this man trying to bend a woman to his will and flatly refusing to recognise failure. With a little shiver she turned her face away from that arrogant figure, etched so clearly in the quivering afternoon glow, and kept her gaze determinedly ahead.

Later, he rescues her when she is struck by lightning in a forest, and he also saves her from her bolting horse. But eventually he has to admit that he considers her to be over-civilised and suggests that if only she were to go camping with him it would make a '*real*' woman of her':

> 'Or a savage,' retorted Patricia.
>   'I suppose that's what you set me down for, isn't it?'
>   'I certainly think you're—primitive,' she returned.
>   'So is God; so is nature. I don't want to be anything else. After all, it's the big, primitive things that count.'
>   She glanced up interrogatively. He was staring out across the moonswept plain, in his eyes a curious dreaming expression so totally opposed to their usual, hard impenetrable gaze that it took her by surprise.
>   'What kind of things?' she said hesitatingly, the question seeming drawn from her almost against her will.
>   His glance came back to her face and rested there.
>   'Birth and death,' he answered quietly. 'Courage to face

life, and love to sweeten it. The first two are inevitable, the beginning and end, and in between, if a man can find the others he's got all that matters.'

'I think you ought to have lived in the Stone Age,' she protested, shying away from the deeps upon which he had touched. 'Your wants seem so few.'

But though his wants are few, they are, as he himself admits, big and primitive wants:

'I love you as I didn't know it was possible to love. I want you in every fibre of my being—so much that it's torture to be near you and not—take what I wanted.'

There was a fire in his eyes—a flaming light of passion barely held in leash that terrified her ... He caught her roughly in his arms. His mouth sought hers, straining against it in fierce, possessive kisses. The love and passion which his iron will had thwarted and held back for months surged over her now in a resistless torrent. The gates had been opened. They could never again be closed.

Though to some extent afraid of this man's unleashed instincts, Patricia ultimately gives in to her own growing love for him, and learns to enjoy his fierce, barbarian, yet strangely gentle kissing:

She lay in his arms, yielding tremulously to the imperious passion that surged over her, conscious only of the utter rapture of his nearness, of the supreme ecstasy of absolute surrender. Nothing could come between them any more. They were together—the dividing wall that had held them apart shattered for ever.

But not entirely shattered, for the chief difficulty of loving a barbarian who believes in the big primitive things in life is that he wants to take her away to discover these primitive things—'right away into the big, clear places of the world where our love won't be stifled and crowded out by a mass of other trivialities', while she still believes wholeheartedly in the civilised English way of life. However, they come to an amicable compromise, agreeing to live six months of the year primitive and six civilised.

The heroine of the thirties was still uncertain whether she wished to be liberated from man or dominated by him. It is indicative of this confusion that she often chooses a lover like the barbarian, who is paradoxically fierce yet gentle, who can kiss with stormy, sudden passion and yet with a simultaneous 'strange and lingering gentleness'. This quality, difficult though it is to achieve, is clearly a very attractive characteristic, for it has been adopted by many present-day heroes, who manage to kiss with a 'fierce, yet tender passion'.

The majority of romantic novelists of this period showed little interest in God. The quasi-Christian religion which had been given a temporary new lease of life by E. M. Dell, Florence Barclay and other revivalists of the romantic-religious theme, finally disappeared altogether from the souls of heroines. During and after the Second World War, comforting religious thoughts, generated out of an atmosphere of fear, doubt, grief and confusion, inevitably had their place. But in the inter-war period, religion in romantic fiction shook off even the pretence of Christianity and appeared in its true light as a religion of erotic love. The state of *being in love* became for the romantic heroine what the state of grace is to the Christian. A person in love was endowed with special immortal powers of perception and universal understanding:

In that never to be repeated or forgotten moment, the young face seemed irradiated from an inner life of communion with Beauty and Knowledge—a pitying knowledge of what was base and mean in humanity, and a triumphant recognition of the fact that though it be dragged through the deepest mire, Love, Truth, and Beauty that is both, must for ever endure.

Mrs. Patrick McGill, *Painted Butterflies*

Where love was sacred, so too was the happiness that went

with it. The personal philosophy of Maysie Greig, based on the somewhat ephemeral quality of happiness, is representative:

> I write *happy* love stories because I believe happiness is the greatest virtue in the world and misery the greatest sin. You can so infect people with your own misery that you can make them miserable when they were quite happy and contented before. To be happy is as though you opened every window in your mind and let in strong, clean sunlight. That is why I think everyone should try to be happy, and read stories that make one happy, rather than those that increase one's sense of futility and despair. If I tried to write a really miserable story I think I should end by committing suicide!
>
> *Why I write Love Stories* (1936)

These beliefs are repeated time and again by the characters in her romances:

> 'Happiness is the most important thing,' he said quietly, 'and love. Not only love of a woman, but love of the whole world you are living in. Why waste time scrambling for worldly goods when but to live happily and simply gives one such an intense pleasure?'
>
> 'Surely the greatest duty of all is the duty each of us owes to ourselves. The duty to let ourselves live as we wish to.'
>
> 'Do you think that God intended any of us to lead a life of miserable self-sacrifice for the sake of others? Do you think He would have given us the power of love if He meant us to deny that love when it came to us? No, Sally, your first duty lies to our love, because that's the most important thing in the world.'
>
> Maysie Greig, *Love me and let me Go* (1936)

Reverence for the happiness of those who were in love was at the core of most popular writers' beliefs. Even for such a

fervent moralist as Gilbert Frankau, the sanctity of the lovers'
happiness could overcome the adultery of their love:

> Love was justified of both by the sheer test of happiness.
> As well accuse the birds of deadly sin as these two who,
> moved by an impulse so overwhelming that to deny it
> would have been a denial of their very natures, had—
> mated.

Gilbert Frankau, *The Love-Story of Aliette Brunton* (1922)

It was not, incidentally, just the popular fiction writers who
were on the inter-war happiness kick. Bertrand Russell, too,
produced his *The Conquest of Happiness* (1930), a book which
explains both why everybody should be happy and how to
attain that state.

Despite the disappearance from romantic fiction of a personal God, and the subsequent though more gradual disin-
tegration of heroines' vaguely Christian feelings, some of the
activities associated with a deity continued to be practised. In
times of elation or distress, romantic characters still resorted
to prayer, though to whom or to what they prayed is usually
left unspecified. Here, in *Love me and let me Go* the wandering artist Rex feels like a moment of prayer before he
carries his girlish bride into their honeymoon tent in the
Lake District on the first night of their rushed marriage:

> She clung tightly about his neck.
> 'Oh, Rex,' she breathed, 'I really *am* scared.'
> He laughed down at her tenderly. 'I'm a bit scared my-
> self, it's ... it's so wonderful, isn't it?' His voice cracked
> slightly.
> She nodded without speaking and pressed her face against
> his coat.
> 'Will it ... will it always be so wonderful, Rex?' she
> whispered.
> He said, a grave note in his young voice, 'Let's pray it
> will be, Sally. I'm not a religious man but I feel like going

down on my knees right now and praying that our love
will always be as glorious as it is now.'

She nodded slowly.

Maysie Greig, *Love me and let me Go*

It is this kind of nonsense, predominating in the thirties, that
went to create the popular, if misinformed, image of romantic
fiction as something shallow, flaccid and unspirited. Much of
the thirties' apotheosis of happiness lacks the 'luxuriant
vitality' and the joyful enthusiasm of, say, Marie Corelli's dotty
religious expositions, and it is as a consequence of this that
so many of the romances of the thirties turned out to be vapid
and empty. But vacuous as it may seem as a basis for a philosophy, this kind of belief in happy love as a beginning and an
end in itself was what the reading public wanted.

Gilbert Frankau, creator of the immortal line: 'That afternoon her sheer physical beauty thrilled him like fine
poetry', was among those popular all-purpose writers who
gave the people what they wanted. He was a newspaper
columnist, romantic novelist, professional intellectual-hater,
and editor of publications like *A Century of Love Stories*.
He was the people's writer, with his finger at the pulse of
the nation. He wrote straight from his heart to the heart of
the world. 'Authorship is not so much a function of the brain
as it is of the heart. And the heart is a universal organ,' he
explained in the *Daily Mail* in 1926. He also claimed that
for a writer, one of the most important things was 'knowledgeableness'. The secret of his technique can only be described as
'superlativeness'. Whatever he was writing about, he wrote
with an exaggerated emotional intensity which was frequently
not only out of proportion to the issue but singularly in-
appropriate. Nothing in his world is ever ordinary. His heroes
are more noble, his aristocracy more genteel, his virgins more
virginal. Even his illicit lovers are somehow more adulterous.
And when it came to kissing, he expressed his superlative
knowledgeableness with excesses of heat and crushing and
aching:

Marie Corelli

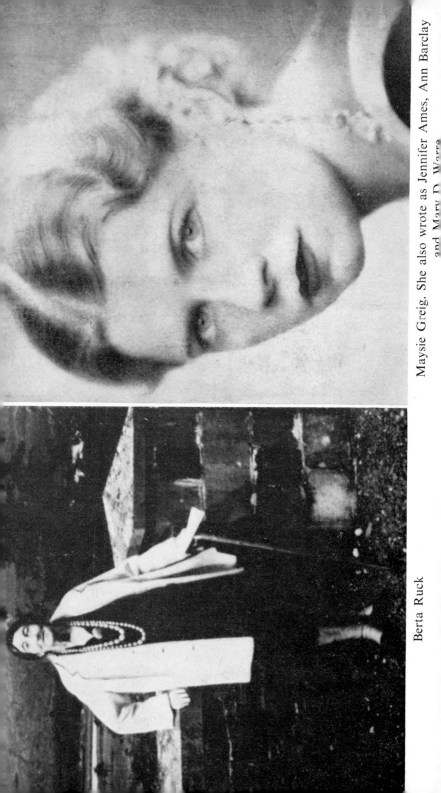

Maysie Greig. She also wrote as Jennifer Ames, Ann Barclay and Mary D. Warre

Berta Ruck

Her lips were fire on his cheeks. The perfume of her was
the fire in his mind. Her arms were chains, chains of fire
about his body. He crushed her to him; crushed her mouth
under his lips. Her whole body ached for him, ached to
surrender itself. A sharp pang as of hatred went through
her body; she hated him for the thing he could not do;
hated herself for the longings in her body.

The Love-Story of Aliette Brunton (1922)

A Gilbert Frankau kiss offers the ultimate religious experience:

> She, too, heard that sheer music which is love. Once more,
> tempest-wise, emotion swept her through and through;
> sweeping away inhibition; sweeping away all false fastidi-
> ousness; cleansing her soul of all instincts save the instinct
> for loving, for being loved. In that one magical self-reveal-
> ing moment, she was conscious solely of joy.

But the continual use of superlatives to describe every character, every state of mind, and every moral indignation, can
lead to a devaluation of all sensation; and in order to sustain,
throughout his prose, the state of erotico-religioso superlativeness, Gilbert Frankau found it necessary to coin new words:
sex-instinct, sex-essence, sex-distrust, sex-awareness, sex-thrill,
sex-duty, anti-sex resolutions, sex-thrilled, sex-foolish, sex-
fool, sex-desire, sex-abyss, sex-craving, sex-issue, sex-outlook,
sex-lesson, passion-hot moment, passion-cold.

Romance has become essentially a woman's world, both for
readers and writers. The fiction of such popular male writers
as A. E. W. Mason or Rafael Sabatini, though in the general
'romance' class, centres on adventure, escapism and excitement rather than matters of the heart. But there are a few
who, like Gilbert Frankau, attempted, and succeeded in writing about low-brow love, among them G. B. Burgin, writing
from the late 1890s until the mid-thirties, author of about
eighty novels, including *The Kiss* (1924), *The Love that Lasts*
(1913) and *Cyrilla Seeks Herself* (1922). But, unlike Gilbert

Frankau's, Burgin's romances are not sex-thrilled. He is openly
sentimental about love, and keeps his heroines firmly on their
pedestals:

> 'Cyrilla, you are divinely, most exquisitely beautiful. You
> are so beautiful that I am afraid of you. You hurt me...
> Don't you see, Cyrilla, don't you know, that you are the
> embodiment of all that is sweetest and dearest in the world
> to me? You're heaven's explanation on earth. You know
> what I mean?'

Another male romance-writer whose immense popularity
makes him worthy of mention is R. W. Alexander, alias Joan
Butler, who wrote from the thirties up to the late sixties. His
view of love is jolly, humorous and light-hearted. In fact,
judging by some of his titles, love is on a par with the state
of the weather: *Set Fair* (1952), *Sheet Lightning* (1950), *Sun
Spots* (1942), *Deep Freeze* (1952), *Cloudy Weather* (1940),
Heat Haze (1949). His style is pseudo-Hemingway:

> 'My only theory is that she got a touch of the sun.'
> 'She's in love.'
> 'Mirabelle is in love?'
> 'Yes. Mirabelle is in love.'
> 'It's not possible!'
> 'It is. She's in love with Paul.'
> 'No!'
> 'Yes, you dope!'
> 'With Paul?'
> 'With Paul.'
> 'You mean that scholarly young character with the glasses?'
> 'I mean Paul Worth.'
> 'And the voice that breathed over Eden is ringing in her
>   ears?'
> 'Like the trumpet-call,' Carrie nodded.
> 'She's promised him her heart and hand?'
> 'Yes. They're going to be married as soon as possible.'

'Then we can chalk it all up to love?'
'I suppose so.'
'It's an amazing business, this love.'

Joan Butler, *Set Fair* (1952)

15

The Relentless Lava of War

> The whole atmosphere was pregnant with a feeling
> of tense realism as though the people knew they
> were living on the edge of a volcano which might
> erupt at any moment to cover them with the
> relentless lava of war.
>> Denise Robins, *This One Night* (1942)

As THE RELENTLESS lava swept over them, the romantic novelists set to work with their pens, as stoutly as the landgirls
with their spades, to do their bit for Britain. In war-time
their function, to bring some romance and happiness into an
otherwise dreary world, became much more apparent, and
they flung themselves at their task with great zest and plenty
of metaphors.

There were two distinctly opposite approaches to romantic
morale-raising. In one method, the war was taken firmly hold
of and made an integral part of the story, with soldier heroes
who are strangely immortal, and make sensitive, yet cour-
ageous remarks about war, and heroines, also in uniform,
who bravely wipe the tears from their eyelashes as they say
good-bye, and everybody comes home smiling.

The other method encouraged the reader to forget the war
altogether and try to think about something quite different.
There was a blatantly sybaritic, escapist quality about many
of these romances, written in a time of lack with their voluptu-

ous descriptions of times of plenty. In *The Captain's House* (1945), by May Edginton, for instance, not only are there chauffeurs, cooks and parlourmaids hovering about in the background, but the heroine samples fresh eggs, fresh cream and fresh strawberries, and observes the softness of the bath towels and the luxurious fineness of the soap.

One example of the kind of approach which encouraged the reader to try to forget about the war is *Rosemary for Forgetting* (1941), by Ruby M. Ayres, a love-story about a rich girl living a stylish pre-war way of life with endless house-parties, cocktail parties, and a Rolls Royce in the garage. Rosemary is the heroine's name; at the time of her birth, her mother had said softly and whimsily and quite irrelevantly, 'Rosemary for remembrance'. The pronouncement, arbitrary though it seemed, turns out to be heavy with irony for, seventeen years later, Rosemary falls irrevocably in love with an unsuitable person. Rosemary's rich father has him sent away and the engagement is broken off. She spends the rest of the book trying to *forget* her childhood sweetheart until at last, on the penultimate page, her rich father now being dead, the lovers are re-united and can be married.

Although this novel was first published when the war had already been going on for a couple of years, there is not a mention of any war. The heroine dashes freely around the countryside in the family Rolls to sort out the complications of her love-life, and her sweetheart is shipped off to New Zealand and back without any danger of being torpedoed. The whole story is so totally lacking in any topicality or historicity that it was able to be successfully re-issued, with only a very few minor changes in the text, in 1966. The only unsuccessful point about this particular re-issue is in the choice of the novel's illustration. In the text, lovely Rosemary is said to live in a large country house a few hours from Paddington Station, and is described as having 'fair hair, and her eyes were as blue as forget-me-nots; her tiny hands and feet were perfect, and when she laughed one corner of her mouth lifted itself a little higher than the other corner in an oddly fascinating manner'. On the 1966 jacket, though doubtless she is oddly fascinating, she is shown as having raven-black hair, coal-dark eyes, and thick symmetrical lips. Moreover, while being kissed on the ear by a man in a lime-green sports shirt, she is standing in front of what is clearly no wealthy Home Counties residence, but seems to be a Canadian log-chalet. This kind of carelessness in presentation has helped to foster the bad image of much of today's romantic fiction.

A splendid example of the other approach to morale-raising, using the war as an integral part of the story, and yet keeping the whole thing cheerful and optimistic, is to be found in Denise Robins's *This One Night* (1942). The war background is thoroughly phantasmagorical, and the politics of war are kept extremely hazy; one of the characters has to travel *incognito* 'because of political matters' but what these matters are is never fully explained. It is the emotions of war, and the metaphors of war which affect the heroine, rather than the reasons for it:

> Europe was writhing and seething in an everspreading war. She realised with a shock that Fascist and Nazi activities in the country from which she had just come were merely small repercussions from the ceaseless blows with which Hitler was hammering at a stricken world.

This One Night opens just at the outbreak of war when the heroine, Tona, a City typist 'with a face like a flower', is travelling on a transcontinental express to a country in the Balkans called 'Gardenia' to do business for her firm. (The name Gardenia is an all-purpose proper noun which crops up here and there in romantic fiction, not only as the name of a mysterious mid-European state, but also as a foreign-sounding surname, or a typically English, female Christian name.)

While changing trains at Istanbul, rather as one might change from the Circle line to the Metropolitan, Tona loses her ticket and handbag. She is rescued by a delightful, handsome, rich man with the unlikely, though fascinating, name of Valentine, who invites her to travel the rest of the way to

Gardenia in his own luxurious compartment:

> Tona sat down and smiled. She found it remarkably easy
> to talk to this young man. The train was already moving
> out of the station, but the coach was so perfectly sprung
> that she scarcely felt any vibration as they passed over the
> points. She looked with shining eyes around the miniature
> *salon*, at the artistically arranged flowers, the heavy rugs on
> the floor and the gold and purple cushions on the sofa.
> 'This is thrilling,' she said. 'It's like a scene out of ... a
> film.'
> 'You make it all very thrilling for me,' he said.
> She gave him a quick look, then changed colour, and
> her long thick lashes dropped. He could see that she had
> the typical English girl's shy reserve. The shyness intrigued
> him.
> He repeated: 'Tell me about yourself.'

Here there are shades of *Stamboul Train* (1932), but while
Graham Greene's tall dark stranger who befriends a stray
girl turns out to be merely a Jewish sultana magnate, Denise
Robins's hero is revealed as the heir to the Gardenian throne.
Graham Greene himself pointed out that the thing about
popular writers is that they do not know when to stop, but
it is unfair to judge Graham Greene and Denise Robins by
the same standards. Berta Ruck provided a better guide when
she wrote:

> Whatever People may feel about their capabilities, what I
> feel about mine is that I am not clever enough to make
> good Art out of a bad show! Always I would rather be
> 'good Bad' than 'bad Good'.

Tona, the typist, and Prince Valentine fall instantly in love,
and all night while the train pounds through the darkness
towards the Balkans, they make mad tempestuous love:

> Now she was sealed fast in his arms. She had no resistance

left. Her last vestige of control snapped and vanished when she felt his heart beat against her own. She would never forget the magic of those arms, and of those lips which brushed her lashes and strayed to her quivering mouth. He was a wonderful, masterful lover. There could never have been, there could never again be such a lover ... She felt herself being lifted into his arms. She knew that she loved him completely and at the same time was aghast at the relentlessness of such love. But she was no longer herself. She was his. All of her. And she wanted him to go on holding her to him and kissing her like this—for ever.

The music played on, until there was only silence, save for the broken, sweet whisperings of love and laughter, and heaven revealed to a golden-haired girl lying in the arms of a princely lover.

The reader, too, may be aghast at the relentlessness of a twenty-year-old typist who flings herself, intoxicated with desire, into the *wagon-lit* of a tall dark stranger in the middle of Turkey. But Denise Robins is never afraid of putting her lovers into bed before they get married, so long as it is all in a good cause and their general behaviour is not promiscuous; she believes that romance is 'a living truth' and that romantic novelists must be 'factual and draw life as it often is'. In *This One Night* the lovers are to some extent forgiven their unleashed passions because they are on the edge of the volcano of war and therefore have heightened emotions. But, more important, the prince and the typist are *in love*. It seems that according to the author's code, premarital sex is wonderful and beautiful so long as it is experienced in an atmosphere of tenderness and generosity, and so long as the love is as wholesome and good as a flower.

'I want something real in life,' says the prince to Tona. 'Something vital like this love which you will give me. You're sweet, good like a flower. I want that flower to wear against my heart for ever.'

And the good cause that makes this unbridled passion pardonable is the cause of Britain and her allies winning the war. For Tona, by her love and devotion, is ultimately to be instrumental in saving Valentine from the Fascists.

Overnight, Valentine learns that, owing to the sudden death of his father, he has turned into the King of Gardenia. He has to abandon Tona in the train and hurry to his throne. When Tona awakens, she is overcome with a terrible blushing. But this is not a post-orgasmic flush, but a blush of *shame*:

> She sat up, her heart pounding and the blood rushing violently to her cheeks as memory after memory of last night returned to her. A scorching blush seemed to envelop her whole body. Fear and ecstasy gripped her. What had she done? She loved this man, but she did not know that love could be so vital, so absorbing, so potent a thing. And he loved her.

Tona struggles on towards Gardenia and once she is there, the war takes on a colourful, glamorous, adventurous Ouida-like quality; it is like an exciting pantomime with everybody in fancy dress. Tona, who is now described as looking as 'fresh as a rose, yet with the languor of a lily', gives up her business for the City firm and instead takes a job as a dancer in a café; she becomes involved with the Fascists; she gives a Royal Command performance at the palace, and dances in front of her king-lover. She is accused of being a spy and is flung into a dark dungeon. She is condemned to death:

> In front of her a line of soldiers, each man carrying a rifle, was standing to attention. The firing squad! A wave of sheer terror gripped her. What had she done? She had chosen to die, to be riddled with bullets, to be hurled into eternity. She had chosen it rather than be helped by a man who might use her against her country.
>
> The officer who was now guiding her to a position against the wall eyed her curiously. He thought he would always be haunted by the classic beauty of that pale young face and by the youthful figure in the shimmering silver cloak which looked so strangely garish in the grey light of the

dawn ... She hung on to her courage desperately. She would show these foreigners how an English girl should die.

Seconds before her execution (wearing little more than a flimsy chiffon dance tunic and a silver cloak) she is rescued. She becomes a British agent. She tries to drug a wicked baron who turns out to be her lover-king cleverly disguised in a false beard and spectacles. Nobody seems to know who is on which side. As espionage is followed by counter-espionage, the reader becomes as baffled as the participants. But no one is quite so confused as Tona. On which side is King Valentine? With his false beard, it is hard to tell. Is he an enemy or an ally of England's? 'The policy of the new King is shrouded in mystery ... some think he's got Nazi sympathies. Most definitely there's a big Fascist organisation in this place.'

Gardenia is so strategically placed that the whole outcome of the war, it seems, depends entirely on which way the King's loyalties lie. It is this question, more than any of her physical sufferings, that worries Tona most; for, deep though her love for Valentine is, her love for her own country must come first. Soon, however, all is made clear, for she is captured by the *other* side and is taken away under close guard to the salt mines. The train crashes and her guards are killed instantly. She escapes and returns to the palace.

After a few more adventures, Tona, by this time pregnant as a result of her night in the *wagon-lit*, is smuggled out of Gardenia by the King's official fiancée, and sent back to England. She moves in with her relatives living in Norwood. She soon hears that a Nazi-inspired revolution in Gardenia has taken place. King Valentine escapes, renounces his throne, and hurries as fast as he can across Europe to Norwood, takes Tona in his arms and, in the final surprise of the book, announces that from now on all he wants is to be an Englishman called plain Mr. Carr, living in a little English house. 'I never wanted to be a king. I wanted what I am going to have now, please God. An English home—an English wife—a son, whom I pray will be born on English soil.'

This moving speech by the ex-King of Gardenia was a glow-

ing tribute to the English people, and must especially have
warmed the hearts of the inhabitants of Norwood.

'Congratulations, ducky. I must say you've done well for
yourself,' says Tona's suburban sister when the marriage is
announced, but Tona replies archly, 'You don't understand,
Kathie. I didn't know he was a king when I first fell in love
with him, and it wouldn't have mattered to me if he had
been one of the footmen at the castle.' Maybe it would not
have mattered to Tona, but it would have made a lot of difference to the story, for who wants to read about a typist marrying a footman?

This story is, of course, quite beyond the bounds of credi-
bility. But this is precisely what makes it successful. Although
the reader can identify emotionally with the heroine, the war
background has very little reality. It is turned into a delightful, exciting charade which does not really frighten anybody.

Ursula Bloom was another writer who, although she incor-
porated the basic existence of the war into her romances, did
not let the horror of it, 'the relentless lava' of it, spoil them.
War was put entirely to the advantage of her heroines. It
was a kind of open-to-all, non-exclusive marriage bureau. By
taking active part in the defence of their country, young
women were able to discover that life is full of surprise and
men. For Jenny, the quite unassuming heroine of *Jenny
W.R.E.N.* (1944), putting on the W.R.E.N.'s uniform opened
up a whole new way of life. In fact, Jenny's chief contribution
to the war effort seems to have been in serving gin and
vegetables to naval officers. But she loved the life:

> She had adored the life in the officers' mess, serving meals,
> pottering to and fro with this and that, handing potatoes,
> handing brussels sprouts, handing cheese. She had thought
> that life had only begun when she had put on the
> W.R.E.N.'s uniform, that the big war (which everybody
> thought to be such a catastrophe) had opened the gates to
> something like heaven for her.

In the Wrens she has the opportunity of meeting delicious

men, sub-lieutenants and squadron leaders, who take her out to have the kind of fun she hardly believed existed, in the Dorchester, Grosvenor House and Claridges. Among her suitors is the dashing, glamorous Robin, R.N., who was perhaps inspired by the naval officer that Ursula Bloom herself married:

> He had dark blue eyes with long, black lashes, completely wasted on any man. He was tanned with that ruddy tan you expect from a man of the sea, he had a curly mouth, with the most outrageously confident smile, and he always gave you the impression that you were *the* girl of girls, the one he's been looking for all his life, and had now found and, oh, how it exceeded what he had expected! He was tall, very tall; he was well built, very well built, and he had that way with him. But was he fickle?

Yes, he is fickle. His fickleness is soon quite apparent to the reader, who is left guessing till the last moment whether Jenny is aware of his fickleness.

The other important man in Jenny's life is a stocky naval doctor with 'harebell eyes' who examines her heart after she has had flu and diagnoses that it is weak:

> The little Doc. was a smallish N.O. He wore his cap at the Beatty angle and he had freckles, surprising freckles on his cherubic face. The little Doc. came from the North, and when he got excited, he burst into Scotch.

It's not till it's too late and the stocky Scot's ship has gone down in the sea that Jenny realises that she loved *him* best of all. But, as the purpose of the story is to raise morale, not sink spirits, she soon hears that there are a few survivors and he is among them.

Basically then, this is the standard tale of the girl with two strings to her bow. But it is given its own particular naval recruiting scheme on account of Jenny's 'dicky heart'. After a fainting fit while serving in the mess she learns that 'her heart has gone bad on her'. 'It does funny things,' she explains. 'It scuttles about. I am never quite responsible for it.' Jenny's ambiguous statements about her own heart offer ample opportunity for her admirers to make remarks about the condition of their own hearts: 'I don't believe there's anything wrong with your heart, but there's going to be whole lots wrong with my heart before long.'

Jenny is sent to see a specialist who says she must leave the Services. This is a dreadful blow to her; the Wrens is life to her and she wants, oh, so badly, to stay. 'Leaving the Wrens would be like dropping out of the war altogether,' she says, but it is no good. She is thrown out of the Navy and has a beastly time but eventually her heart improves and she gets back in. The message of the novel is that if plucky little Jenny with her dicky heart is willing to work for the war, how much more willing should able-bodied girls with strong hearts be to serve potatoes to naval officers.

Another of Ursula Bloom's wartime romances, *Romantic Fugitive* (1943), gives the reader an insight into British courage as observed by the Norwegians. Thiska, a Norwegian girl whose village has been occupied by the Nazis, escapes by sea with her childhood sweetheart, Ola, in a small open dinghy. They are picked up by a British destroyer and Thiska, a mournful, humourless girl with the twilight gloom in her blood, is shocked by the English sailors' apparently flippant and carefree attitude to war. 'It's the greatest fun. Coming to sea in a jolly fine gun room, then getting this war. A bit of luck getting this war so early on,' says one of the sailors who hauls her up out of the dinghy.

> That was the English all over! Everything she had ever heard about them came back to her. They laughed at death and danger, they thought it was fun. A curious nation, she didn't suppose anybody could understand them.

But, when she has settled down in war-ravaged England, Thiska gradually learns to understand them; she discovers that the whole secret of their indomitable courage is their gaiety, their sense of humour, and their laughter in times of crisis. Thiska falls out of love with her gloomy Ola, and into love with the cheery English sailor.

The essentially light-hearted, escapist touch of a Denise Robins or an Ursula Bloom romance was necessary to prevent the wartime story from sinking into tragedy. The romances which tried to give a 'truthful', realistic war background usually ended up on a note of appalling hopelessness.

So Long as We're Together (1943), by Sophie Cole, is a 'realistic' account of the courtship and marriage of a Canadian fighter-pilot and a London secretary, but the story does not stand a chance. The theme of the story is that young lovers will always find happiness so long as they're together. But, as disaster follows disaster, as more and more characters get killed off in air-raids, there really does not seem to be anything to be happy about. Eventually, even when they are together there's no happiness, for the heroine is pregnant and has nowhere to live, and the fighter-pilot goes slightly mad from strain, and attempts suicide. By the end, the situation seems so dreary that the story has to take a quick side-track into the specialised realms of the psychic world. The only ray of hope for the lovers, for London, and, it is implied, for the whole of humanity, is to be found in crystal-gazing. One of the characters gazes into her crystal ball and conjures up a 'vision of the future' of the lights of London turning on again 'just as they used to do in the streets at twilight before the war'.

> 'The lights of London!' he said, and there was a touch of awe in his voice. 'They aren't put out for ever! We shall see them again, Anna.'
>
> She sighed. 'It was a dream,' she said, and pushed the crystal from her.
>
> 'Call it a vision of the future,' he suggested, 'and pray that we'll see them together.'

When the war was over, the world was found to be much changed. Many romantic heroines seemed confused and upset, not least Marlene, heroine of *Where are you Going?* (1946), by Ruby M. Ayres. 'She asked herself sadly the question, "Where are you going?" and failed to find an answer,' explains the blurb; but Marlene, in spite of her metaphysical questing, luckily manages to find a partner who is equally unsure where he is going, a tired-looking, discharged soldier with a slight limp:

> Not a handsome man—not like Hugh—but there was something about him, something she could not explain, but which again gave her that curious feeling of kinship, as if they were not strangers, so that it seemed the most natural thing in the world to speak to him and to ask,
>
> 'Where are you going? Can I give you a lift?'
>
> 'Where am I going?' he smiled ruefully as he repeated her question. 'I wish I knew, but I haven't the slightest idea.'

These two lost souls eventually find their way towards a romantic attachment with one another which is based on 'complete sympathy and understanding', a relationship which is respectable, thoroughly sensible, and altogether dull.

The war had finally killed off any of the last remaining traces of the reckless spirit of E. M. Hull and E. M. Dell, or Elinor Glyn. Heroines were never again to know the wild sweet joy of mad, passionate love. Such experiences began to be classed out of romantic fiction and into pornography. From this point on, the aim of popular romantic novelists was to make their fiction respectable, in both the literary and the moral sense. In the attempt it began to lose much of its earlier vigour.

16

Aseptic Love

THE HOSPITAL ROMANCES, easily distinguished from the straight romances by their self-explanatory titles—*Hospital of the Heart, Ward Nine at St. Jude's, Doctor Divine, Doctor Delightful, The Adorable Doctor, The Doctor's Favourite Nurse, Nurse in Conflict, Doctor's Slave, Night Nurse in Peril, Part-Time Nurse, Free-Lance Nurse, The Mind of a Doctor,* etc. etc.—make a specialised study of the intimate lives of doctors and nurses.

Breathless embraces are snatched in the dispensary and rueful looks exchanged across the beds of the dying; emotions run riot and love flourishes particularly well in the aseptic, but apparently appealing, conditions of the operating theatre. 'Theatre was a magic place where most of the goings-on still held mystery and glamour,' as the heroine of *The Rebellion of Nurse Smith* (1967), by Elizabeth Gilzean, observed. All the nice girls may be waiting for sailors, but what all the nurses are waiting for is tall, cool surgeons with skilled, sensitive fingers. 'It was obvious he was a surgeon, even at fifteen yards. Surgeons—those under forty, at any rate—have a look of immediacy about them, a special kind of alert fitness.' Kate Norway, *The Bedside Manner* (1971).

Lucilla Andrews, herself an ex-nurse, and subsequently a successful exponent of the hospital romance (*Nurse Errant* (1968), *The Light in the Ward* (1966), *Hospital Circles*

The Barbarian Lover by Margaret Pedler, 1923. Jacket picture
of Hodders Ninepenny Series

Flight to the Stars by Pamela Kent.
Mills & Boon Paperback Edition

Yesterday's Love by Hermina Black.
Coronet Paperback Edition

(1967)), explains why a love-story with a hospital background is such a good idea:

> Though (the) technicalities can be tricky, there are ... great and obvious advantages if one uses a hospital background. Any hospital is an enclosed community. In any enclosed community, propinquity will accentuate personal characteristics; there is bound to be some incompatibility of temperament; and since—in a teaching hospital—90 per cent of the medical and nursing staff will be under 30 and single, sex will flourish openly. Conflict will be inevitable. Conflict is the essence of drama. Drama makes good copy.
>
> *Books and Bookmen*, November 1967

But why, one may ask, should people prefer to read about the 'accentuated personal characteristics' and the 'openly-flourishing' sexual adventures of nurses and doctors at work, rather than any other group of young, single people working in an enclosed community? Why is there an established convention of the hospital romance, but not a romance of schoolteachers or hairdressers?

The particular brand of drama that makes for what Lucilla Andrews calls the 'good copy' of the hospital romance is the drama of *human suffering*.

The hospital romance frankly relies, for at least some of its appeal, on the fact that the reader will experience a certain thrill in witnessing, in the safety of her own home, something rather appalling happening to someone else. In this, hospital romances fulfil some of the same requirements as the Victorian penny dreadfuls or the present-day sex and violence thrillers, though on a less crudely sadistic scale. All the human sufferings of the hospital romance can be perpetrated without resort to physical violence. The dramas and horrors that occur are entirely socially acceptable, even commendable. So, possibly, the appeal is that, in identifying with the patients and having the vicarious experience of rare diseases, broken legs and abdominal incisions, readers gain a magical protection from these actually happening to them in real life.

In *Doctor's Quest* (1971), by Kate Norway, there occurs a particularly gruesome drama which seems curiously out of place in a 'love-story'. The heroine-nurse, a probationer, is in love (or thinks she is) with the surgeon's assistant. Between them, the two handsome, bachelor surgeons have just cut open the patient's stomach, the incision having been described in some detail. Suddenly, something goes wrong. The patient has an 'aortic aneurysm' (a swollen-up artery). It bursts, or else is punctured by the surgeon's knife. Blood goes everywhere. The man dies. It is the heroine's first d.o.t. (death on table). She is aghast:

> Then everything stopped. The breathing had stopped long before. Tim Frost ripped off his gloves and flung them across the theatre, saying: 'Damn, damn, *damn!*' Sister, no longer bothering about asepsis, put her gloved hand over her face. Staff Coutts and the junior simply stood there, staring at her. David walked out of the scrub-room, and heaved over the first basin he came to. And now I could see that there was blood just about everywhere. The table sheet, the towels and Tim's gown were all drenched, and when Sister dropped her hand again there was a great smear of it on her forehead, between her turban and her mask.

Hardly surprisingly, the heroine-nurse realises that she isn't in love with the surgeon who performed the fatal puncture of the artery (he goes mad at the end anyway), nor with the other surgeon who, it transpires, was probably bribed to kill the patient, and she finds a more handsome, more successful surgeon instead.

The National Health Service started in July 1948, and it was following this, during the fifties, that the hospital romance established itself as a definite genre in its own right. Of course, nurse love-stories have been popping up here and there since the 1900s, and most of the well-known authors of straight romantic fiction have written the occasional nurse story too; Berta Ruck: *The Bride Who Ran Away—Nurse Henderson* (1922); Maysie Greig: *The Doctor Is a Lady* (1962); Denise

Robins: *Something to Love* (1951), for the nurse-patient relationship is an ideal situation for the development of an
intimate bond of affection. In the Victorian romances it was
by nursing a sick lover that many a heroine found the right
outlet for the *sacrifice* that she felt it was necessary to make
before she was worthy of being loved. By stroking the forehead of her ailing sweetheart, a girl is able to demonstrate
her love, her tenderness and her efficiency.

But few of the early nurse-heroines felt a definite calling to
the vocation. More often they slipped into the temporary role
of nurse when the situation demanded, as for instance Amy
in the first romance, *The Heir of Redclyffe*, or Jane in *The
Rosary*.

One Edwardian heroine who did actually make a career in
nursing (though a fairly short-lived one) was Emily, heroine
of *The Parish Nurse* (1905), by Mary E. Mann, a girl with
wide clear eyes and rich, auburn, plentiful hair, who prided
herself on her practical good sense and her quality of level-
headedness, though even she only put on the uniform and
went to care for the needy poor in the country in order to
escape from a broken heart. The only qualification necessary
was that she should be 'a lady by birth and education' as she
would be in 'daily association with the family of the clergyman' who was employing her. The ailments and accidents
she had to cope with, though not described in gory detail,
were every bit as horrifying as an aortic aneurysm, and ranged
from a woman who died of a broken neck, and an old man
suffering from 'senile decay' who, while wearing his deceased
wife's frilly nightcap, tried to kill himself by hitting his own
head with a hammer, down to curing the festering sores on
the village children's heads and faces. For the treatment of
her patients, Nurse Emily has little more to offer than tiny
tots of whisky for the old man with the hammer-hole in his
head, and instruction in the uses of personal hygiene and
fresh air for the rest. The implication of the book is that the
poor are dirty, stupid, careless and drunk, and eventually
Nurse Emily, despite her level-headedness, has to admit, 'I
really hate them. I hate their ignorance, their roughness, their

habits; I hate the smell of them, the touch of them.' Luckily, love catches up with her in the person of the local squire, and she takes off her uniform and goes back to being a gentle-woman.

Today the production of hospital romances is a flourishing and highly specialised business. Most of them are issued only by those publishing houses which specialise in romance, (John Gresham, Hurst and Blackett, Robert Hale, the Romance Book Club, Mills and Boon, Arrow, Fontana), in special library editions. A recent innovation by Robert Hale and John Gresham has been to replace the traditional, often some-what crudely painted, jacket illustration, by a glossy coloured photograph of the doctor and nurse lovers of the story, a touch which is presumably intended to convey 'authenticity' to the hospital setting. Today's writers of hospital romances are myriad; among the many are Julia Davis, Jeanne Bowman, Renee Shayn, Sonia Deane, Vera Craig, Marjorie Rylstone, Kay Talbot, Quenna Tilbury, Juliet Shore, Gern Shepherd, Linda Curzon, Petra Sawley, Clare Cavendish, Elizabeth Sei-fert, Rona Randall, Jean S. MacLeod, Olive Patterson, Joyce Dingwell, Jean Dunbar. Among the various themes which come within the scope of the convention are: plastic surgery (*The Beauty Surgeon*), the hospital thriller (*Nurse in Peril, Doctor of Fear, Mystery Clinic*), the life of the district nurse, the doctor's wife (*Julie Barden, Doctor's Wife*), the lady doctor (*The Romance of Dr. Dinah, The Doctor is a Lady*), the Alpine clinic, and the dying child. This is a theme which in-spires immediate compassion, though sometimes the attempt to hold the reader's pity goes just too far and becomes ludi-crous, as in *The Rebellion of Nurse Smith*, by Elizabeth Gil-zean, in which a young boy suffering from osteomylitis (cancer of the bone) is entrusted into the care of the probationary nurse-heroine:

'The point is, are you tough enough to give him the support he needs? I'll not pretend that it will be easy. There'll be many a time when you want to run away and cry. For the boy's sake you must not ... I'll not blame you if you feel

you can't take it, but I'm begging you to think of the boy . . .
Can you do it?'

Nurse Smith agrees to take on this great responsibility of the
boy's life. So far, so sentimental. But then follows an extraordinary situation in which Nurse Smith, young and very
inexperienced as she is, is asked to sit on a stool in the operating theatre and hold on to the boy's leg while it is being sawn
off. 'Just hold it steady, Nurse, and be ready to take the
weight.'

Strangely, hospital romances seldom feature the love-lives
of those doctors and nurses who work in the maternity wards;
this is possibly because, although surgical operations are acceptable, confinements are felt to go beyond the bounds of
propriety. Furthermore, a confinement is a reminder that
sexual relations have taken place.

The four main essentials of the hospital romance are the
doctor, the nurse, the dreadful illnesses or operations, and
the kiss. The doctor has intrinsic glamour and sex-appeal
because, by the very nature of his profession, he is allowed
access to the body. What the reader is subconsciously hoping
for is the touch of those gentle yet capable hands doing intimate and dreadful things to her. In the life and death situation, the reader/patient must subjugate herself completely
to the doctor, which, though it is not so explicit here as in the
Sheik-type novels, is what every reader/heroine really wants:
total subjugation to her man. The reader's identification with
the heroine is vitally necessary for all this. Quite often the
nurse does actually end up in one of her own hospital beds,
usually as the result of a car accident, something clear-cut
and definable, rather than illness, which does make things
easier.

But the nurse of romantic fiction is a tricky heroine because
her real-life counterpart, underpaid and overworked, is already such a ready-made heroine. When her training, her long
working day (or night), her tired feet, her low pay, her irregu-
lar off-duty periods, her lack of freedom (the figure of Matron
is always hovering ominously in the background), her sense of

vocation, are put into print, she seems almost too virtuous to be true.

The fictitious nurse has two aims in life. One is to pass her exams and so win the approval of her chosen doctor; the other is to be kissed by him. These rapacious women appear to have an insatiable desire for kisses.

Because she is fulfilling a vocation, she does not suffer from the same wanderlust, glamour-cravings, search for fame and glory, as other romantic heroines. And so any glamour or excitement which has not been found in the operating theatre, must be provided by the kiss.

It is what they are all waiting for; and they become neurotically disappointed if they do not get it. In *Nurse Errant* (1969), by Olive Patterson (there is another *Nurse Errant* by Lucilla Andrews), the doctor, a Scot called Fergus, takes his nurse for a walk in the countryside to an interesting bird-watching spot. He wants to show her the birds' nests. 'The eggs are hatching now, and the trees should be filled with young birds,' he says enticingly. But Nurse Beth is completely uninterested in bird-filled trees. All she wants is to be kissed and she can't think why he doesn't get on with it. 'She felt the urgency of her thoughts gathering in her breast, and longed to feel his arms about her,' and then, 'She could feel the emotion engulfing all else inside her, and she moistened her lips as they dried out under the pressures of her gathering emotions.'

When Nurse Beth realises that at last she is going to get a kiss, in the rapture of expectation she becomes so confused that she forgets everything she has been taught about human physiology. 'As he came towards her, she felt her emotions rise up in her throat in an encompassing wave.'

Many good nurses forget, too, the advice offered by so many fictional matrons about not letting their feelings run away with them:

'You have the right temperament for a nurse, my dear, but remember you need control too. You're a little over-emotional at times. A good nurse never shows her feelings.

She can't afford to. She needs to be very phlegmatic.'
Denise Robins, *Something to Love* (1951)

The proper kiss, nurse-style, when it *does* come, is powerful
stuff:

> Then he ran his long, sure fingers into my hair and began to
> kiss me.
> It was a long kiss, and it seemed to be controlled by some
> kind of rheostat, like the twelve-position graduation of the
> dimmer switches in the wards, which bring up the lights
> from a mere hint to a full blaze. It began with a gentle
> brush of his lips, and then the current steadily surged until
> there were drum rolls and flashes of scarlet and gold, and
> somewhere, I could have sworn, there was a full orchestra
> poised ready to play the Ravel *Bolero*.
> I don't know what would have happened if we hadn't
> been interrupted at that point, because he was about to
> step forward again, and I am quite sure I couldn't have
> done much about it. He might have been able to control
> the situation, but I should have been helpless.
> Kate Norway, *The Bedside Manner*

There is such reverence attached to kissing that even afterwards a nurse is in a state of wonder and awe about it. 'She
lifted trembling fingers to her lips and pressed them gently,
filled with wonder, and inside her mind there were great
patches of raw excitement.'

Considering the extraordinary effects these kisses have on
the nurses, one might have expected the doctors and surgeons
to take advantage of the situation and, while their nurses are
still helplessly enjoying their dry lips, raw patches in the
mind and encompassing waves of emotions in the throat, to
follow their love-making through to its ultimate conclusion.
But, in fact, their sexual behaviour is without blemish. Indeed, some of them totally misinterpret the nurses' behaviour
and become as worried about overdoing the kissing, as the
nurses are about not getting it. In *The Doctor's Prescription*

(1970), by Lorna Page, the fear that he might have kissed Nurse Jenny too much troubles the new surgeon all night and the following day, and in the end he has to call on her to check up that she is all right:

> 'Did you mind me kissing you last night?' he persisted.
> She shook her head slowly. 'No! I didn't mind.'
> 'You would rather I didn't act so forward?' There was anxiety in his tones.
> 'I was quite happy,' she admitted.
> 'That's all I want to know!' He sighed as if with relief and Jenny watched his face with all her intense emotions spreading through her mind.

Although the author can blow her mind when describing the mysteries of a surgeon's kiss, when it comes to writing about the patients' ailments, accurate research is essential; Lucilla Andrews, in her advice to other would-be hospital novelists, insists that all medical facts must come from modern, up-to-date textbooks:

> God help the writer using a hospital background who does not verify facts and keep up to date ... If a diagnosis and symptoms are mentioned, both must be correct and memory can err. To give a specific treatment is to get on very thin ice. Treatments, and particularly drugs, change with such speed that even last year's edition (of a medical textbook) can be out of date and even dangerous. I usually try to stick to general nursing points, but check them, too. Readers have a disconcerting habit of using a hospital novel as a guide book on Home Nursing. Just one example: a teenager in Northern Australia wrote and told me she had just nursed mum and two kid sisters through measles with one of my books with a measles scene open at the particular chapter throughout.

Not just the writing and publishing of hospital romances, but the reading of them, too, requires considerable specialised knowledge. Many of them, in their endeavour to be accurate and to set the authentic tone, are written in a style which is quite aneurysmal with medical jargon. The medical world is anyway notorious for its use of initials, and the reader who has no previous experience of the real hospital world may well be totally mystified by the terminology. For instance, within the first few chapters of *The Bedside Manner*, by Kate Norway, there are references to P.T.S., C.H.S., S.M.O., S.S.O., b.p., O.P.D., C.H.S., S.R.N., S.E.N., p.p., d.o.t. and S.E.E., often without any clue, least of all context, as to their meaning.

But for those who *are* in the know, this use of the code of the medical world all adds to the mystique, and they can nod wisely and knowingly when the heroine of *The Bedside Manner* announces that she is off to prepare her patients for a query abdomen laparotomy, a chole-cystectomy, a choledocho-motomy and a two-thirds gastrectomy. Occasionally, though, Nurse's remarks are more than self-explanatory even to the uninitiated; and on such occasions the reader might almost wish they were not, as when she announces brightly, 'I'm supposed to be giving Mrs. Potter a rectal wash-out.'

In order to maintain the tone of sickness and suffering throughout the novel, the healthy characters in the story are often described by specially-coined medical metaphors which seem to refer either to operations or to varying states of ill-health, as for instance, 'He had a faintly puzzled expression, as though he'd just opened up an alleged appendix and discovered a double intussesception instead,'
or,

> Tim looked at me over his mask as he helped me to get the gastrectomy man on to the trolley. He has small brown hypermetrophical-looking eyes which are half an inch too close together.

Even the off-duty love-talk between doctor and nurse is on a quasi-medical level:

> 'Your feet,' he said. He picked up the one without a slipper

and ran his fingers over the instep. Then he flicked the sole
gently and elicited a beautiful plantar reflex. 'Nice flexor
response,' he said. 'I don't think we need to try to look for
any Oppenheim's sign, do you?' ... 'As I was saying, your
feet have the most perfect metatarsal arches I have ever
seen.'

While Kate Norway and others attempt to blind the reader
with science in this way, other hospital novelists remain staggeringly vague about the nature of the patients' illnesses and
the treatments for them. *The Doctor's Favourite Nurse* (1971),
by Julia Davis, purports to be about radiation. Nurse Shirley
goes to work in a special clinic where sleepy-eyed Doctor
Gavriel is conducting some 'brilliant research' into the effects
of radiation. The clinic is situated in a remote mountainous
district of Scotland (where the locals speak a strange cockney
dialect), and there are dark hints about the extremely dangerous nature of the work and the dedication of the nursing
staff who are sacrificing their own health and lives to work
there. 'I'm not afraid of the type of work,' says Nurse Shirley
with a sudden show of spirit, for, 'She was not a shy modest
violet but a creature whose fires were hidden but could come
to light at the touch of a spark.' Her hidden fires are, of
course, sparked off by Dr. Gavriel, but as to the nature of
the dangers they are all exposed to there is no hint. In fact,
to judge by the kind of nursing that Nurse Shirley does for
the radiation-victims, the effects of exposure to radiation are
similar to a mixture of common cold, indigestion, insomnia
and the general need to be cheered up. One night Nurse
Shirley goes to take over the night duty from Nurse Jones.
Nurse Jones greets Nurse Shirley with relief. 'I'm so glad to
see you, nurse,' she says. For, though it is nearly midnight,
the patients are still awake and very restive. Nurse Jones is
unable to settle them; she knows that it is only Nurse Shirley,
with her wonderful way with radiation victims, who will be
able to quieten them:

Shirley went from bed to bed. The men all knew her. She

said a quiet word to one, joked with another, fetched a glass of water for a third. One blew her a kiss, another called her his girl friend.

Soon the ward was quiet. Most of the men had fallen asleep.

The reader's identification with the nurse-heroine is made particularly easy in a story like this, where Nurse Shirley's dangerous but vital work is really no more than the 'mothering' that most wives have to do every day. But in the atmosphere of the radiation clinic, the dull routine tasks of domestic life—making the beds, fetching drinks of water, clearing up the meals, tucking up the children—take on a new importance. Moreover, the heroine's family—the leg-amputees, the sufferers from polio of the brain (sic), the radiation victims—never answer back rudely as families tend to, but lie quietly and tidily in their beds and are terribly grateful for even a sip of cold water.

The climax of *The Doctor's Favourite Nurse* comes after an atomic explosion in Finland when a whole load of Finns are flown in by helicopter to the clinic in the Highlands. It is so dangerous, and the Finns' condition is such a threat both to themselves and to the nursing staff that Dr. Gavriel has them put in quarantine in a hut in the clinic grounds. He courageously shuts himself up with them:

Dr. Gavriel had selflessly decided to shut himself away with them in an attempt to save their lives ... It was yet another example of the devotion men and women gave to their fellow human beings through their exacting profession.

Several anxious days later he emerges triumphantly, calls together his staff in the canteen and tells them he will explain 'the real nature of his research' and 'exactly what's been going on in the past few days'. At this, the reader may well expect some astounding twist in the plot, such as that the radiation story was a cover-up and all along Dr. Gavriel has really been conducting horrific brain-transplants in the hut. But there is no such excitement. Dr. Gavriel's 'explanation' of his important work is to say that 'The poor fellows who were flown in from Finland the other night are likely to get better'. On hearing this all the staff cheer like mad and Nurse Shirley realises how very much she loves him.

Although the hospital romance is a post-National-Health phenomenon, many of the stories are, paradoxically, set in privately-run hospitals and clinics.

The hospital in *Theatre Sister at Riley's* (1964), by Hermina Black, for instance, is a private one so that there will be 'no government red tape to get tangled up in'; it is, nonetheless, the reader is assured, a 'real hospital', but one 'without the deadening hand of bureaucracy'; the doctor-hero approves of the N.H.S. up to a point but is 'too much of an individualist to stand being kicked around as his colleagues are'.

The busy general N.H.S. hospital would offer neither the time, nor the conditions, nor the right opportunity for the unorthodox behaviour of the romantic doctor and nurse. As Hermina Black says: 'I have a great respect for the medical profession though less now since the National Health.'

17

Sort of Sensitive, with Standards

BY THE END of the 1950s the romantic hero and heroine were
becoming increasingly stereotyped and had to conform to
what was the authors' idea of the readers' ideal.

Valentine Llewellyn, speaking on *Woman's Hour*, gave a
summary of the ideal couple. 'I like a hero to be a man of the
world. I like him to have been around and to be his own
master. The girl I like fairly young and not too innocent
and I'd like her to have a will of her own, and not be involved
with too many relatives.'

Violet Winspear was even more explicit in the *Radio
Times*:

I think all women like to dream about marvellous men.
You know, real hero types. I've never met any of them
myself, I doubt if anybody has...

I get my heroes so that they're lean and hard muscled
and mocking and sardonic and tough and tigerish and single,
of course. Oh, and they've got to be rich and then I make
it that they're only cynical and smooth on the surface. But
underneath they're, well, you know, sort of lost and lonely.
In need of love but, when roused, capable of breath-taking
passion and potency. Most of my heroes, well, all of them
really, are like that. They frighten but fascinate...

I have to make the heroine innocent and untouched. I
try not to make her too soppy, I get it so she's sort of sensitive, with standards. Preferably with both parents dead so

there's only her to hold fast and say No. That's until she gets the ring on her finger. I have thought about having a heroine who's been around a bit already, as it were, but then I reckoned she wouldn't be saying No and I'd be left without a plot altogether.

The standard hero has come a long way from the timid, soul-searching perfection of Sir Guy in *The Heir of Redclyffe*. He is now a far coarser, harsher character. Steely strength (only half hidden by well-cut tailor-made clothes), swift decision-making and cold blue eyes, are more important attractions than any of young Sir Guy's chivalrous sensitivity. But, though he has discarded the inheritances from Sir Guy, the modern hero has retained many of the qualities of the sheik and barbarian-type lovers of the twenties. He is, however, more likely to be wearing a 'well-cut suit that did things for his figure' than Arab costume or riding breeches, and to hold a high-up, well-paid professional job, possibly in advertising or independent television, than to be dashing about on horse-back quelling the natives. The ideal hero is a soft-centred savage in city clothes. 'I could crunch you between these two hands of mine' boasts the well-dressed hero of *Kiss in Sunlight* (1956), by Maysie Greig; it is not hard to believe, for the cut of his dark suit 'accentuated his height and powerful shoulders'.

The typical hero has thick unruly hair and a determined-looking jaw. In *Flight to the Stars* (1959), by Pamela Kent, 'his square jaw looked both mutinous and sullen', and in *Kiss in Sunlight*, by Maysie Greig, one of the female admirers observes 'he looks aggressive tonight. See the way his lower jaw is thrust out almost savagely.' The hero is athletic and physically fit; his sport tends to be the sort that is expensive to play: he yachts, plays polo, car races or flies his own aeroplane. He might even, like Rick Vandraaton, hero of *Flight to the Stars*, excel in so many directions that even the junior secretary, Melanie, has heard of his successes:

Melanie knew that he played polo magnificently, and that

he had sailed his own yacht across the Atlantic. That he could never be deceived about horse-flesh, and maintained a regular string of horses at his Berkshire home—which was merely a rented home, but famous for week-end parties —in addition to his polo ponies. And having once seen him riding in the Row she knew that he could become part and parcel of a horse. He drove a long, sleek Jaguar at hair-raising speed, and had recently been involved in a car smash. But he had escaped unscathed, and with a clean licence, because it hadn't been his fault. Nothing was ever his fault that was a matter of precision and skill and nerve.

Pamela Kent, *Flight to the Stars* (1959)

It used to be possible for a hero to be considerably younger than the heroine, notably, of course, Paul in *Three Weeks*, and a number of Florence Barclay's heroes. But by now such an idea has a hint of wilful non-conformity, even of obscenity about it. It is better if the hero has passed beyond the first fine glow of youth, and he must definitely not be younger than the woman. 'He was 35, it was the age when a man became really interesting and from then on could be increasingly attractive.' Hermina Black, *Theatre Sister at Riley's*.

By this age men apparently know how to treat a woman and make her feel like a lady; they stand up when women come into a room and they open doors for them, and perform 'all those little things that mean so much'. For, despite the jutting jaws and powerful shoulders, the heroes are, above all, conforming to an ideal of middle-class gentility and prim pleasantness.

The heroine is, of course, attractive; even plain heroines are lovely in their own unusual way. But, whereas once classical statuary provided the ideal model for heroines with their 'finely chiselled' features or marble-white skins, now the metaphors to describe female perfection are drawn from nature. 'Her eyes, under slender brown brows, were the smoky colour of rain-washed lilac.' (Anne Duffield, *Violetta*) or, even more ambiguous and curious, 'Her eyes were the colour of clouds.' (Guy Trent, *Woman Lovely Woman* (1951))

The heroine is in her early twenties, probably an orphan, and a virgin by intent and not by accident. But although she may be spirited (red hair) and have a will of her own, it is also a matter of common understanding that she is a likeable girl:

> She had always been happier when thinking of others, and it was difficult to realise that she had a problem of her own. Not a problem exactly; it was beginning to ache at the back of her consciousness like a grief.
>
> Kathryn Blair, *The Dangerous Kind of Love* (1964)

The concept of the evil heroine in the manner of E. M. Braddon is now out of the question. The modern heroine does not steal, cheat or murder, and only tells lies when absolutely necessary to save someone else's honour.

Romantic heroines are not worried by acne, flat feet, ingrowing toe-nails, too-small bosoms or large bottoms, and they are never black. Nor are they worried by the same spiritual problems as earlier heroines. They are safe and moderate in all things, except beauty; although they may occasionally be not just 'lovely', not just 'unusually lovely' but 'outstandingly lovely', they are seldom outstandingly clever. Thus, Violetta in *Violetta* had a fragile, flower-like appearance but she was 'not over-burdened with intellect', whereas Clare, a top model in the same story, who had 'brains as well as beauty', is not at all a nice type of girl; she is, in fact, in the opinion of the heroine, 'a cat'.

If heroines were too bright, they might start to think and even develop doubts, neuroses and personality problems. But although they do not think, they do sometimes *wonder* fleetingly about things, like who they are, or why they are who they are. Then they turn to their dressing-table mirrors—this occurs in almost all romances, sometimes even two or three times—and see reflected a blonde, or brunette or whatever, either petite, or of a pleasant medium height, and they are thus totally reassured of their own existence:

> Julie studied her reflection critically in the mirror of her

dressing table and gave a half-rueful smile. She was ready,
and she hoped she would not let Paul down. Tonight was
important to him, and she wanted to please him. Her dress,
white lace over pink taffeta, complemented her creamy complexion, and was short, revealing a slender length of shapely
leg. Her eyes, brown with tiny green lights in them, sparkled
at the prospect of the evening ahead of her, and she cupped
her chin on one hand as she wondered why tonight seemed
so full of promise.

Anne Mather, *Dangerous Enchantment* (1969)

Julie, of *Dangerous Enchantment*, has a job selling expensive
perfume in the cosmetics department of a large store. Curiously, selling expensive perfume is all right; and selling anti-
ques is all right for the more bohemian heroines, but selling
sweeties is not. Heroines also have jobs as governesses, secreta-
ries to business directors or solicitors, and other office jobs,
which sound rather unglamorous, but the heroines seem to
find satisfaction from a job well done.

From the thirties onwards, great importance was laid on
the quality of a girl's eyelashes. They had begun to take on
almost the same importance in the story as hair had in the
romances of Ouida's time. Modern heroines flutter their eyelashes, and blink them and glance surreptitiously out from
under them and, if they are long and dark enough, even use
them like an extra limb and sweep the floor with them. They
can be a mark of innocence: 'her long childlike lashes'; a
signal of intense emotion: 'she blinked; he saw the flutter of
her lashes and noted the barely perceptible pause before she
turned to him, her eyes two limpid pools of innocence'. The
eyelashes of the heroine of *Violetta* (1960), by Anne Duffield,
are particularly hard worked, and their rapid movements
even indicate to her admirers when that poor girl, who is anyway not overburdened with intellect, is trying to think. 'He
saw the flutter of her lashes which meant swift thinking and
arriving at a decision.' The whole of this heroine's romance
is conducted by a series of tell-tale glances and meaningful
ocular exchanges between Violetta and the various men she

encounters while staying in the South of France.

In the romantic authors' attempts to keep romantic fiction refined, the breathless embrace was rapidly giving way to the fleeting glance. It was meaningful looks from their heroes, rather than kisses, which now set heroines' heartbeats pounding. Many of these romances are morally quite irreproachable, and often have no more than one demure kiss right at the end and no dangerously throbbing thoughts to accompany it. Instead, there are incessant exchanges of the eye; the characters never stop looking at each other. In *Violetta* there are speculative expressions, rueful looks, laughing glances, doubtful smiles, meaningful winks, startled stares, nonplussed gazes. When a story concerns a lovely, lilac-eyed young girl of nineteen falling in love for the first time on the Côte d'Azur in summertime, and yet conveys no sense of any youthful, exuberant, enthusiastic desire, the final result seems curiously coy, as though something is being kept from the reader. At moments in the narrative when one might expect the heroine to admit, if only to herself that she has taken a fancy to the hero, she stifles such thoughts as though even the state of being in love were lewd. When she catches a fleeting, but unexpected, glimpse of him coming into a café, she pretends to her companions that she's been 'pricked by a fly'. This statement sounds oddly out of place because although flies may irritate they surely do not prick?

'Oh!' Violetta uttered an involuntary ejaculation and the faint colour in her cheeks deepened. Her companions looked at her in astonishment.

'What is the matter?' Lucius demanded.

He saw the tell-tale flicker of her lashes that seemed the outward symbol of some swift mental process.

'Just a—a prick,' she answered. 'A mosquito, or maybe a fly—.'

Such ambivalent uses of vocabulary are apparently quite unconscious.

The archetype for many modern heroines is Amy, from

The Heir of Redclyffe. The sanctity and purity of a young girl's love is one of the conventions of today's romantic novel. But Amy's simple virtues, when superimposed on to modern heroines, appear, not as innocence and purity, but only as coyness and false modesty. Amy's 'maidenly qualities' reflected her author's own innocence. Today, romantic novelists are not innocent, nor in all probability are the majority of their readers. So the authors have deliberately to crush any sexual feelings they, or their heroines, may have.

One romantic novelist who has acknowledged that there is sexual hypocrisy in modern romance is Violet Winspear:

> I don't really think that romantic novels should be called 'romantic' really. Between you and me, I think they're basically twisted sex stories. I mean, it is a bit sadistic, isn't it, to be reading about a man blowing his top with frustration because he can't get it. And I think women love reading all this stuff because it gives them a bit of a thrill to think about it . . .
>
> I put all these cruel manly words into these men's mouths, and then work so's he makes a grab for the girl. And then she's half fainting, you know what I mean, with a burning desire, which she doesn't even understand herself. And then he's bruising her mouth with his urgent demanding kisses and he's got this strange steely light in his eyes. And I get it so's the girl says to herself, 'What does it mean, what does it mean?' Good God, I tell you, honestly, sometimes I get so worked up myself writing the stuff that I don't know what to do.
>
> Violet Winspear

Modern romantic fiction does not see romantic love carrying on into marriage as it did in earlier novels, but expects it to end at the altar. There are, of course, some exceptions to this, such as the love-life of the young widow, or the discontented wife who spreads her wings but flies home to her husband in the end. But on the whole modern novelists feel that only the

thrills of courtship are romantic, whereas post-marital love is
not:

> It is not, and never has been, the function of a romantic
> novelist to continue further than the first dawning and final
> declaration of true love. To take the next step would be to
> enter into an entirely different field. I am glad this is so.
> It would take the gilt off the gingerbread to follow the
> idyllic dream with realism. How sad to watch the heroine,
> now married and pregnant, trying to do up her shoes. Her
> expression of mystery would be replaced with a look of
> grim determination to eat mustard pickles at all costs. And
> how on earth can she give light lilting laughs while speed-
> ing to the loo for a bout of morning sickness? Her frantic
> search now is not for the blossoming of love, but for a
> packet of indigestion tablets. No! Penelope is best left
> where she is—wide-eyed and happy and quite, quite beau-
> tiful in her wedding-gown.

Irene Roberts, romantic novelist, writing in *Books and
Bookmen*, 1967

While early romantic writers can certainly not be said to have
given a realistic account of married life, they seldom assumed
that all problems ended at the altar. The glamour of their
romances is provided, as the convention demanded, by descriptions of food, faraway places and clothes. Faraway
favourites included the Australian Outback (with exciting
bush-fire nearly at the end) or the Canadian Rockies (exciting
dam disaster) for the fresh-air outdoor types, Italy for art
lovers, Paris or Venice for dreamers, Majorca in springtime
(with the almond trees in bloom) for Mediterranean lovers.
By the end of the sixties such geographical exotica was no
longer the exception but the rule; the interesting foreign
background had now become virtually obligatory for the successful romance. Here are some of the faraway titles from
just one Mills & Boon catalogue: *Carnival at San Cristobal*
by Nan Asquith, *The Rustle of Bamboo* by Celine Conway,
Bauhinia Junction by Margaret Way, *It Began in Te Rangi*

by Gloria Bevan, *A Castle in Spain* by Eleanor Farnes, *Raintree Country* by Violet Winspear, *A Kiss in a Gondola* by Ketrina Britt, *Parisian Adventure* by Elizabeth Ashton, *Spanish Lace* by Joyce Dingwell, *Moroccan Affair* by Irene Dickens, *The Cruise to Curaçao* by Belinda Dell, *Honeymoon in Delphi* by Elizabeth Holland, *The Legend of Katmandu* by Isobel Chace. There are also a fair number of interesting islands: *The Forbidden Island* by Sara Seale, *The Enchanting Island* by Kathryn Blair, *Golden Apple Island* by Jane Arbor, *Isle of Pomegranates* by Iris Danbury, *Love Hath an Island* by Anne Hampson, *Island of Secrets* by Henrietta Reid, *Journey to an Island* by Hilary Wilde, *Isle of Song* by Hilary Wilde, *Paradise Island* by Hilary Wilde, *Island Affair* by Hettie Grimstead.

As to the food content of romances, it is part of the magic that heroines are not bothered by putting on weight; but even when a heroine is prevented from eating by extreme emotion, the missed meal is nonetheless described for the benefit of the reader:

A footman entered carrying a huge silver tray on which reposed a number of different dishes. There were truffles in aspic, ortolans decorated with asparagus tips and *pâté de foie gras*, lobster with a golden mayonnaise, and many other strange and delicious-looking concoctions to which Gardenia could put no name. The footman set the silver tray down on a small table beside her.

'But I couldn't eat all this!' she exclaimed.

'Eat what you can,' Lord Harcourt advised. 'You will feel better afterwards.'

Barbara Cartland, *A Virgin in Paris* (1966)

There is a certain timeless quality about ortolans in aspic, but the obligatory descriptions of the heroines' dresses tend to date rapidly. There is nothing so *un*appealing and *un*glamorous as last season's full black taffeta evening gown with frilled net bodice, or as a 'long-skirted amber-coloured jersey dress fastening with gold flower-shaped buttons on the shoulders, cut high to the throat in front and much lower at the back' whose 'glowing tones emphasised the lovely matt ivory of her skin that needed enviously little make-up' in a season when high backs and bare bosoms are in vogue; the more meticulous the attention to detail, the more quickly do the clothes become dated. Although sometimes the details of the heroine's attire are placed quite perfunctorily and incongruously in the text, most authors do at least try to incorporate the necessary details into the narrative by such ingenuous tricks as: 'I must say you look good in that dress, Annette—different somehow', or, rather more curiously: 'She had worn her plainest, darkest dress, in a deep wine shade that luckily toned with the carpet.'

One author who overcomes the problem of rapidly dated clothes while at the same time including detailed accounts of them is Barbara Cartland, who gives her romances an 'old-fashioned' background. Indeed, in her quasi-historical world, descriptions of pretty clothes virtually take over. Her heroines are quite unashamedly as flimsy and gauzy as the dresses they wear:

It was indeed a day-dress such as she had dreamed of possessing—of soft, very pale green crêpe, embroidered with braid and with draped chiffon. It gave her a diaphanous appearance as fresh and young as the spring itself. The hat to wear with it was of green straw, encircled with a small wreath of daffodils. It was very simple, very young, and made the Duchesse draw in her breath when she looked from it to Gardenia's shining eyes and parted lips.

A Virgin in Paris (1966)

Later the same girl puts on another dress; the colour of the crêpe and the type of flowers have changed. The description and the eyes have not:

She had put on her most attractive gown for the occasion, and she knew that the rose-pink crêpe, with its touches of azure-blue ribbon on the neck, the wrists and on the wide tight waistband, was exquisitely becoming. Her almost childish hat, trimmed with a wreath of roses, framed her excited face and sparkling eyes.

One of the characters, Monsieur Worth, Parisian couturier, warns the virgin heroine, Gardenia, 'Remember, clothes, however gorgeous, are only a frame. I cannot re-make or create the person inside them.' It is a noble sentiment, and Barbara Cartland lives up to it; clothes form the frame, not just of the heroines but of the whole world. Paris, for instance, is seen as a great number of garments promenading around a vast wardrobe. Thus, when Gardenia drives down the Champs Elysées for the first time, there are no cafés, no shops or Arc de Triomphe; instead, it is described in terms of what people were wearing:

> There were ladies in summer dresses and lacy parasols sitting under the trees, talking to men with their trousers creased down the side in the fashion that had been started by King Edward and wearing high satin cravats decorated with sparkling, jewelled tie-pins.

There was, of course, something quite safe and reassuring about the clichés and stereotypes of the romances that followed this convention; readers could be sure of finding an easily recognisable hero, a heroine to identify with, and a situation she understood. But some romantic novelists were aware that the whole scope of the romantic novel needed stretching:

> Romances need to break away from long-established formulas, while retaining their optimistic outlook. Now that there are so many opportunities for women in the way of careers, travel, study, it seems strange that comparatively few writers make use of such material.
>
> Claire Ritchie, *Books and Bookmen*

As a reaction against the inherent silliness of a lot of romantic fiction, a number of writers did try to cope seriously and conscientiously with the problems of the day, just as the popular writers at the end of the nineteenth century had often done as a matter of course. The result is a number of seemingly anti-romantic romances which, instead of being about lovely young girls falling in love with the right person in a glamourous situation, are about unhappy people and their big, real, universal crises.

Maynah Lewis, twice winner of the Romantic Novelists Association Major Award for a romantic novel, was one who reckoned that 'with the widening of horizons, the scope of the romantic novel is undergoing a change'. In her view, the romantic novel was already far less restricted in 1967 than it had been ten years before; consequently, she chose suitably unrestricted subject-matter:

> In my first novel my heroine didn't get her man, in my second the heroine was 64 years old, my third was romantic suspense set behind the Iron Curtain, my fourth had no wedding bells, not even in the far distance. And now I have a book about a nun who cannot take her final vows, and comes out into the world to face a cruel testing time, physically, mentally, and spiritually. The setting is a slum and I had a hard job keeping it from becoming a sociological study on why people bet!

Although the widening of horizons did take in distressed nuns and cruel testing times, the dominant themes of the anti-romantic romances of the 1950s and 1960s were marital problems. The dreaded peril of permissiveness was threatening to sweep away all that the romantic novelists believed in. The reaction of some romantic novelists to the increased liberty and the changing attitudes to sex was to tighten up fictional virtue even more, to put heroines on even higher pedestals, and to make virgins superlatively virginal. Barbara Cartland believes that:

> Women should be elusive, mysterious, and chaste. And I

think that every man's ideal—even though they pretend it isn't, today—is to find the wonderful, charming, delightful girl who will surrender to them ... The girls today are so stupid ... they forget ... that every single young man has a mother who says nice girls don't.

But other novelists attempted to find a *solution* to permissiveness, to bring all the 'modern' problems out into the open and have a look at them. There was a wave of neo-realistic novels about adultery, unhappy wives, ugly girls on the shelf—'There must be someone—somewhere—who will really want me one day' wails the lonely orphaned heroine of *Runaway Heart* (1967), by Pat Dacres—men married to flighty girls, and restless women married to boring men.

The treatment for this type of novel was to offer psychological insight into the characters' problems. *Light from One Star* (1956), by Netta Muskett, is about the older man who is captivated by, and mistakenly marries, a much younger, extrovert glamorous television personality. 'Too late, he discovered his mistake that he had married the wrong woman.' There is a realistic, yet terribly discreet, treatment of the various sexual difficulties that the couple encounter. To begin with, the television star does not want to give her husband 'what he wants', although she feels that it is fair 'payment' for all the expensive presents he has given her. She is thus very relieved when they have to spend the first night of the honeymoon on a train with separate sleeping compartments. She is less grateful and relieved when they check in to their luxury honeymoon hotel and he insists on having their dinner (with champagne) served to them upstairs in their own private suite (with balcony overlooking the blue waters of Lake Lucerne):

> 'I want to show off my clothes,' she said, like a child. 'How can I, if we stay up here and there's only you to admire me?'
> He laughed.
> 'No one will ever admire you more,' he said, 'but have it your own way. I shall have something to show off too—my beautiful wife,' taking her in his arms and kissing her

with something new in his embrace which made her struggle a little, her face flaming.

'Did I frighten you?' he asked very tenderly.

'Well, I—of course we're married, but I—I shall have to get used to it, shan't I?' she asked, turning away.

She never does get used to it. But some months later, having failed as a television star, she decides that she ought to try to be a 'good' wife to Sir Blaine. Whether the marriage has been consummated yet is not altogether clear. But it is by now too late. He has lost interest:

'Well—how about it? Blaine, don't you *want* me any more?' with a pretty little lift of her head and an inviting look in her eyes.

He laid the book down carefully on the bedside table before he replied, slowly, thoughtfully, not looking at her. He gave no impression of his profound discomfort.

'You don't want me, Virginia,' he said at last. 'I've realised that for a long time. You never have wanted me. I'm not blaming you, my dear. I ought to have known. As a doctor, I ought to have realised before it was too late, but I was very much in love with you, and I thought—believed —that you felt the same towards me.'

The omission of the finite verb in the first sentence is intentional. The neo-realistic romances are often written in a special, hasty, semi-documentary style with verbs left out and random adverbs and commas thrown in.

Shopping for a Husband (1967), by Berta Ruck, is even more breathless than *Light from One Star*. It is written in a quasi-stream of consciousness, staccato style which leaves out not just finite verbs but also definite articles and pronouns and instead makes the fullest possible use of italics, capital letters and unusual punctuation. The novel is dedicated to Heather Jenner, principal and founder of one of the largest marriage bureaux in the country and it is the story of bed-sitter Kate, who is on the shelf in her late twenties and is desperately lonely and longing to have a husband:

> '*My husband says*' ... '*Mine's just the same*' ...
> These women had found husbands. Which meant com-
> panionship. Someone *there*, who wanted the woman to be
> there with him. Romance, that broken reed which leaves
> cruel splinters in the palm! May have passed them by.
> Never mind. Men have married them. Most of them are
> nothing to look at, either. Now, *there's* a sample...
> Over shoulders of the impeding crowd Kate had caught
> sight of a dejected female head in the limpest of scarves.
> No hair, all face. Nose mauve with cold, otherwise no
> colour, no shape. *She's* married ... *Heavens! Is it?* ...
> Kate had just seen that *it* was. The reflection of herself
> in a plate-glass shop-window. *My god!* Am I all those years
> older?
> Like a cold wave there surged in upon Kate that Terror
> of The Closing Door. This swamps a woman's morale with
> the conviction *I'm 'getting on' and I'm not 'getting off'.*
> *How much longer before I lose the last vestige of attrac-*
> *tion I've possessed for men?*
> The door is closing, closing. It'll shut, and I shall have
> had it.
> ... STOP! she urged herself. *This is morbid. Positively*
> *vulgar, too. Not 'you'!*

Kate is finally driven, as the title suggests, to go shopping
for a husband. With the help of 'The Match-Maker' at a
marriage bureau, she works her way through numerous men
on the bureau's books (details of whom sound as though they
had been copied off Heather Jenner's filing card system), and
finally falls for John Oppenshaw, a staggeringly rich north-
country, Bentley-owning, steel magnate:

> 'Before lunch we have to look in at Cartier's; choose your
> engagement-ring. Which you'll please to wear at once to
> show there's no more of this Shopping for a Husband.
> You've got him. Ready?'

She took down The Coat. He held it for her to slip into the tiger-stripes that emphasised the russet hair, the goldy-brown gaze, the classic shape of her. She turned and saw by his eyes that she did not look like just a film-star. She was a Queen. His.

'Yes. I'm ready. Let's go, lad.'

The door of the empty bed-sitter slammed behind them.

Finding a husband through the services of a bureau is thus proved to be as legitimate and wonderful a way of discovering true love as any. And, according to Heather Jenner, young people *are* becoming much more practical and down-to-earth in their approach to love. In a recent book, *Men and Marriage* (1970), which makes use of her years of experience in the field of love and marriage, Heather Jenner describes 'What the Modern Man Looks for in a Wife':

Our modern young man is practical; too practical to love the unattainable. He does not yearn for a mysterious goddess, wrapped in veils of elusive glamour. She would scare him stiff. The wife he wants is, as much as possible, like the girl next door ... Education has become the new yardstick in class distinction. Degrees and qualifications are regarded as more important than social standing, ancestry or wealth. Know-how is the new golden key to the hearts of millionaires and aristocrats alike. The young Britisher is becoming more indifferent to high rank. He prefers to marry a girl who has been well-educated, but has no interest in how well-born she is ...

The whole social concept of marriage has changed, but a man still seeks a wife who fits in with his background and who comes of wholesome stock.

Untrue love is a part of modern life, too, and there are a number of restless bored heroines whose disenchantment with marriage is as pressing a problem as the lonely spinster's. But after a fruitless search for extra-marital excitement, these discontented women usually realise that what is really wrong with their marriages is not their dull husbands but their own selfishness. The heroine of *Spring Fever* by Paula Lindsay, for instance, rushes off to have an affair with 'a glamorous stranger', but just in time she discovers her husband's true worth:

> She had been foolish, unappreciative of the love Giles gave so freely and gladly—but she had realised her folly before she lost everything in life that she valued. Never again would she be restless, bored, discontented—she had learnt to count her blessings with a full heart, and the greatest blessing that life had bestowed upon her was the deep and lasting love of the man she had married.
>
> Paula Lindsay, *Spring Fever*

Julia Daunt, heroine of *Restless Heart* (1954), by Denise Robins, is another self-centred wife in search of illicit kicks, and she does, after a lot of talk, suspense and worry, actually get to bed with her lover. She has been married for five years to a well-off, pipe-smoking, gardening, dog-loving chap called Bill. Outwardly, she would seem to be happy enough, but inwardly Julia is very dissatisfied. Bill is a 'little solid and British, and a little lacking, perhaps, in that spice of the devil which she had always liked in men'. Julia's life seemed to lack fulfilment. 'She began to wonder if she would ever know that glorious, thrilling madness which the poets sang about, and called "love".' She manages to find it with Ivor Bent, a brilliant though erratic, half-French, London painter, also married, who has already noticed and been attracted by Julia's lovely tobacco-coloured hair:

> 'I've never seen hair like yours before,' he had said, *à propos* of nothing, during the middle of dinner, and he had leaned forward and looked at it closely: 'It's a most pleasant change after all the artificial curls and waves. It's almost straight, isn't it? And the colour of a cigar ... It isn't like a cigar to touch. And it isn't soft and silky. It's vital, buoyant hair. Like the mane of a young wild pony. I'd

like to paint you standing on a moor in the wind holding on to the neck of a moorland horse. How well you'd blend.'

She had thrilled strangely to the touch of his finger and had laughed to cover a certain confusion which the intimate gesture roused in her. And she had said:

'Do you think I look a horsey woman?'

'God, no! But there's something about you which has the aura; a slim brown thoroughbred, with sensitive nostrils, and that rough brown hair of yours.'

They embark on a *grande passion* and, though Julia knows it is wrong to betray old Bill, Ivor Bent persuades her that it would equally be a crime to let such a vital and wonderful love as theirs go unfulfilled. She agrees to spend one night in a hotel with him but by the next morning she begins to realise the insidious truth; her feeling for Ivor Bent is not really love but only a hot infatuation. 'The house of dreams which she had built about her lover was collapsing.' But it is too late for Julia to undo what she has done. Having already embarked on the sea of adultery and deception, the waves of sin have been set in motion. Julia and Ivor are involved in a car crash with a lorry as they leave the hotel and so the truth of their relationship is out. Many sore trials ensue and it is a long time before Julia can regain the trust of Bill and the sweetness of marriage. But at the end of it all, she is older and wiser:

'I'm beginning to think,' said Julia, 'that sex experience and big thrills aren't of any value. At least, not the kind that entail intrigues and deceptions, and taking risks with other people's happiness. I don't think I gained anything through that night with Ivor, and I lost everything when I lost Bill.'

The heavy-handed moralising is necessary if romantic fiction is to be an effective argument against the evils of promiscuity. But Denise Robins never makes any pretence about the attractions and sweetness of illicit love. In Julia Daunt's one

night at the hotel, for instance, she experiences all 'the un-
imaginable poetry and fire' of Ivor Bent's loving. And in
More Than Love (1947), Denise Robins tells the story of a
girl's affair with a married man ('her fate was to fall in love
with a married man'), and despite all the pain and agonies
of being not wife but mistress to Richard Corrington-Ashe,
Rosalinda Browne admits that she had no regrets:

> If back comes the old question ... 'Has it been worth-
> while ... ?' The answer is still *'Yes'*, a thousand times. For
> the sake of the years we have loved each other; for the
> sake of the hours we have spent together ... for the sake of
> our love ... this love that is *more than love* which we have
> for each other ... *YES!*
>
> *More Than Love*

But when there is adultery, the penalty must be paid. And
the penalty is death. Like Tristan and Iseult, Rosalinda
Browne and Richard Corrington-Ashe must die; he is killed
in a plane crash; she is run down by a bus in the Old Bromp-
ton Road. Strictly speaking, Julia Daunt and Ivor Bent in
Restless Heart should have been killed, too, in their car smash
when they left the hotel, but Julia was already beginning to
regret her affair so she is let off with bruises and cuts. For
modern romantic fiction has always to reflect the 'spirit of
optimism which is an essential part of the romantic outlook'.
—Alice Chetwynd Ley.

18

Romance and the Reader or Cheerful and Relaxing

CHARLOTTE M. YONGE was read by parsons, students and pre-Raphaelites. Marie Corelli was read by Tennyson, Queen Victoria and the Dean of Gloucester. Elinor Glyn said she was read by bishops and crowned heads. But these are among the exceptions; such a broad readership of romantic fiction is limited mostly to romantic novelists of the last century. It has always been implicitly understood, especially by the highly educated, that the bulk of romantic fiction is read by semi-literate working girls—especially housemaids—and by crabbed old spinsters. This view has even been held by some of the romantic novelists themselves. In *The Master Man* (1920), by Ruby M. Ayres, there is a touch of self-mockery in the portrayal of a kind-eyed, sentimental 'under-housemaid who was young and romantic and devoured every novel she could get hold of'. And in *Arabella the Awful* (1918), by Berta Ruck, awful Arabella is at her happiest when lying on her bed in floods of tears over a 'lovely, natural' book called *Good-bye, Sweetheart* (by Rhoda Broughton).

In 1968 Peter Mann, a sociologist at Sheffield University, in collaboration with the romance publishers, Mills & Boon, conducted a questionnaire survey among readers on the Mills & Boon mailing-lists. The results showed that a high proportion of readers were not sloppy-minded juveniles nor unmarried old ladies, but reasonably well-educated, married women in the twenty-five to thirty-five age group, at home with young children.

> These women are not intellectuals by any means ... but they are by no means unintelligent (as many written-in comments show) and they are definitely a cut above the square-eyed, television-fixated, and pulp-magazine level. Many of the romance readers are female 'white-collar' workers rather than merely manual workers, and it is quite noteworthy how large a proportion are of the semi-professional or lower professional occupations. One reader wrote, in answer to the questionnaire, 'Between the covers of your books I can ignore the T.V., the transistors, politicians and the weather. I thank you most sincerely for the happiness your books have given me.'

As Dr. Mann pointed out in his conclusions, 'What publishing house in this country could ask for more?'

Among the Mills & Boon readers there was a high level of what Dr. Mann called 'reader loyalty'. Many readers, in replying to the questionnaire, 'took the opportunity to say a very sincere "thank you" to Mills & Boon for the pleasure that the romances gave them.'

> I can't say why they are so popular with me except that once you start reading one of them you can't stop until you reach the end. Some other publishers' books get boring half way through, but I have never yet been bored with a Mills & Boon book.

> My husband has had to build two cupboards to store my Mills & Boon books. I have about 500 or so.

> They are clean and wholesome without any unpleasant sexy stuff. They all leave one with a sense of pleasant and hopeful existence. I find them cheerful and relaxing.

But such enthusiastic reader loyalty is not spontaneous. There is no doubt that over the last decade, popular romantic fiction went into a decline. Sales of novels, though still enormous compared to other standards of reading-matter, dropped. A recent look at the news-stalls on London's main stations showed that although there were plenty of thrillers and novels of violence and of the supernatural, there was no straight popular romantic fiction. In the past three or four years many publishers have either cut down drastically on the amount of romance on their lists, or even dropped it altogether. With the closing of such private subscription libraries as Boots (Harrod's is now among the very last of the private sub-scription libraries), this regular outlet has ceased to exist. The librarians of the free public libraries are not able, or willing, to spend so much of their funds on romance.

As sales have become less reliable, those who do continue to publish romantic novels have had to woo their readers carefully. Mills & Boon, well documented in Peter Mann's *Books, Borrowers and Buyers*, provide a good example. Their retail and library outlets are augmented by a postal selling scheme called 'Miss Jane Lovell' which sends out regular catalogues and offers a steady nine new titles a month. Just as important is their attitude to the postal readers for, according to the Peter Mann survey, 17 per cent of readers regularly bought romances by post.

The selling motto of Mills & Boon is 'Books that *Please*', and they try to give the impression that they are a public service rather than a commercial enterprise.

Through the cosy chat and extracts from readers' letters in the catalogue, they build up a rapport with readers and establish themselves as something of a world-wide friendship club. 'We are always conscious that we are something more than publishers and that we are also a link between readers all over the world who are united in a common interest.'

Having discovered through Peter Mann's survey that many of their readers are of a higher educational standard than was previously suspected, Mills & Boon have been able to incor-porate this into recent promotions. The theme of one recent catalogue is the 'educational merits' of Mills & Boon romances.

'We believe that we are continuing to be successful in achieving this goal,' says the catalogue, and their claim is supported by extracts from numerous readers' letters all over the world (including a professor in the Philippines), extolling the high educational value of the novels. 'They are just great. They are very interesting, exciting, educational,' says a reader from Trinidad. It is significant that she describes the books as 'educational', 'because she echoes the opinion of many other readers who say that they learn from the Mills & Boon series'. They make a point of mentioning this 'because there are still people who are quite unaware of this fact and still have a misconceived idea of the value of the novels'.

Robert Hale, Hurst and Blackett, The Romance Book Club, and Collins are among the other publishers selling romance through mail order. Hodder and Stoughton have recently joined them, opening their *Coronet Romance Club* in 1972, which has a bi-annual *Club News*, the first number of which included a letter from the Club President, Denise Robins, a short story by another popular romantic author, a list of new romantic titles available, and a correspondence column with a £5 prize for the best reader's letter.

Among the various difficulties facing publishers today is also the shortage of good new romantic novels. One leading agent for romantic fiction explained that this shortage is because younger promising writers are not being tempted by this medium:

The younger age group of writers on the female side are too realistic in their outlook on love and sex to write to the traditional romantic novel recipe. This is left to the older writer to supply ... One of the reasons why the older writer has been able to supply this type of fiction for so many years, was that between the wars, due to the shortage of marriageable men, many young women with any sort of writing talent created their own romances as a large percentage knew the chances were they would never marry. This age produced a great upsurge of romantic fiction writers. Today's young girls with the balance of the sexes in their favour, don't need this outlet. They can *live* their romances.

In order that, despite the shortage of good new romantic novels, they can offer readers a full list of dreamy-sounding titles, many publishers have resorted to the re-issuing of old novels, sometimes as many as twenty years out of date, but updated and with new dust-jackets and titles. From a list of seven 'New Romantic Titles' announced in the *Coronet Romance Club News*, only one is, in fact, a new unpublished novel, the other six all having been published before.

The movement of the romantic novel now is away from the straight love-story to the 'thriller romance', in which a lovely innocent heroine finds herself in 'circumstances of danger' or is caught up in a web of intrigue and suspicion.

There is also an increasing demand, both in this country and in America, for the Gothic and historical romance. In Gothic romance, often set in Cornwall or Wales, the characters are dressed in eighteenth- or nineteenth-century costume, and a background of quaint country customs is provided by gypsies and rustics who have a knowledge of local folk-lore, herbal recipes and magic. Modern Gothic romance shares some affinities with the eighteenth-century novels of Mrs. Anne Radcliffe in that there is a combination of ruined buildings, fear and innocence, and they use Mrs. Radcliffe's well-known technique of arousing fear and suspense by events which are apparently supernatural but afterwards are explained by natural means.

Popular historical romances re-tell the love lives, real or supposed, of historical figures, often English royalty, for example, *Here Lies Our Sovereign Lord* (1957), by Jean Plaidy, on Charles II. Mary Queen of Scots is one of the most popular monarchs for this treatment. The background details of contemporary costume and daily life for historical romances are usually meticulously well researched, and in reading the novels one often has the impression that the author was loath to omit any of the carefully discovered facts, however irrelevant.

Although there does at present seem to be this slight swing away from the straight romantic novel, Alan Boon, director of Mills & Boon, is optimistic about predicting the future prospects of romance:

> I think that of all categories of fiction, romantic fiction is now the most popular. This is not only in the U.K., but it extends all over the world ... (They are) more successful than any other category of British fiction, surely that entitles them to the esteem of people. There are no comparable writers in the world compared to the best of most successful romantic novelists. I think a good romantic novelist has to be sincere and also have a wonderful technique. This technique is really impossible to define, but which we can see or recognise when we see it.
>
> Woman's Hour, B.B.C.

Denise Robins, called the 'Queen of Romance' by one of her publishers, also remains optimistic:

> No matter what winds of change have blown through the world, romance has never changed. At the root it is unalterable. Its source lies in the heart of every human being. The outward presentation may alter at times—as fashions do—but it is rather pleasant today for us to realise that there is a definite increase in the demand for romantic literature and that the ugly pornographic vicious trend is fast coming to an end.

This mood of continual hope for a cleaner, nobler future, is common to all today's romantic novelists:

> I am certain that the romantic novel has a future ... After all, the student protest marcher of today is the responsible parent of tomorrow; the public must eventually tire of naked sex on stage and printed page, and the 'eternal verities' will still be there for us to write about. Their appeal has endured since the first book was printed.
>
> Alex Stuart

Popular romantic fiction offers the reader more than just the 'eternal verities', whatever they are. It offers escapism into a rose-coloured world, vicarious experience, wish-fulfilment and, for the bored young mother, even justification for her way of life stuck at home with small children. She is living the 'happily ever after' of falling in love that the romantic novel promised.

Romantic fiction also offers a belief in something. Readers still want, or need, the 'vague warm surges of feeling' that Q. D. Leavis found in the best-sellers of the twenties.

The following passage, entitled *All You Need is Love*, was published as the 'Star Letter' in a women's glossy monthly magazine, and was written, not by a romantic novelist, but by a reader:

> The union of a man and a woman who love each other in the true sense of that much abused word is a many splen-doured thing. It is of the earth, earthy, yet it can soar into the mysterious realm of the spirit. It may be an expression of mutual love such as no words can convey, which so strengthens and sustains love that those who have experienced it can feel closest to each other at times when intercourse is out of the question, such as during illness or childbirth. Yet many modern writers attempt not only to describe this wonder but to reduce it to a technique. This is like trying to catch a moonbeam.
>
> I believe a woman should give herself to her husband as simply and unselfconsciously as a flower opens its petals to the sun. No book can teach her how to do this. The knowledge must come from her own heart.

Although they may no longer believe in God, readers do still believe in love. The romantic novelists are not propagating or even perpetuating any new ideas about flower-petals and the mysterious realms of the spirit. Such ideas are already among the eternal verities in readers' minds. The romantic novelists are merely fulfilling an already existing demand for this sort of thing, in an easily recognisable, non-pernicious form. Gene

Stratton Porter, popular novelist of the 1920s and 1930s wrote, 'There is one great beauty in idealized romance; reading it can make no one worse than he is. It may fire thousands to higher aspiration than they ever before have had.' While the second half of the statement may be over-optimistic, it does seem to be true that, if there is a readership which finds satisfaction in reading romantic fiction, while it may not give them any positive benefit, may not make them nobler or wiser, it is very unlikely to corrupt them. As Margaret Drabble said of Eric Segal's *Love Story* (1970), 'It's an innocently selfish fantasy ... it won't do anyone any harm, so good luck to the nine millions.'

19

Romance and the Writer or Compassionate Hearts and Understanding Minds

POPULAR ROMANTIC NOVELISTS are a supremely confident type of writer. They seldom appear to suffer from doubts or lack of faith about their usefulness.

Q. D. Leavis pointed out that it was partly a question of education, or lack of it. Education and a cultured background tended to get between an author and her 'spontaneities', and to suppress her ability to write with such sublime confidence and vivacity.

Their enthusiasm for their 'spontaneities' has led some romantic novelists on to shameless arrogance about them. Writers like Ouida or Marie Corelli did not think of applying external critical standards to their own novels. While humility was a quality sometimes bestowed on a heroine as she peeped coyly out from beneath her eyelashes, it was not often shared by her creator.

Marie Corelli considered herself to be a 'prose Shakespeare', and was annoyed that nobody else took this view. Ouida considered her work to be that of 'an inspired genius' and regarded each latest book as a masterpiece. Charlotte M. Yonge compiled a list of 'Books to lend and to give' and included as 'safe reading—fit for those who need to have their ideal of love and courtship elevated and refined' seven of her own books. Though none of today's romantic novelists see themselves as latterday Shakespeares, some of them do dismiss other contemporary literature as permissive rubbish, while suggesting that their own reflects a spirit of truth. 'The romantic novelist is almost alone in presenting a picture of true love, decent and honourable conduct, and the happiness which is the result of these "old-fashioned things",' writes Claire Ritchie in *Writing the Romantic Novel* (1962), and another romantic novelist, Clare Breton Smith, says that 'For this difficult form of writing you must have genuine love of your fellow creatures'. Hermina Black states simply and categorically that 'A love-story is the most important thing in the world ... I think a woman in love is a terribly important thing'.

Another indication of the exalted view which some romantic novelists have of their calling is expressed in the romance *Uncertain Journey* (1967), by Berta King. In this story the heroine goes to work as secretary to a writer, and discovers that this male writer is the author of a series of well-known and successful novels which are published under a woman's name. She is at first appalled, but on reflection the real truth of the matter comes to her:

> No person without the necessary warmth and sincerity could have written the Jane Calton stories. They couldn't be built like a house from toy bricks. Every fibre and fabric of those novels had been devised by a compassionate heart and an intelligent and understanding mind.

Their obvious concern for the 'most important thing in the world' causes many romantic novelists to become authorities on the subject. One of the ancillary activities of writing romantic novels has often been to provide advice or practical help on love and its related topics—beauty, sex, homeliness, woman's role in the home; e.g. in 1893 there was Annie S. Swan's *Courtship and Marriage, and the Gentle Art of Love-making*, and the very popular romantic novelists also had their own widely-selling 'birthday books', such as *The Berta Ruck Birthday Book* (1920), or *The Marie Corelli Birthday Book* (1897), or, better still, *The Marie Corelli Calendar* (1913), which had a quotation from the works of

Marie Corelli for every day of the year. There was no Elinor Glyn birthday book.

Elinor Glyn was a self-proclaimed authority on love in its widest sense. In 1920 she published *Love: What I think of it*, and then in 1928 went still further and produced an 'academic treatise' called *The Philosophy of Love*. She began by defining the various kinds of love—Ideal Love, Platonic Friendship, Love out of Marriage—and then described how to cope with them. There is discussion on such topics as *The Advantages of Being a Mistress, Motives for Marriage, Is the Problem of Marriage more acute than it was?* and on *The Nature of Woman*. '*The Three Classes of Women*: We can very well class women into three distinct root types, from which further amalgamations branch, of—The Lover Women—The Mother Women—the Neuter Women.' In the last hundred years, she adds, there seem to be more of the last root-type than before. At the beginning of her paper she apologises if it all 'sounds a bit highbrow'. The general tone goes like this:

> Being *in love* is merely a physical state of exaltation; *loving* is the merging of the spirit which at its white heat has glorified the physical instinct for re-creation into a godlike beatitude not of earth. Loving throbs with delight in the flesh; it thrills the spirit with reverence; it glorifies into beauty commonplace things.

Probably more helpful to the reading public than Elinor Glyn's effusive nonsense are the agony columns which are often run by romantic novelists in the women's magazines. Ruby M. Ayres was answering readers' problem letters in *Home Companion* in the 1950s, and today Denise Robins performs a similar service in the magazine *She*. Denise Robins' column was originally called *Straight from the Shoulder*:

> It was a great joy to me and over the years has proved a stimulating job. Letters come from all over the world. They bring me in close contact with human beings in all kinds of

trouble. It is my privilege to help and counsel.

The outer woman as well as the inner comes within the scope of the romantic novelist. Elinor Glyn, for instance, wrote *The Wrinkle Book: or, How to Keep Looking Young* (1927), and in more recent years, in the same vein, there has been Barbara Cartland's crusade for natural health and beauty achieved by means of honey, health food, and regular bowel movements. Barbara Cartland also advises that 'if you want to be a good lover you have to eat eighty grammes of protein a day—eggs, meat, fish, cheese, soya flour'.

Practical advice on enhancing one's life was particularly abundant during the lean years of the late 1940s and 1950s and included a comprehensive series from Ursula Bloom—*You and Your Fun* (1950), *You and Your Dog* (1949), *You and Your Holiday* (1946), *You and Your Looks* (1949), *You and Your Needle* (1950), *You and Your Life* (1950).

In more recent years to the books of home-spun philosophies and advice on beauty and home-making have been added several handbooks written by romantic novelists which set out the rules of romance and offer advice to others on how to write it:

> You must yourself believe that good ultimately triumphs over evil, that happiness comes when we try to make others happy, and that Love, or 'sweet charity', as someone has described it, is the greatest power in the world—stronger than trouble, disaster, separation and death ... You have the opportunity to provide mental refreshment, a holiday in spirit, for women weary of the monotony of daily cares; to paint for them a picture lit by sunshine under a clear sky. Is not this a privilege of which you should be proud?
>
> Claire Ritchie, *Writing the Romantic Novel* (1962)

The two authors of another handbook, *Romantic Fiction* (1960), Anne Britton and Marion Collin, explain that there are certain strict taboos in romantic fiction, among them mixed marriages (no blacks), and drunkenness; also:

> ...deformity is very unpopular ... of course, there have
> been some very moving stories about blind girls, and girls
> with a slight limp who fear that love is not for them, but
> this kind of plot is not easy to put over sincerely ... never
> a heroine with one leg...

There are instructions on *How to Convey Emotion, Building Love Scenes*, and the *Use of Endearments*, with examples of the right and wrong way. These authors treat romance with great respect and impress upon would-be romantic novelists that Love is no subject to laugh about:

> It is absolutely imperative that authors realise from the
> outset that in dealing with romance you are handling a
> quality or a state of mind which enters the lives of the
> majority of people in the world in some form or another.
> Individual attitudes towards romance may change with
> age and outlook, but while it lasts in the individual's mind
> that romance is *real*.

Emotion, explain the authors, plays a very important part in all forms of fiction; they give an example, 'She stretched out her arms towards the sun. "Oh, Martin, it's all so wonderful I just want to sing."' But although emotion is important, endearments, they explain categorically, do not make good reading, and in dealing with love scenes the 'indirect approach' is considered better. They give examples of the direct (wrong) approach to emotion, and the indirect (right) approach:

Direct approach:
(1) He kissed her with sudden, unexpected passion.
(2) The intensity of his kiss bewildered her, even frightened her a little.

Indirect approach:

(1) He took her in his arms. After a moment they drew apart, smiling at each other, slightly dazed.

(2) He touched her hand, then gently drew her towards him. There was no longer any need for words between them.

The authors qualify their choice of examples:

All these examples convey the mood of the scene fairly briefly and with some subtlety. After all, a reader's imagination is often stronger than any words would be.

There is a thin border-line in a romantic story between good and bad taste, that shade of difference between gently sensual writing and sheer crudity ... Poor taste is perhaps best illustrated by an example of the lines followed by some of the earlier romantic fiction, so often about sheikhs on Arab steeds in the burning desert!

His strong brown arms held her in an iron-like grip and her breast was pressed against his. Through the thin material of her dress she could feel his heart pounding against his ribs.

In contrast, here is the author's version of a more subtle, tender love scene:

'Now you know how I feel about you,' Mark said almost roughly. Maria did not answer. In all her dreams about this moment she had not imagined that Mark, normally so gay and confident, would be so solemn and uneasy.

There are many people who find the existence of popular romantic fiction extremely disquieting. Romantic novels have been accused of 'exploiting housewives', of 'breeding dissatisfaction and disillusionment', of encouraging the habit of 'fantasying' which could lead to maladjustment in later life, of implanting dangerous ideas of female subjugation into the minds of helpless, unsuspecting women.

This sort of nonsense not only helps to keep women in a

state of mindless, admiring subjection—it is in its shallow-
ness, and its lack of intelligence, an insult to those who
believe that a valuable function of literature is to illumin-
ate the realities of life,

wrote one reviewer in *Books and Bookmen*. Moreover,
'romance sanctions drudgery, physical incompetence, and
prostitution', says Germaine Greer in *The Female Eunuch*.

Romantic fiction champions cosily domestic and bourgeois
values, which are the very antithesis of the aims and aspirations of Women's Liberation, and for this reason some of the
opposition to romantic fiction is understandable. But it does
seem incongruous that something which has been described
by Peter Mann as being of 'impeccable moral purity' should
also be accused of 'encouraging prostitution'. The violent
antagonism towards romantic fiction is due not only to disapproval of the message or literary standards. It is due also
to a fear of the unknown, a fear of something whose appeal
and power over millions of readers they cannot share or com-
prehend. The barriers between intellectuals and non-intel-
lectuals are much higher than are often supposed:

Nearly all bookish people are snobs, and especially the more
enlightened among them. They are apt to assume that if a
writer has immense circulation, if he is enjoyed by plain
persons, and if he can fill several theatres at once, he cannot possibly be worth reading and merits only indifference
and disdain.

Arnold Bennett (1928)

Romance-knocking is, of course, nothing new. Both the books
and their authors, and occasionally the people who read them
too, have always been laughed at or scorned. Ouida was frequently ridiculed in the comic papers of the nineteenth century, and criticised in the serious ones. Lord Strangford,
writing in the *Pall Mall Gazette* in 1867 threw contempt not
only on Ouida, but on anybody who read her, too. 'The taste
for Ouida's novels confirms what we know from other sources

of the curious ignorance and vacuity of mind of the English middle-classes.'

Rhoda Broughton's *Cometh up as a Flower* was described by a publisher's reader as being, 'coarse, vulgar and very objectionable'. Rhoda Broughton tried to divert attack on her work by herself mocking in one of her novels the very thing she was writing about:

> What absurdly false pictures novels do give one of love, the drawings they make of it are so out of perspective! They represent it as the one main interest of life, instead of being, as it mostly is, a short unimportant little episode. I declare it is enough to give one a disgust for the whole concern.

But she was among the few romantic novelists to have got her subject-matter in a true perspective. Marie Corelli, some twenty years later on, was a huge joke with the serious critics. Like an angry child, she was never sure which was worse, to be derided or ignored. Her first novel, *A Romance of Two Worlds*, though it was an enormous popular success, received only four reviews, all of them brief and unfavourable. After her next novel, *Barabbas*, had been, as she saw it, unfairly received by the critics, she tried to forestall all future criticisms by not allowing review copies of subsequent novels to be sent out at all. Instead, she had the following notice, printed in red, inserted inside all copies of her books:

> SPECIAL NOTICE—No copies of this book are sent out for review. Members of the Press will therefore obtain it (should they wish to do so) in the usual way with the rest of the public, i.e. through the booksellers and libraries.

She claimed not to approve of 'self-advertisement', and tried to keep gossip and photographs of herself out of the newspapers, but then seemed upset when she was not mentioned.

Elinor Glyn, too, claimed that her novel *Three Weeks* was misunderstood and misinterpreted by 'nearly the entire Press and a section of the public'.

Perhaps the man who has in this century been harshest on romantic love is E. M. Forster. In his *Aspects of the Novel* he decries love in any form appearing in fiction:

> Love. You all know now enormously love bulks in novels, and you will probably agree with me that it has done them harm and made them monotonous ... If you think of a novel in the vague you think of a love interest—of a man and woman who wanted to be united and perhaps succeed. If you think of your own life in the vague, or of a group of lives, you are left with a very different and more complex impression.

In real life, he wrote, people are *not* in love the whole time, though they may experience moments of passion or intensity. He suggests then, that this 'constant sensitiveness of characters for each other', 'this constant awareness, this endless readjusting, this ceaseless hunger' is really no more than the reflections of novelists' own states of mind while they compose. It is, he says, an unfortunate, but unconscious, fault of novelists to be in this 'love-hungering' state of mind while they compose. In fact, for many writers of popular romantic fiction, far from being an unconscious fault, this 'love-awareness' is an induced state, a conscious belief. While E. M. Forster may feel that too much emphasis is given to love in novels, Gilbert Frankau believes that the novelist has a positive *duty* to write about love:

> I hold that love—using the word in its accepted sense—being the forerunner of birth, cannot possibly be excluded from any novel or any story which attempts to depict life whole.
> I hold that it is the novelist's duty—even if it be not his pleasure, for there are many things which I personally find far more interesting to write about—to depict love as he sees it at work on the lives of others, and as he feels it at work in his own.
> I believe that the novelist who does not study, and con-

stantly, the peculiarly intricate relation between mental and physical aspects of love will never succeed in creating living characters; and his work will be unconvincing, the very worst fault which any literary craftsman's work can display.

It is one of the romantic novelists' persistent complaints that they do not make the money they are reputed to, and do not receive the respect they deserve. So, in 1960, two romantic novelists, Denise Robins and Alex Stuart, decided to form the Romantic Novelists Association in order to protect romantic love from the mockers and knockers. The aim of the Association is to use 'all the means in its power, individually and collectively, to raise the prestige of Romantic Authorship'.

There have been many efforts to bring about its (romance's) destruction because those who turn their backs upon romance seem to become extraordinarily bitter. They like to sneer at and deride romantic love. Book critics try to toss aside the works of the romantic novelists. Knowing this, Alex Stuart and I decided to found the *Romantic Novelists Association*, and we did so because hundreds of other romantic novelists resented the recent attempt to belittle our type of work. We have been striving ever since to raise the prestige of it.

Denise Robins

The Chairman of the Romantic Novelists Association, Alice Chetwynd Ley, defined the romantic novel as 'a novel which relies on imagination and emotion rather than fact and realism'. The best definition of romantic fiction, as the Romantic Novelists Association likes to see it, was the 'accurate and honest assessment' made by an admirer when the Association was first founded, and quoted in their newsletter celebrating their anniversary ten years later:

Romantic novels are novels which deal with love rather than sex, with courage rather than cowardice, with clean living rather than crime, with decent people rather than degenerates, with questions of right conduct rather than social problems, with the eternal verities rather than fashionable psychological theories, are written with humour that does not depend on impropriety, in traditional English rather than imitation American; and because of these disadvantages, are seldom reviewed, though read by a vast and respectable section of the community.

> *Daniel George,*
> *Romantic Novelists Association*
> *News,* Autumn 1970.

Speaking to the Association on their tenth anniversary in 1970, Alex Stuart reminded members that during the next decade romantic fiction must be of even more value 'as an antidote to the persuasive preaching of the permissive society to which, by its very nature, it is actively opposed'.

The romantic novelists, even if sometimes confused, are thoroughly sincere in their aims. They insist on the importance of the *ideals* of romantic fiction, though the precise nature of these ideals is not always any clearer than it was in Elinor Glyn's day when she explained that:

> Romance is the glamour which turns the dust of everyday life into a golden haze ... But romance cannot exist without ideals, and ideals are the creations of the spirit and so are shrouded in mystery. They are not commonplace facts which jump to the eye!

More recently, Hermina Black has tried to express her ideals of romance:

> I feel very strongly that Romance not only supplies a need, but expresses a truth. In a society where Love is too often replaced by other four-letter words, this truth badly required recognition.
> ... Love is not only a biological urge, and while sexual passion is a very strong and necessary part of it, there's a

lot more to it than that. That has become an excuse for just sleeping around, the logical outcome of a spiritually barren and promiscuous society. The romantic novel points to an idea, and is worthy of respect.

The ideals of most of the early romantic novelists were based loosely on Christianity. There are today still some novelists who admit freely to specific Christian beliefs which they try to incorporate into their novels, notably, Bethea Creese, who says:

> I do believe that people read for entertainment and to get out of their own lives. I think that's one of our purposes. But I think we have another purpose. We can put over good living, and I myself try to do my little bit in a very subtle way to bring people to think of Christ. And Christianity. And I don't do that at all obviously. I do it by— perhaps I might send my heroine to church, or make her sing in the church choir, or the hero. Well, it might just occur to some girl or some young man reading it that it wasn't a bad thing to do.

But the majority of today's romantic novelists are far less specific about the motivating ideals behind their work. Their ideals tend to be undefined spiritual qualities. Barbara Cartland's ideal is a rainbow. She concludes one of her autobiographies:

> I have called this book *I Search for Rainbows* because this is what I have been doing all my life. However black, however miserable events have been, there has always been inside me the knowledge that I was not alone. There has always been hope and faith ... There is such a tremendous amount still to do—an increasing battle against injustice, hardship, ignorance and sickness. Sometimes it seems to me overwhelming, impossible, terrifying!
> But always there is a rainbow.

For Denise Robins Romance is an ideal in itself, which encompasses the animal as well as the human kingdom:

> It is a living truth. Something that an imaginative writer puts down in words because he or she has participated in it or, if not, seen it—watched the experience of others...
>
> It is to me the *primary* emotion—physical love combined with spiritual yearning. Desire, walking hand in hand with affection and friendship. It is the dream of youth, the beginning of courtship and marriage and the consolation of the aged ... It is as necessary to the human heart as food to the hungry ... And romance exists not only among human beings but in the world of animals. One reads strangely moving tales of the love and loyalty among the beasts of the field and the birds of the air. It is an *essential*, basic and immovable, and capable of stirring the hardest heart.

Until recently the success of popular romantic fiction has usually been attributable to the fervour with which the author has expressed her 'message', the most successful and readable of the romantic novelists being those who were driven by the most ardently held (although possibly absurd) conviction.

The modern popular romantic novel seems to be losing some of its early vitality and conviction. The romantic novelists have a set of rules for decorous behaviour, rules for tender tasteful love scenes, and an association to keep them together. The reduction of romance to a neat formula is not, by itself, necessarily such a destructive thing; formula writing can, after all, be extremely good, as in the case of detective stories and cookery books. But the genre as a whole seems to be without positive values.

Instead of the passionate, daring defiance that was part of the message of a Rhoda Broughton or a Marie Corelli, today's romantic novelists have come to see themselves as a restraining, conservative element in society, upholders of proper standards of public morality. No longer pioneers, they have become the curators of a tradition, and the formation of the Romantic Novelists Association shows that they are conscious of this altered role.

Today's novelists are undoubtedly sincere, but the problem is whether they have anything daring or positive to be sincere about. Can one write daringly and passionately about rainbows, and loyalty among birds.

Measured in terms of world-sales figures, popular romantic fiction continues, despite the predictions, to be an unqualified success story. But it will only continue to be an interesting genre if its authors can rediscover a passionate belief in their convictions, the total commitment to dotty ideals which once gave to that inimitable prose style its power, emotional drive and luxuriant vitality.

Index